Case Management and the Elderly

Case Management and the Elderly

A Handbook for Planning and Administering Programs

Raymond M. Steinberg
Genevieve W. Carter
Andrus Gerontology Center,
University of Southern
California

LexingtonBooks
D.C. Heath and Company
Lexington, Massachusetts
Toronto

Library of Congress Cataloging in Publication Data

Steinberg, Raymond M.
    Case management and the elderly.

    Includes index.
    1. Social work with the aged—United States—Handbooks,
manuals, etc. 2. Social work administration—United States—
Handbooks, manuals, etc. I. Carter, Genevieve W. II. Title.
[DNLM: 1. Health services for the aged—Organization and
administration—Handbooks. WT 30 S819c]
HV1461.S83   362.6′042   82–17127
ISBN 0–669–06089–5

Second printing, June 1984

Published simultaneously in Canada

Printed in the United States of America on acid-free paper

International Standard Book Number: 0–669–06089–5

Library of Congress Catalog Card Number: 82–17127

Contents

v

Contents

Tables

Preface

The purpose of this book is to present the complex subject of case management with the frail elderly from the perspective of the planner, the administrator, and the evaluator. For some audiences, these three roles are carried by three separate persons who rarely see a frail older person but who make important decisions affecting the lives of the elderly. Other readers will be case managers or supervisors who carry all three roles within a small program while working directly with clients.

The book is an outgrowth of a three-year research project at the University of Southern California's Andrus Gerontology Center and funded by the Administration on Aging (AoA grant 90-A-1280). The project was titled "Alternative Designs for Comprehensive Delivery through Case Service Coordination and Advocacy." It was a search for models, best practices, and guidelines for program development. Methods and findings are outlined in chapter 9.

A program model usually describes a set of structures and procedures that represent a standard of excellence worthy of imitation. This book does not deal with models. It deals instead with a variety of components of program design that are mixed and matched to suit particular purposes in particular environments.

The perspective is that the program designer takes stock of the initiating circumstances, the givens, that call forth the new program and that set limits on possible choices. The planner or administrator then reviews the options and makes decisions. The evaluator, in turn, must have a clear understanding of the choices that have been made in order to assess the degree to which decisions are being carried out and the degree to which the program's intentions are being achieved.

We have chosen to organize our discussion of case management from the bottom up. Although we recognize that crucial program decisions do not often begin with clients or patients, we have found that the concept of the client pathway provides a simple, unifying structure for examining variations in organization and activity at all program levels. As we move from the client pathway of chapter 1 through the chapters dealing with organizational bases, mobilizing resources, planning steps, funding, staffing patterns, and information systems we present a series of tables that comment on design choices in each of these content areas in terms of their relationship with the client pathway. The client pathway is visualized in five columns representing phases: entry, assessment, goal setting and care planning, care-plan implementation, and evaluation of client status.

In the early stages of writing it became clear that the many variations in components and related decision steps were so numerous that we had to break away from the temptation to cite the research findings or to reference all the sources that influenced the ideas expressed in this book. We also decided to omit descriptions of specific programs across the country, or in other nations, because all these are in constant change. We would not want to promulgate models or practices that are sometimes abandoned by the time their reports are printed. We concluded that if this volume were to be of practical use to planners and administrators in the field it must be a brief-as-possible distillation of issues, questions, and some answers. The research project has produced eighteen reports that more fully describe findings, attribute new ideas to their respective authors, describe particular demonstration programs, and reference nearly 1,000 project reports and interproject research studies that increased our knowledge of the subject.

The potential importance of case management to at least one million older Americans as well as to thousands of policymakers and practitioners whose careers may hinge on making informed choices prevented us from editing down to the point of oversimplification. For example, the first chapter outlines about seventy-five considerations in designing client pathway functions and describes over sixty planning alternatives and their consequences.

The Elusive Definition of Case Management

There is no one common definition of case management, nor is there any one best model for a case-management program. During the life cycle of an agency, the structures, practices, and staffing pattern undergo changes, as does the agency's definition of case management.

The use of the term *case management* should be reserved for programs with the following essential characteristics:

The defined goals and target groups are appropriate for the level of skill of the service staff and the capacity of the organization.

Orderly procedures exist for case finding and screening of clients.

The program is recognized for its expertise in mobilizing services and other resource options needed by its clients.

The program incorporates a balanced perspective on the client's physical and mental health as well as the client's social, environmental, and economic condition.

Comprehensive assessment procedures are well defined.

Care plans derived from the assessment process reflect the unique needs, conditions, and participation of the aged client.

Case recording reflects planning, action steps, and services procured.

Provisions exist for follow-through, a supportive relationship, and reevaluation of the client and the client's situation.

Attention is paid to interorganizational linkages with participating service providers.

The program's administrators and case managers are committed to service system improvement goals as well as to individual client goals.

In this volume we impartially scan a wide variety of uses of case management in different contexts. Although we present no judgments, we recognize that increased attention to design, administration, and re-search of case management can be expected to center on the reform of long-term care. We do not believe that all the variations described are suitable when dealing with the vulnerable elderly who are the principal concern of long-term-care systems. In the use of case management as a key component in a long-term-care system, two important requirements must be met. The case managers and the resources they control must meet high standards. And the continuum of different levels of care must span not only the home-based and community-based options but also residential facilities for long-term care. The more that a system succeeds in diverting some people from inappropriate institutionalization, the more attention must be paid to the linkages with and programs within those facilities that care for people whose impairments are greatest.

Acknowledgments

The authors are indebted to a committed professional staff who helped to conduct the three-year study in the Social Policy Laboratory of the Andrus Gerontology Center. Rachel Downing brought to the project a rich background of clinical experience with the frail elderly and provided sensitive, conceptual insights about case managers' roles and practices that permeate this volume. Monika White contributed greatly to the clarification of program design concepts and the validation of guidelines for program development. Dr. White also continued to provide crucial collegial support to the authors after the project terminated, in the organization and editing of this volume. Joe Kuna provided leadership around the history and evaluation of past case-coordination programs. Valerie Jurkiewicz executed the National Survey of Case Coordination Programs for the Elderly and, through key informant interviews in six cities, greatly increased our knowledge of the impacts of community environments and interorganizational linkages on program implementation.

At various points in the project the authors had the privilege of utilizing consultants as sources of information and as sounding boards for emerging concepts and conclusions. Julia Carpenter, Nathan E. Cohen, Neal E. Cutler, Stewart Greathouse, Barbara Schneider Ishizaki, Ed O. Moe, Robert Morris, Alex Norman, Marijo Walsh, and Edna Wasser were sources of inspiration and support.

Neither the project nor this book could have been realized without the cooperation of administrators, case managers, and service providers across the nation. Over 300 different programs participated in the National Survey of Case Coordination Programs for the Elderly in addition to over 100 who cooperated in the telephone and pilot surveys and 35 agencies in 6 cities that sampled cases for the site studies. Major contributions to our practical knowledge of case coordination programs came from the 16 members of the Administrators Task Force and the 12 case managers who participated in the project's intensive Symposium of Front-Line Practitioners.

Although we are deeply indebted to many people who helped to mobilize an information base for this handbook, we alone are responsible for the selection and use of the information, which has been sifted through the filters of our personal biases and combined seventy-five years of professional experience.

1

Alternative Approaches to the Client Pathway

Case management is a valuable and versatile approach to meeting the service needs of the home-bound elderly and other people with complex situations that place them at risk of diminished independence. It may be viewed from a variety of perspectives. For the clinician, case management may be one of the intervention options in psychosocial or medical treatment. For the administrator, case management may be a central component in a program seeking to provide a continuum of care for a target population. For the program developer and legislator, case management may be the rationale controlling a communitywide long-term-care system.

This book approaches policy development, program planning, and administration from the bottom up. It begins with what happens to those who are to benefit from the programs. This is not merely an ideological stance, although the older people who are the consumers of case-management services are indeed the most important component of the programs or long-term-care system. The main reason for starting with the client pathway in this book is that numerous project reports and inter-program evaluations have highlighted the importance and practicality of using the case-management component and the client pathway as the principal frames of reference in formulating policy and designing organizational and interorganizational structures for a coordination project.

Organizational Capacities Required for Client Pathway Functions

In this chapter, eleven client-level functions are described in detail with the focus on the decisions that must be made by planners and administrators (and sometimes board members and legislators) in order to have an appropriate organizational structure and capacity. The eleven functions are grouped as follows into five client-level phases for purposes of simplified tables that appear throughout the chapters:

Functions	Phases
Case finding	
Prescreening	Entry
Intake	

1

Assessment	Assessment
Goal setting	
Care planning	Goal setting and service planning
Capacity building	
Care-plan implementation	Care-plan implementation
Reassessment	
Termination	Review and evaluation of status
Maintaining relationships	

Although the functions outlined in table 1–1 are often referred to as steps in the client pathway, it is commonly understood that any one task of the worker (whether a home visit, consultation, or contact with relatives) may serve several purposes. The sequence of tasks may vary with individual client situations, such as emergencies or fearfulness or strong capacities for self-help, and with different program contingencies, such as agency waiting lists, staff vacancies, and funding regulations. The full client pathway is not covered for all clients. Some clients are steered ("channeled" or "triaged") to alternative programs or, by choice, exit from the program before the full cycle is completed. In some programs the entire client pathway has a single case manager serving as helper and broker throughout. Other programs divide these functions among different personnel. (See chapter 6.)

The specific organizational structures, divisions of responsibility among personnel, and program methods vary from community to community, but all case-management organizations must have *capacities* for

1. *Case finding, in order to reach all the people who need help* in maximizing their strengths and in obtaining multiple services in a coordinated way in order to live in the least restrictive environment and to experience a maximum feasible quality of life.
2. *Prescreening, in order to respond to those who most need and can benefit most from the case-management service* without inappropriate referrals or excessive waiting time.
3. *Intake, in order to engage the client in a dignified way* to assure that the nature of the case-management service is understood, demonstrate that the personnel are competent and trustworthy, and involve the client in the service.
4. *Assessment, in order to understand the client as a whole person* and *be aware of all aspects of the client's situation* that threaten everyday functioning and longer-term well-being.

5. *Goal setting, in order to develop clear expectations* about what is to be achieved through the case-management service consistent with the capacities of the program and consistent with the aspirations and preferences of the client.

6. *Care planning, in order to arrange an individualized package of services* and other supportive activities suitable to the client's needs and values.

7. *Capacity building, in order to maximize the potential of-the client* and of the client's informal support network to function independently and when necessary to obtain, coordinate, and monitor services on their own.

8. *Care-plan implementation, in order to assure that high-quality services are found and delivered* quickly and smoothly and that the client is suitably utilizing the available services.

9. *Reassessment, to keep current* regarding the status of the client and the suitability of the current care plan.

10. *Termination, in order to phase out the case-management service* when it is no longer necessary for the well-being of the client, and;

11. *Maintaining relationships, in order to remain accessible to former clients* in the event that case-management services are needed at a later time.

Each decision regarding how a program will provide itself with these eleven capacities is not only a matter of which structures, personnel, and procedures work best, but also a question of costs, interorganizational relations, and acceptability to clients.

Phase 1: Entry

Case Finding: Deciding on an Appropriate Strategy

Case finding is a process through which a program identifies and establishes contact with individuals who need the services provided by the program, especially those for whom its unique services are especially suited. Since a program usually has limited resources, it is imperative to develop an efficient and effective case-finding strategy to reach the intended users. Inadequate case finding means that the program will handle requests from many individuals and families who do not need case management and who can be served directly by providers. Moreover, inappropriate or borderline clients may receive service while more appropriate candidates from the target population are denied service or placed on waiting lists. It means too that many home bound and vulnerable elderly

Table 1–1
Program Functions at the Client Level

Entry	Assessment	Case Goal Setting and Service Planning	Care-Plan Implementation	Review and Evaluation of Client and Program Status
Purpose	*Purpose*	*Purpose*	*Purpose*	*Purpose*
To identify and enroll clients most appropriate for objectives and capacities of program.	To understand the client as a whole person and be aware of strengths and needs in client's situation.	To clarify expectations and agree upon an individualized plan of services and other problem-solving activities.	To arrange and ensure that services and other help are provided and utilized effectively.	To update knowledge of client and situation for possible revisions in client plan or for management of agency resources.
Guidelines	*Guidelines*	*Guidelines*	*Guidelines*	*Guidelines*
Select casefinding approach.	Conduct comprehensive standard agency assessment if required.	Formulate goals and plans according to agency format requirements.	Make service search using resource inventory, own experience, and confirm inquiries.	Reassess client needs.
Prescreen potential clients, in and out.	If standardized assessment is not required, select assessment scope and conduct client assessment according to client or situation giving consideration to	Formulate goals and plans according to client or situation, giving consideration to	Explain request, negotiate, advocate, and procure needed services.	Revise care plans as indicated.
Engage client in intake process.		stating case goals or focus;	Confirm initiation of service and confirm client utilization.	Prioritize cases for caseload management.
Refer client to proper resource if indicated.		outlining optimal solutions and alternatives;	Monitor service delivery.	Terminate cases no longer needing active coordination service.
Handle immediate emergency as needed.	presenting problem;	negotiating tentative care plan with client;	Provide encouragement to service provider and to client.	Encourage reopening when client needs help again.
Explain agency service.	physical health problems;	clarifying tasks of client, worker and informal network members.	Mediate conflicts or misunderstandings.	Maintain agency relationships with past clients.
Enroll applicant as an identified agency client.	psychosocial functioning;			Evaluate program capacity to meet needs of target clients.
Obtain consent forms from client.	values, preferences, interpersonal style;			

Table 1–1 Continued

Entry	Assessment	Case Goal Setting and Service Planning	Care-Plan Implementation	Review and Evaluation of Client and Program Status
Arrange next contact.	informal support system;	Review goals and needed services to clarify intended intervention focus:	Make changes or adaptations indicated.	Review needed changes in policies, structure, procedures and distribution of agency resources.
	economic and geographic factors, including eligibility factors;	assist with instrumental/ environmental help;	Create new service; locate new resources.	Identify the barriers to prompt, qualitative program implementation.
	diagnostic information from other agencies and significant others;	offer some affective support;	Identify and report service gaps.	
	use of consultation experts, medical or social.	work toward capacity building objectives	Provide direct service if within own agency policy.	
	Determine next steps— immediate priorities, supplemental information needed, timetable, and so on.	with client, with natural support network, or with service system.	Develop client participation and self-reporting.	
		Determine sequence and priorities in service delivery.		

persons fail to obtain case management and direct services that they need, because neither they nor others in their social network know that such services exist or how they can be useful. Among the mechanisms for case finding are outreach, information and referral, agreements with referral sources, outstationing, and public information campaigns. Further discussion of some of these mechanisms appears in chapter 3.

Considering the Givens that Influence Choice. In selecting an appropriate case-finding strategy and tactic, the planner or administrator must consider a variety of organizational and community contexts in order to develop a design adapted to the particular setting.

Organizational Constraints and Capacities

the specificity of the target population as defined by funding sources, sponsors, or community needs studies;

the image of the target population to be established locally;

the numbers of clients who can be handled effectively in the near future;

the degree to which the agency already has contact with and access to the target population through internal referrals;

the extent and nature of the program's relationships with other agencies who work with the target clients;

the possible legal liabilities for inappropriate screening out of clients who want service;

the personnel available within the case-management agency to perform case finding and prescreening functions in general and with respect to special subgroups based on such factors as language or location.

Community and System Conditions

existence of other case-finding and referral agencies that already reach out, visit, or attract the target population;

existence of other case-management programs responding to a special segment of the target population (the handicapped, members of a certain ethnic group, residents of a certain community, and so on);

degree of public and service system awareness of the need for the program;

technical capacities of other referring agencies to identify and refer appropriate clients to the program;

existing patterns of service utilization by the target population (who are the unconnected?);

geographic proximity and residential density of potential clients as they may affect staff travel time for home visits:

extent to which communication channels exist for reaching and informing nonagency case finders (such as associations of clergy, lawyers, doctors, law enforcement officers);

subgroups who will need special approaches to overcome community barriers based on ethnic discrimination, geographic isolation, lifestyle intolerances, jurisdictional rivalries, ageism, or sexism.

Design Choices in Case Finding. After consideration of the organizational and community contexts, three basic design decisions can be made concerning the extent to which there will be (1) reliance on other agencies for case finding; (2) specificity in client selection; and (3) formalization of the referral process. If the program relies primarily on other agencies or community agents to do the case finding, then it may be necessary to negotiate a written referral agreement or to supplement the resources of the other agencies through purchase-of-service contracts. If case finding is to be retained in the agency, then appropriate personnel assignments must be made for the case-finding function and time allocated for the tasks.

The more specific the criteria for client selection, the more pinpointed the search for appropriate clients must be. Some types of clients may be so hard to locate that a wide sweep will be necessary to establish contact followed by a prescreening of those identified.

Regardless of the choice of who does most of the case finding, a certain number of clients always find the program through referrals by others. Some programs promote the use of written referral forms, ''sign-offs'' from medical personnel, or other documents assuring eligibility and indicating the presenting problems.

Too many programs formalize the referral process too much in an attempt to appear businesslike and to simplify the assignment of new cases to appropriate workers. Formality can be a barrier to clients as well as to workers in other agencies. In soliciting referrals or in referring out to another agency, a brief and informal but polite note of introduction (with a copy to the person being referred) can communicate respect for the client and for colleagues in other agencies and attention to detail, reassuring the older client.

One other important but often neglected consideration is whether the case-management agency is committed to notify the referring agency formally about acceptance of the case and progress of the client. This courtesy has a cost but may pay off in the long run by assuring referral agents that their cooperation is valuable. This process also helps to keep the originating agency involved in preparation for the day when the client may no longer need case management but may need still need occasional contact with that agency.

Prescreening: Deciding on Criteria and Methods

Prescreening is a process by which a preliminary determination is made regarding the suitability of the program for the person who is directly or indirectly applying for case-management services. Effective prescreening saves the program from investing in unnecessary intake and assessment steps with people whom the program is not designed to serve. More important, it saves older people and their helpers from undergoing a partial induction experience or a waiting period that may lead only to a referral to another agency. Programs with multiple funding sources often use prescreening to determine to which funding source particular cases should be assigned.

Establishing Prescreening Criteria. Different programs utilize different combinations of prescreening criteria depending on their goals, resources, and the condition of their waiting lists. At an early stage, a program tends to have broad criteria that are liberally interpreted in order to accept as many new clients as possible. After a program and referring agencies gain more experience and the flow of appropriate clients is established, the trend is to narrow the criteria and encourage personnel to screen out clients who may not be the most needy or who cannot benefit from the program. Examples of prescreening criteria for targeting and referral of people for case management are the following:

Is the person about to enter institutional care?

Is the person suffering from a recent loss of a spouse or significant other?

Do the person's needs for assistance in daily living tasks exceed the supply of help available from the natural support system?

Is the person seeking service for the first time?

Does the person need two or more services or have multiple or complex problems?

Is the person home bound and can he be seen only at home?

Does the person have a 3-inch thick medical record?

Is the person's behavior regarded by others as too deviant to tolerate?

Does an information and referral (I&R) worker note that information alone will not meet the client's needs?

Does the I&R worker sense that something is wrong with the situation, or can the worker not get a clear picture of the situation?

Has a guardian or conservator been appointed?

Depending on whether they are relevant to eligibility requirements or priority populations, prescreening criteria may also include income level, handicaps, place of residence, ethnicity, or age.

Some Prescreening Methods. Frequently programs distribute referral forms for others to use. Such forms include essential identifying information about the client and a brief introduction to the presenting problem. Because inevitably not all referring agents adapt to the program's wishes for a neat and uniform procedure, the program must be prepared to use a variety of information sources for prescreening.

The program's referral form must contain the information most useful for prescreening decisions. The program may also have an in-house format for logging potential clients based on information received in such ways as a telephone conversation with or about the potential client, a referral form unique to the referring agent, a segment of the referring agent's case file or medical record, or a printout from a computerized client-tracking system. In all such transfers of information about the client, prior consent should have been obtained from the client. In case the information about the client obtained from others is insufficient, programs often provide for a prescreening home visit by one of their own staff members.

In time the program's personnel develop useful shortcuts to prescreening. They develop confidence in the ability of particular referring agencies or particular workers within other agencies to make good prescreening judgments. Confidence may also develop in particular physicians or clergy. In such cases no further prescreening work is done, and the case manager is assigned to complete the intake process and to begin the assessment procedures.

Design Choices in Prescreening. Three basic design or procedural choices to make in prescreening concern (1) the breadth of the prescreening criteria (2) the degree of formality of the prescreening process, (3) the level of professional skill needed to make prescreening decisions. The choices may change depending on whether the program has reached its capacity to serve a finite number of clients at any one point in time. Perhaps the greatest influence on these choices, however, is the program's funding source. Not only do different funding sources have different goals and entitlements, but they also have different reporting requirements. Some sources require case-by-case accountability whereas others permit the program to aggregate information about cases and assign costs to each funding source on the basis of aggregated data.

The administrator must also make choices regarding the level of effort to be expended to provide checks and balances in prescreening and in periodic monitoring and evaluation to assure uniform compliance with policy. The ultimate concern should be whether the prescreening is in effect making it possible to serve first those whom the program is committed to serve and that no relevant subgroup is being inequitably screened out through personal prejudice or systematic but unintended bias in the procedures.

Intake: Committing the Program to Serve and
Engaging the Client in the Planning Process

In most case-management programs, intake is a barely distinguishable step in the process. For many programs intake is accomplished when the worker knocks on the door and gains entry into the client's home for the first time. For other programs intake is accomplished when the client (or a caretaker) signs a form consenting to an exchange of information among agencies or to apply for entitlement to service under Title XX of the Social Security Act or Medicaid.

What Is Accomplished at the Intake Step. Most commonly intake is seen as the starting of a case record (or reactivating an old case record) with implied consent of the client. For purposes of this book, intake is seen to include

learning the client's expectation (why did the person come?);

showing the program's respect for and interest in the older person;

explaining what the program can offer, how it works, and what conditions or responsibilities will have to be accepted by the client;

assuring the person or kin of rights of choice and control;

obtaining the person's agreement to become a client;

confirming to the client that the program has accepted responsibility
and will do its best;

assessing the relative urgency of the case and characteristics that may
influence which worker will best fit;

handling emergencies if necessary;

arranging appointments for routine next steps; and

notifying other previously involved agencies.

Admitting the client into the program system initiates both agency
and client responsibilities. Case accountability begins here. It is important
for the administrator to allow enough staff time for intake and staff
preservice training to ensure skills in doing intake so that clients are not
made to feel that intake or assessment is a test of their competence or
compliance and that their individuality is being reduced to bureaucratic
case numbers.

Another important task that is sometimes accomplished as part of
intake is the notification of the referring agent and of other agencies that
may be concurrently serving the client that their client has been accepted
into the program. Such notifications must formally be noted in the case
record since these and other agencies may be named by the client later
during the assessment and care-planning phases.

Design Choices for Intake. The planner or administrator must remain
conscious that intake policies have a significant impact on agency–client
relationships. Accuracy of information and expectations as well as motivation and participation of the client may hinge on the intake experience.
The administrator must weigh these client-oriented concerns against the
bureaucratic necessities and cost constraints impinging on the quality of
intake. Specifically, the quality of intake will be affected by administrative decisions regarding:

which personnel handle intake;

how much independent decision-making discretion will be delegated;

which administrative tasks must be accomplished at intake (internal
and interagency);

what degree of attention will be paid to legal constraints, determination of mental competency to consent, and clinical considerations
regarding which member of a family is the client;

whether intake will include the determination of which worker will be assigned to the client and the basis of the assignment (worker specialization); and

the extent to which intake must be concerned with research-oriented tasks or accountability to funding sources.

Phase 2: Assessment for Care Planning

Many case-management programs claim to bring to the traditional service network a holistic approach, which is symbolized by a comprehensive and standardized assessment instrument. But the whole-person commitment must be reflected in all the tasks at the client and organizational levels. The whole-person concept does not have to be put into effect in one day's time. It is a philosophical viewpoint with an integrated medical-social stance. Its implementation may be incremental, and diagnostic comprehensiveness may be achieved in cumulative phases. The search for the ideal instrument to assess the whole person must include consideration of program goals, staffing patterns, target populations, capacities to formulate and implement care plans, and evaluation needs. Planning concerns must be balanced. There is little point in having a comprehensive individualized assessment if the care plans all look alike. There is little point to a standardized assessment if its excessive length and privacy-invading style drive needy clients away.

An increasing number of good references discuss assessment of the elderly from the perspective of the clinical practitioner and from the perspective of the researcher. Therefore the following discussion is focused on issues that affect the design choices of program planners and administrators rather than on clinical issues.

Obtaining Information about the Client. There are many sources of information to help the care planner to understand the client and become aware of the strengths and needs in the client's situation. The first is the observation of the client at home. Then the skilled clinician will use informal interviewing techniques to assess the feasibility of various courses of action. Which problem most places the client at risk? On which problem is the client most ready to work? Which solutions will best fit the client's values and beliefs? What can be expected from the client's natural support network? A clinically oriented assessment interview permits the worker much discretion regarding which topics to cover in a first interview and which to avoid or defer to later interviews.

A contrasting approach is to guide the interview by means of a standardized list of assessment questions commonly called an assessment tool. Such a tool not only ensures that all relevant topics will be covered but also organizes the answers so that they may be more readily accessed later by the case manager and other relevant personnel. Some programs that use a standardized assessment tool permit the interviewer to adjust the sequence of topics to fit the client's pattern of recall or perceptions of the relative importance of topics. Standardized tools that have summary measures of functional status also make it easier for the agency to compare clients with one another and track the client's progress by means of successive assessments.

In both types of assessment it is possible to test the mental status of clients through indirect questions dealing with time and place orientation, ability to recall, and manipulation of numbers. In both types of assessment, even when there have been advance reports of senility, incompetence, or depression, the experienced worker begins with the client as the primary source of information, then turns for supplementary information to family and friends as needed, with the permission of the client. Beginning with the client is important not only for obtaining relevant data but also for communicating to all concerned that the client has basic rights of privacy and self-determination regardless of being old or ill. If, indeed, the client is too ill to give information or informed consent, then special steps must be taken clinically and administratively to protect the client's interests.

Additional assessment information sources are physician's reports, medical records, agency case records and, in some cases, newspaper accounts or complaint letters from neighbors. Sometimes the worker may request that the client be seen by a specialist for supplemental assessment of problems that are beyond the expertise of the case manager. A worker may also wish to obtain consultation (for which the client is not seen directly by the specialist) for advice or confirmation of conclusions reached on the basis of client responses in the assessment interview.

Categories of Information and Limitations of Assessment Tools. Different programs give varying emphasis to the physical as compared with the psychosocial components of assessment. Increasingly case-management programs are seeking to balance these concerns in recognition of the interrelation of these components in assessing well-being or the risk of institutionalization.

Virtually all assessments cover the presenting problem; some formats make necessary distinctions as to whether the record shows the words of the client or the summary judgment of the worker. There is usually a review of physical health, impairments in activities of daily living, psychosocial functioning, and economic conditions. Some assessments have formal provisions for measuring morale; virtually none deal with the

client's values and interpersonal style, which can be very important to
the care plan. All assessments include some information about family
and friends, but only the rare assessment tool provides for differentiating
helpful from harmful relationships. Most assessments pay attention to
housing conditions and whether the client lives alone, but not whether
living alone means isolation or whether it means liberation for that person.
During the problem-oriented interview the skilled assessor is also measuring the client's capacities for self-help and willingness to take an active
role in the planning and action process to come, but standardized tools
rarely provide a place to record these positive capacities. Most assessments find out whether the client is currently receiving any services; few
assessment forms provide space to record the client's attitudes toward
services currently received or received in the past.

One dilemma faced by the administrator is what compromises to
make so that the assessment is acceptable to the client—a prime goal.
It should also be accomplished within a reasonable period of time, obtain
sufficient information for comprehensive care planning, and meet information needs for administration and program evaluation.

The Worker: The Most Important Assessment Tool. Since any choice of
policy, procedure, and design for client assessment is a compromise, the
case manager, who performs or coordinates the assessment, should be
as highly qualified as the program can afford. A skilled clinician is able
to individualize the client's situation, is sensitive to pertinent questions
not included in standardized assessment formats, and can adapt interviewing techniques to the particular client and situation. It is the case
manager who must use the assessment for formulating a care plan. Often
planners and administrators of new programs underestimate the interviewing skills required and the effectiveness and efficiency of having
case managers who can establish trusting encouraging relationships with
clients. Many administrators report that over time they recognize that
better paid, more highly skilled workers are essential and seek to upgrade
the classification level of the case manager. Specific differences that skill
levels make in assessment are discussed in chapter 6.

Common Misperceptions about Assessment. Only 25 percent of the programs in our national survey of case-management programs for the elderly
utilized a standardized list of written questions for assessment. However,
a great deal of interest exists in the concept of a comprehensive assessment
and a great many unrealistic perceptions about how it works. Three main
misconceptions concerning the selection and maintenance of assessment
policies and procedures are common:

Misperception 1. One comprehensive needs assessment by the case-management agency will make it unnecessary for each service provider to make its own assessment.

It is important to distinguish between the case manager's assessment of service needs and the kind of assessment that the provider uses before offering a particular service such as day health care or home chore. At first glance it may appear that the case manager can determine the need for an instrumental service such as transportation and home-delivered meals, but it may be desirable to supplement the initial assessment with a careful diagnosis of the extent to which these helps would be more desirable when coming from relatives, friends, or neighbors. The extra assessment step will lead to better judgments regarding the level of formal service to provide whether it be meals, visiting nurse service, or psychotherapy.

Misperception 2. The most desirable assessment tool is one that has been tested and validated by research.

Administrators must take care to ensure that the selected assessment instrument or method adopted or adapted was developed for the *same purposes* as one's own program. Some instruments were developed to answer research questions and were not designed to serve clinical purposes (such as instruments for community-need surveys). Other existing instruments are compromise solutions to conflicting dual needs of demonstration programs to provide case management and at the same time evaluate the effectiveness of the program. Other instruments, which were tested as clinically oriented assessment tools, and which are abundantly available in project descriptions, were replaced during the life of the project on the basis of experience. Administrators interested in obtaining another program's version as a model for their own programs should be certain to get the version that emerged after an implementation period of trial and error.

No known assessment instrument equally well meets the needs of the clinician, the administrator, and the researcher. There is no point in using an assessment form that primarily meets research requirements of another agency unless you have the same program and research objectives.

Misperception 3. A fully comprehensive assessment should be obtained on the first visit.

Evidence is mounting that elderly respondents do not give as accurate information during their first contact with an agency as they do in subsequent interviews. Administrators and the case managers often face pressures to cover the entire comprehensive assessment before any service is provided. Some of the pressures develop from program realities as when, for research purposes, the clients must be assessed before they are assigned to different experimental subgroups or when the assessment is done by a team or a specialist before the case is assigned to another person as service coordinator and hence service cannot begin until the comprehensive assessment is completed. Pressure also occurs when many service referrals require information about clients' income and assets, questions about which are placed near the end of the instrument, so that the whole instrument must be completed (if a uniform sequence is required by research policy) before those services can be requested.

Some demonstration programs use a research-oriented instrument by a research interviewer on a first visit, then have a separate service-oriented assessment conducted by the case manager. Other programs, which have no research design to follow, reduce the original assessment instrument to a "minimum data set" needed for the management information system and such additional questions as prove meaningful for services to the majority of clients.

Some programs use a miniassessment. This assesses only aspects of the client related directly to the presenting problem or only those problems about which the agency can offer help in the short range. The use of a miniassessment for a faster initiation of service does not preclude incrementally expanded assessment over time. Some miniassessments have "trigger" questions that indicate whether or not supplemental assessments should be made on medical, social, psychological, environmental, or income factors beyond those explored with the average client. Triggering or branching assessment approaches save unnecessary wear and tear on both clients and workers.

Of more recent origin are attempts to have the client (with the help of others if needed) fill out a self-assessment instrument in advance of the first interview. In these instances the case manager need only deal with the more sensitive questions. This technique is modeled after the medical history fact sheet used in many clinics and waiting rooms of physicians.

Common Causes of Incomplete Assessments. As previously noted, it is common for programs to have some problems with judging the capacity of the clients to be the primary source of information. Other problems include the degree to which the length of the instrument becomes a barrier to the client and the degree of discretion that can be delegated to front-line workers to deviate from standardized procedures. Still another kind of problem has to do with the slippage that often takes place among workers with respect to completeness and accuracy of the assessment information. Workers tend to "fudge" on information that is never used or that deals with needs for which they can never find a solution. Some workers are uneasy about dealing with questions about drinking habits, sexual activities, mental illness, or the recent death of loved ones and are provided with no opportunity to identify their blocks and work them through. When workers recognize questions that are for administrative use only and become aware that the administrators never use that information, they may begin to ignore them rather than call attention of superiors to systematic wastes of time. Finally, when rules of confidentiality have been violated by the program or no such rules exist, workers who respect the right of privacy of clients will avoid recording any information that may adversely affect their access to service.

Choices in Assessment Design. In summary, a number of choices deserve the consideration of designers or administrators of programs:

To what degree is the assessment primarily for clinical purposes, administrative purposes, or research purposes? What will be the assessment pace (mini-, incremental, immediate comprehensive) and which assessment instrument, if any, will be used (scope, standardization, uses of summary classification)? Which variables from the assessment need to be logged into a client-tracking or management information system?

Which personnel will conduct assessments of clients? The common variations are (1) case manager alone, (2) case manager with assistance as needed from specialists, and (3) multidisciplinary assessment team. The degree to which assessment is viewed as a sensitive, clinically oriented, diagnostic process will affect decisions regarding the professional qualifications of the case manager.

If assessments are to be conducted by an individual staff member, to what extent will there be case reviews by supervisors or consultants to ensure completeness and accuracy and to discuss implications of the assessment for care planning?

What policy and procedures will be established to obtain and use assessment information from sources in addition to clients? What formal provisions will be made to protect client rights?

What provision will be made to evaluate the assessment process over time and, if necessary, modify the design to improve its utility?

Phase 3: Case Goal Setting and Service Planning

Setting Goals

Theoretically a care plan begins with formulating and negotiating goals
or objectives with each client. In practice administrative policies to have
records contain an explicit goal statement for each case are frequently
weathered away. Many programs report that writing goal statements is
not a comfortable step for clients or workers. Clients reportedly prefer
to state problems to be solved rather than ultimate aims. Workers reportedly prefer to state the services to be obtained rather than the anticipated results.

As a practical matter no evidence exists that case or program outcomes
are achieved when case goals are made explicit. Experienced clinicians
tend to advocate the use of explicit goal setting, especially with the frail
elderly. Frequently, different agencies have different objectives; expectations of the worker, the client, and the client's significant others may
all differ, leading to disagreements about the proposed solutions. Some
workers are committed to goal setting as a useful clinical technique for
engaging clients to participate actively in their own care planning and
follow-through.

Administrators and program evaluators find case goal statements or
objectives to be essential in judging goal attainment of the overall program. For example, the program goal may be to reduce inappropriate
institutionalization. If the program can be evaluated only by aggregate
data on the percentage of clients who are institutionalized, the findings
fail to take into account those clients for whom institutionalization may
have been the most appropriate solution. Case goals are one way to
consider clients in clusters for measuring achievements of the case-management program.

Specifying Attainable Objectives. Case goals, like program goals, must
be operationalized in terms of achievable objectives, which in turn are
translated into action priorities. Goals state broad aims such as "rehabilitation," "quality of life," or "independence." More specific guidance for the care plan is expressed in attainable objectives such as
"protection," "alleviation of stress," "maintenance at home," "diminished isolation," or "improvement of long-term custodial care." The
most commonly used goal statements by case managers, if goals are made
explicit at all, are at the level of securing services such as "to obtain a
homemaker," "to obtain psychotherapy," "to connect the client with
social activities." Lists of services to be obtained do not make clear the
objectives to be achieved. Therefore case records should specify the

objectives for which services are being secured: "to develop a better living arrangement," "to strengthen family ties and care-giving," or "to help client to adapt his life-style to cope with new chronic impairments or social losses." These kinds of objectives provide a base for the care plan and specific action steps discussed later in this chapter.

Issues of Goal Congruence. Whether case goals are implicit or explicit and regardless of the level of specificity of goals, case managers inevitably encounter goal conflicts, which must be acknowledged and if possible resolved. These conflicts arise with respect to objectives and action steps rather than at the level of broad goals. Disagreements may develop between worker and client; between family members and the client or worker; between case goals and program goals; between case goals and prevailing community values; or between different agencies working with the same client. The first two examples of goal conflict are exclusively a clinical concern and are discussed elsewhere in casework literature and in this project's publication, "Case Coordination with the Elderly: The Experience of Front-Line Practitioners." The other three examples will be illustrated here because they may call for assistance from the supervisor or administrator.

Case Goals and Program Goals. As noted earlier, the program's goal may be to avoid institutionalization, but in particular cases the goal may be to help the client to obtain institutional services. Another example is when the program's goal is to prove that comprehensive noninstitutional care can be provided at 75 percent of the cost of institutional care. In some cases there may be many catch-up costs, however, for previously neglected clients such as dental care, psychiatric consultation, and home repairs. Most programs have some provision for case review to authorize greater than average short-range expenditures for particular clients and for other special cases in which case goals appear to conflict with program goals or policies.

Case Goals and Community Values. Some cases are brought to the attention of the agency by neighbors, law enforcement personnel, and others who are convinced that the older person must be removed from his home. The precipitating condition may be filth, fire hazards, an excessive number of troublesome pets, wandering, threats to the safety of passersby, or suspected physical abuse by relatives. The case manager may conclude that the client's goal to stay at home is a feasible goal and proceed to take incremental, alleviating steps. The complainants may be insisting on immediate remedies, the newspapers may be pressuring for a prompt humane resolution, and regulatory agencies may be unwilling to delay actions that would undermine the case goal. Administrators must be prepared to handle the mediation of such conflicts. Meanwhile the case manager faces dilemmas regarding how much to deal with neighbors, law enforcement agencies, financial institutions, and alienated family members on behalf of the client without violating ethics of confidentiality and client consent.

Interagency Disagreements on Case Goals. Implicit or explicit conflicts over goals generally occur between agencies around different perceptions about whether the assessed conditions can be improved and around the degree to which client dependency is to be avoided. Other incongruities arise when the case goals lead to case plans that conflict with normal operating procedures of another agency. For example, some home-delivered-meals programs will provide meals only on a uniform schedule of days per week and require that the client be home to receive them. Meanwhile the case manager arranges for the client to spend one day a week at an adult day care program or wants to preserve the care giving of a relative who has been regularly visiting one day a week to prepare a meal. Such disagreements are often resolved in regularly scheduled or ad hoc interagency case conferences (see also chapter 3). Occasionally the administrator must present the test case to the other agency's executive or board in order to obtain a change in policy for cases like these or resort to a class action legal suit.

Implications of Case Objectives for the Care Plan. Practitioners sometimes have difficulty verbalizing their thoughts and decision patterns in translating assessment information into a care or service plan. One of the steps in the translation is a conscious or unconscious setting of case objectives. For example, assume that the case manager has found in the assessment that the client needs assistance with the activities of daily living. The worker has a choice as to whether to recommend or authorize a home-chore service or a home-health aide service. The case manager may make the choice on the basis of which kind of assistance will be most consistent with long-range goals. If the client has been resistant to the use of social services, the uniformed health aide may be more acceptable and pave the way to other needed personal care services. On the other hand, if the client needs to be weaned away from the sick role in order to regain a measure of independence, then the worker may choose the home-chore aide to avoid a medical image.

The type of service having been selected, the case manager may also recommend different intensities of service not based on physical functioning alone but on objectives related to the case goal.

If the main objective is to maximize the client's potential for self-care, the amount of service may be kept to a minimum.

If an objective is to strengthen the care giving of the family or friends, the amount of service will be modulated to fill gaps in care.

If an objective is to reduce depression in the client and among family members whose physical or emotional capacities are stretched to the limit in providing care, the amount of service will be increased to provide respite.

If an objective involves new major demands on the client and family to effect a basic change in the client's situation, the amount of day-to-day personal care service might be increased for a while in order to free energies of the family to carry out the more comprehensive and demanding tasks.

Such gradations in levels of care require good communications about case goals and objectives, not only between workers of different agencies but also among workers in the same agency. This is especially so when there are checks and balances to monitor the use of purchased service or competition among case managers to access scarce resources for their respective clients.

A troubling trend exists for administrators to ignore the possibility of modulating services in individualizing case goals. Some program administrators are seeking ''algorithms'' or standardized care packages that can be prescribed on the basis of quantified data in the assessment. Such efforts seek to reduce the use of human judgment in care planning and make it possible to use inexperienced workers as case managers and to make case costs more predictable. This trend overlooks the facts that the same impairment profile will have different meanings for different clients and the same service package will have different potential benefits for individuals whose perceptions, trust, natural support network, and coping styles differ. Until better predictive measures of client attitudes and behaviors are devleoped, we must rely on well-qualified clinicians to combine quantifiable information with intuitive judgment to explain variations in case outcomes. To this end administrators should keep internal lines of communication open so that workers can bring attention to instances in which program policies such as cost limits, time limits, and preplanned service packages have unintended negative consequences on case achievements.

Choices in Case Goal-Setting Policies. In summary the administrator has several policy choices to make:

To what extent will explicit case goals or objectives be required?

To what extent will the program require that case goal concurrence be formalized—signed by client, agreed to by family, and distributed to cooperating agencies as part of the care plan?

To what extent will case managers be delegated discretion to exceed care-plan norms in order to achieve individual case objectives?

To what extent will statements of case objectives be utilized as a variable in the management information system or in evaluative research?

How much effort are the program's administrators prepared to invest in in-service training, supervision, and staff meetings to develop worker's skills in formulating and negotiating statements of case objectives?

The Care Plan

The care plan is the action agenda for all concerned. Many case-management programs use a standardized written service plan for each client which is then shared with the other agencies involved. Others use written plans only in-house. In some programs no formal plans are written at all. Whether care plans are formal, standardized, written or not, the principal problem for administrators as well as for case managers is to preserve as much time as possible to search out the options and engage all relevant actors in the planning process.

What the Care Plan Contains. Presently there is no uniformity across the country with respect to formats or scope of service plans. The medically oriented programs tend to use case files that combine assessment and care plan information in a problem-oriented record. Few if any care plan formats allow for the fact that the original plan drafted by the case manager undergoes many changes in the process of gaining client consent and obtaining commitments from service providers. Few service plan formats allow for recording actions or services that would have been ideal but that were not feasible and the reasons why. Many programs use a "service plan" that deals only with formal services to be obtained for the client. In general, the care plan should record

the desired outcome (objectives);

what is to be done by the client (such as signing documents, informing relatives, requesting services directly, self-care);

what is to be done by family, friends, or neighbors;

what is to be done by the case manager;

what is to be done by other workers within the agency;

what is to be obtained from other agencies (in what sequence, for what duration, how paid, whether additional specialized assessment is needed, what desired but not available); and

what events will trigger a new step in the plan, reassessment, or a revised plan.

The Functional Scope of the Care Plan. The functional scope of the care plan is related partly to program policy, partly to the skill level of the case manager, and partly to the needs and trust of the client. In almost all programs the plan focuses on the *instrumental needs* of clients such as income, help with activities of daily living, home maintenance, mobility, and access to medical care for physical needs.

Programs with significant psychosocial emphasis also address the *affectional needs* of clients in both care plans and worker activities. Service packages tend to include counseling, psychiatric day care, socialization services, or friendly visiting. Worker activities are likely to include frequent meetings with the client and telephone contacts to provide moral support and to keep clients engaged in the planning and action process.

Case managers in many settings report that they select services and focus their own activities on *helping to build capacities* in and around the client so that long-term case management will not be needed. Case managers may hold "network" meetings of relatives and friends, counsel or teach significant others how to take care of the client, refer spouses or adult children to services they themselves may need, arrange for neighbors to be paid as caretakers, and, most important, teach the client how to take over the referral and monitoring functions of the case manager and to discontinue services where they are no longer needed (see also chapter 7 regarding worker roles and tasks). Programs that include affectional needs and capacity building within the scope of the case manager's functions take a developmental view that goes beyond problem correction to educational and other enabling interventions to enhance the client's potential.

Considerations in the Selection of Services. The following checklist presents considerations of which the administrator should be aware in evaluating care plans and in developing interorganizational linkages for needed services (see chapter 3).

the case objectives (based on presenting problem and comprehensive assessment);

the services already in place;

the inappropriateness of any client requests that may be due to misinformation or lack of awareness of better alternatives; that ignore eligibility criteria such as income, geography, or functional status; or that may produce more dependency than needed.

client values and preferences and how these affect the client's readiness to act.

which plan would produce the least drastic changes in the client's normal life-style (an incremental approach, for example);

whether the needed kind of service exists in the community. If it does not exist, can it be created? It may exist but

> has too long a waiting list;
>
> may require medical but not social or emotional necessity as basis for eligibility;
>
> is too deficient in quality of service,
>
> does not respect the referrals from case managers,
>
> exceeds cost limits of program; or
>
> the client refuses it on the basis of past experience or prejudice.

Design Choices in Care-Plan Administration. Many of the choices of the administrator are the same as in previous steps regarding level of staff expertise required; the degree of formalization and standardization of format; the extent to which written plan is to serve clinical purposes, administrative purposes, or research purposes; and the extent to which plans will be subject to review by supervisors, staff groupings, or interagency committees. In addition, choices in care plans include the following questions:

> To what extent will the written plan be used as a "contract" with the client, significant others, and with cooperating service providers?
>
> To what extent will the written plan be used to identify gaps in available services for action at the system level?
>
> To what extent will the case manager be provided with support personnel to search for, negotiate for, and create needed services?

To what extent are case managers encouraged to go beyond planning for instrumental needs alone and become involved in affective and capacity-building concerns?

To what extent will care plans be monitored to balance demands for services among cooperating agencies?

To what extent are case managers also to provide direct services?

Monitoring of care plans is also a way to identify worker biases that develop in favor of purchased services and in avoidance of hard-to-get services when such biases run counter to the interests of clients.

Phase 4: Care-Plan Implementation

The characteristic that most distinguishes good programs from mediocre ones is thorough plan implementation—the breadth, intensity, and skill of follow-through. Generally case managers know much more about implementation than they use. They are often constrained by time and budget. They are discouraged by administrators who evaluate personnel by their performance in other tasks but not in care-plan implementation tasks. They are discouraged by administrators who transmit implicit messages that workers should avoid conflict. Aggressive care-plan implementation sometimes calls for risking conflict and always bears the risk of making mistakes. At the same time the troubleshooting, problem solving, and task achievements in care-plan implementation are the most gratifying parts of the case manager's job. Needless to say, implementation is the key to client satisfaction and benefit.

Examples of Implementation Tasks. When the service or care plan is ready for implementation, a number of tasks need to be performed with the client and the client's natural support system, with other agencies that will be providing services and within the case management agency (see also chapter 7). The tasks of implementation include the following:

Working with the Client and Natural Support System

giving information about services to come;

modeling behaviors in how to secure services;

providing support or sharing responsibility for obtaining services;

counseling on understanding problems, seeking solutions, carrying out plans for change, evaluating changes;

helping out with a specific task or doing it for the client;

confronting the client with how he may be exacerbating own problem;

engaging clients and others in monitoring services in the home;

preparing for reductions or termination of services.

Working with Service Providers

informing agencies about the case manager's work with the client;

purchasing services (if provided in program);

encouraging providers;

monitoring the delivery of service;

mediating conflicts between providers or between client and provider;

becoming an advocate or ombudsman when necessary to obtain or correct a service;

correcting resource files (or service directory) to reflect actual performance of providers;

creating new service for a client or class of clients;

identifying and reporting barriers to service delivery;

troubleshooting arrangements with landlords, utility companies, tax officials, zoning or sanitation departments;

requesting progress reports from providers as needed.

Working within the Agency

informing ancillary personnel as needed;

reporting barriers created by agency policy or procedures;

making and updating reports essential for case records, administration or evaluation;

obtaining consultation if needed.

Design Choices in Administering Care Plans. Once again the conditions and policies set by the administrator will determine the breadth and intensity of the case manager's ability to follow-through. The conditions will be affected by the answers to these questions:

To what extent does the case manager carry sole responsibility for implementation. Conversely, to what extent are support personnel provided—such as resource procurers, staff specialists, case aides, fiscal and file clerks, secretarial services, and courteous, well-informed receptionists at the telephones to channel calls?

To what extent are there interagency linkages to facilitate access to services (see chapter 3);

How much importance does the administrator communicate regarding follow-through as compared with other agency tasks?

Phase 5: Reassessment and Termination

Reassessment may consist of a full replay of the original assessment process or a partial update of the conditions most central to case goals. In a highly clinically oriented program, assessment is a cumulative, incremental process; therefore it may be said that in such programs reassessment is being done by the case manager or counselor on a continuous basis. In programs in which the case manager has responsibility for controlling purchased services or has guardianship responsibilities with some clients, a formal, periodic reassessment is usually required to assure that costs are justfied and that the client is assured maximum independence commensurate with his condition.

The purpose of reassessment is to determine whether services need to be changed in any way. Changes may include replacement of one service by another, modification of intensity of service, or termination of services. These considerations apply not only to the services obtained through case management but also to the service of case management.

Reassessment may be precipitated in a number of ways:

at standardized intervals prescribed by agency policy—six weeks, three months, or six months;

on a schedule written into the care plan based upon the case manager's expectations;

when a new worker is assigned to the case;

when the continuing worker thinks that a better level of trust has been established than at the outset, as when the presenting problem has been resolved, alleviated, or redefined;

when a planned service is discontinued by the service provider or the client;

when there is planned withdrawal of a service and a need to help the
client to see the change in a positive light;

when a new, unanticipated crisis or impairment befalls the client or
family or there is an unanticipated improvement in the client's situation;

when there is agency pressure to terminate improved or stable cases
to make way for new, waiting clients;

when there is a change of living arrangements. (For example, visiting
nurse services generally reassess a client two days after the client
returns home from the hospital, nursing home, or home of a relative.
Client capacities for self-care often improve greatly.)

In addition to updating the status of client functioning, reassessment
provides an opportunity to obtain feedback on the client's satisfaction
and commitment to the existing care plan.

Design Choices in Reassessment. The various administrative choices described under assessment also apply to reassessment regarding purposes,
personnel, and degree of formalization. In addition, the administrator
must decide the following:

To what extent will the frequency of reassessment be standardized
by policy or left to the discretion of individual workers?

To what extent will reassessment findings, by policy, determine continuation of the case or level of costs, and which data will be essential
for updating the information system, if any?

By what method will information obtained during reassessment (client
satisfaction, barriers to services, unintended consequences of program's policies and procedures) be reported to administrators?

Reasons for Termination

In our study of case loads in six cities, the majority of cases were regarded
as long-term clients. Front-line practitioners expressed a reluctance to
terminate cases when there are improvements in the situation because it
is then very cumbersome (with new paperwork) to reopen the case if
changes occur later. At the same time practitioners agreed that in selected
cases termination not only helps to reduced excessive caseloads but also
makes it possible to "graduate" a client to a renewed level of independence.

The more successful a program is in targeting to the most vulnerable elderly, the greater percentage of the caseload is carried for the long term. There are a number of occasions, however, when cases are terminated. The following list represents the most common reasons for terminating clients:

The client himself terminates.

The principal service provider recommends termination.

The case goals have been achieved.

A single service provider accepts comprehensive responsibility for the care.

The client enters an extended care facility, hospice program, or dies. (Some programs, fortunately, are able to continue case coordination service while the client is temporarily hospitalized or lodged in a nursing home; others do not.)

The client insists on services that the case manager thinks will be counterproductive or refuses recommended services plans or in other ways is considered so uncooperative as to waste resources or risk the agency's credibility or liability. (Some practitioners use a last-resort threat of termination to precipitate a crisis in order to reengage the client in the case management process.)

The presenting problem has been alleviated and the case manager thinks that the client or caretaker can carry responsibility for the service procurement and coordination tasks.

Demands for services and scarce resources make it necessry to set priorities among clients and withdraw services from those who can still benefit but whose needs are less hazardous than others.

For the administrator there are two problems that are endemic in termination. One is the understandable desire of workers to hold on to some of their successful cases as a respite from many frustrating cases. Administrators must have empathy for the workers' needs to balance their case loads while distributing limited resources equitably.

The second problem is a related one of helping staff to maintain their morale in the face of inevitable failures. On some occasions case managers will have to accept the fact that in spite of all they do, they will not be successful with all of their cases. No system known can adequately meet the needs of everyone who needs help. At the same time the administrator must provide avenues of advocacy for the workers and the program's leaders to change those societal or system limitations that are not inevitable.

Design Choices Regarding Termination. The administrator, probably with the involvement of the governance body, must clarify to what extent the various reasons for termination will be recognized by the program. Related to these decisions is a basic stance regarding whether or not to establish a waiting list when program capacities no longer can stretch beyond existing caseloads. If the program wishes to avoid having a waiting list, it inevitably must set priorities for which clients it will retain and which new clients it will accept beyond the prescreening phase. To the extent that terminations may result from client initiative or impasses between workers and clients, the administrator may establish a policy whereby a separate case manager, a supervisor, or a case-review committee investigates the circumstances to see if there are misunderstandings or mismatches of personalities before formally terminating a case for these reasons.

Maintaining Relationships with Former Clients

While most programs must mobilize all their resources for serving the clients at hand, some programs regard it as a wise investment to maintain a communications link with former clients. This kind of follow-up helps to reinforce client achievements, track program results, and keep access open to old and new clients when adverse changes occur.

Purposes of Extended Contact. Specific purposes for ongoing communication after case termination or deactivation include

keeping the door open for former clients whenever the case-management service is needed again;

facilitating the referral by former clients of new clients;

providing feedback to staff regarding client progress (for staff morale) and extending a gesture of continuing interest and friendliness on behalf of workers;

providing ongoing moral support to clients (they do not need to get worse to get attention) as an intervention with its own value to the client;

supporting the ongoing service provider, if any, by recognizing the value of their continuing service to the client and showing the programs' readiness to assist when necessary;

ensuring the earliest possible alert to clients' pending discharge from a hospital or nursing home for which case management may be needed; and

giving "drop-out" or service-rejecting clients a second chance. (Some older persons refuse service for fear that control of their lives will be taken out of their hands. After they have tested the agency's acceptance of their right to refuse, many will accept service when a second opportunity is offered.)

Some Methods for Keeping Access Open. The basic choice for the administrator is whether or not to allocate any resources at all to maintaining relationships with former clients. While there are some values to such follow-up being done by each client's case manager, there are also options that call for well-oriented clerical personnel, use of volunteers (especially retired professionals), and surveys by university students in professional schools. Precautions must be taken to respect former clients' rights to privacy. Some of the methods for follow-up include

referring clients, before termination, to ongoing programs of telephone reassurance or friendly visiting whose workers are aware of the case management program should the need arise at a later time;

routine mailings of greetings at a holiday season or on the client's birthday or on the anniversary of leaving the program;

routine offering of a short-term service, for former as well as current clients such as assistance with annual tax forms or senior discount identification cards;

periodic consumer satisfaction surveys or evaluation studies of client status;

periodic requests to other agencies that have continuing contact with the program's former clients; and

including former clients on the mailing list for the program's newsletter.

Summary

A generic client pathway has been outlined and many of the techniques used by past and present programs listed. We have highlighted many decision issues for the program planner and administrator. A recapitulation of the client-level functions appears in table 1–1. The following chapters and tables describe issues and program choices to be made by planners, administrators, and governance bodies concerning the client level, the organization level, the service system level and, sometimes, the legislative level that directly or indirectly affect what happens to clients of a case-management program. Decision makers will need to mix and match these design choices in the light of what is desirable and feasible in their own settings.

Suggested Readings

Austin, C.D. "Case Management in Long-Term Care: Options and Opportunities," *Health and Social Work* 8, no. 1 (Winter 1983):16–30.

Beatrice, D.F. "Case Management: A Policy Option for Long-Term Care." In Callahan, J.J., Jr. and Wallack, S. (eds.), *Reforming the Long-Term-Care System,* Lexington, Mass.: Lexington Books, 1981, 121–161.

Center for the Study of Aging and Human Development, Duke University. *Guidelines for an Information and Counseling Service for Older Persons.* Durham, N.C.: CSAHD, 1973.

Frankfather, D.; Smith, M.; and Caro, F. *Family Care of the Elderly.* Lexington, Mass.: Lexington Books, 1981.

Grisham, M.; White, M.; and Miller, L.S. "Case Management as a Problem-Solving Strategy." *PRIDE Institute Journal of Long-Term Home Health Care* 2, no. 4 (Fall 1983).

Hageboeck, H. *Training the Trainers Manual: Iowa Gerontology Model Project.* Iowa City, Iowa: University of Iowa, 1981.

Kahn, A.J. "Perspectives on Access to Social Services." *Social Work* 15 (April 1970):95–101.

Kane, R.A., and Kane, R.L. *Assessing the Elderly.* Lexington, Mass.: Lexington Books, 1981.

Steinberg, R.M. "Access Assistance and Case Management." In Monk, A. (ed.), *Handbook of Gerontological Services.* New York: Van Nostrand Reinhold, in press.

Stumpf, J. *Case Management with the Frail Elderly: A Training Manual.* Vols. I & II. Long Beach, Calif. SCAN (Senior Care Action Network), 1981.

U.S. Comptroller General. *Information and Referral for People Needing Human Services: A Complex System that Should Be Improved.* Washington, D.C.: General Accounting Office, 1978 (Report to the Congress, HRD-77-134).

2 Organizational Influences

Responsibility for a coordinated community care program is usually lodged in an umbrella organization or lead agency. The lead agency may retain the case-level coordination function (case management) or delegate it to one or several case-management agencies. On the other hand, many case-management agencies are not a formal part of any wider community care program.

In this chapter we ask readers to consider five influences on case-management organizations and to apply the discussion to whichever agency type may be their focus of attention. The principal influences are (1) primary mission, (2) organizational setting, (3) authority base, (4) professional reference groups, and (5) target populations. Additional organizational influences will be listed in this and subsequent chapters. This chapter will illustrate how these influences result in different configurations of organizational structure, capacities, and policies that in turn affect the focus, functions, and abilities of the case manager to help clients.

Primary Mission

Generally case-management programs have three organizational levels: the community service system, the operating agency, and the client–worker level. Each level has organizational objectives, but one or two will be given priority based on the program's mission. For example, a research-based experimental program will serve needy clients, but its primary mission is to produce knowledge as a basis for policy, program planning, or innovation in practice. Such a mission will require the organization to make a larger-than-average commitment to researching outcomes. Provision must also be made for considerable demands upon staff to participate in national and local information sharing and planning. In demonstration research, the organization must provide itself with expertise for data gathering and evaluation, and its case managers often must sacrifice client-service time to data-generating tasks, and accommodate to standardized procedures that may create barriers to rapport between worker and client.

Another example of a primary mission would be the coordination of services on a programmatic as well as client-level basis in order to influence the distribution of human service resources and to work toward the modification or development of other services. In this case the program will need to engage in an ongoing planning role, mobilize control over the funds of other agencies, and engage in community organization activities far beyond the average client-centered program.

By far the majority of case-management programs for the elderly are primarily client centered. At earlier points in their history many of these were initiated as model projects or demonstration programs addressed to testing policy, improving practice, or developing a comprehensive and coordinated system of services at the local level. In some communities, as programs progressed toward continuity and stability, they moved into new auspices prepared to continue the program on a long-range basis. Although leaders of a client-centered program may be involved in providing assistance to local, state, and national efforts to improve policies or work toward system change, the major consideration in program design and the first consideration in allocating agency resources is the degree to which that organization can succeed in serving the clients well on a one-by-one basis.

In our study as well as many others no significant differences in the objectives or performance of organizations were found on the basis of whether they were governmental, private nonprofit, or quasi-governmental. Rather, differences appear to be based on the autonomy of the case-management program relative to its host agency setting and the sources of its authority. Table 2–1 illustrates ways that program goals influence functions at the client level.

Organizational Setting

Another kind of influence is the type of home base the program has—the original sponsor or auspice of the program. Examples vary with respect to the relative autonomy of the case management unit within a larger program. Seven types of settings are discussed here: (1) the freestanding agency, (2) special unit in a planning agency, (3) special unit in an information and referral (I&R) agency, (4) special unit in a direct service agency, (5) special unit in an institution or multifunctional agency, (6) a consortium or federation, and (7) membership associations. The advantages and disadvantages of each type are addressed.

The Freestanding Agency

A relatively infrequent type of organization is the freestanding agency; it has no other major program than case management and has an auton-

Table 2-1
Comparison of Program Goals in Relation to Program Functions at the Client Level

Entry	Assessment	Case Goal Setting and Service Planning	Care-Plan Implementation	Review and Evaluation of Client and Program Status
Purpose To identify and enroll clients most appropriate for objectives and capacities of program.	*Purpose* To understand the client as a whole person and be aware of strengths and needs in client's situation.	*Purpose* To clarify expectations and agree upon an individualized plan of services and other problem-solving activities.	*Purpose* To arrange and ensure that services and other help are provided and utilized effectively.	*Purpose* To update knowledge of client and situation for possible revisions in client plan or for management of agency resources.
Guidelines If the primary program goal is "comprehensive service delivery to most highly vulnerable" (at risk of institutionalization) or "cost containment" or "equity for underserved groups" (ethnic, rural, or low income), then casefinding is narrow and focused; prescreening and intake criteria are highly specific. If the primary program goal is "improving access to services," "enhancing service coordination (build system)," "filling gaps and increase supply of services," then entry activities and intake	*Guidelines* If program goals include advancing policy or practice by "evaluation and other research," then assessment may need to include additional data not needed for practice. If program goals do not give importance to "system-building," then assessment can be limited to problems for which program has remedies; otherwise assessment is comprehensive (holistic), even though some remedies may not be available at a given time. If program goals emphasize "comprehensive	*Guidelines* If program goal is "cost containment," then service packages tend to be limited to instrumental and most crucial needs. Justifications for high-cost services must be documented. Program goals such as "improving access," "enhancing service coordination," "comprehensive services," "equity," and "long-term care" require extending beyond instrumental needs of clients and take into account affective needs and opportunities for capacity building among clients and significant others so	*Guidelines* Regardless of goals, best practice maximizes available services before resorting to purchase of service or creation of new services. Some demonstration programs with ample resources for purchased services experience pressures to spend dollars within fiscal year, thereby undermining goals such as "long-term care," "system building," "cost containment," and "avoiding dependency." When program goals emphasize "improving access" or "equity for the underserved" or when	*Guidelines* If program goals include "gap filling," and "system building," then periodic analysis must be made concerning the relative use of different services, obstacles to service access, and unavailable needed services. All client-oriented goals require systematic review of such variables as who utilizes the program; which target groups are missing or drop out; variations in case plan and worker activities based on worker or client type;

Table 2–1 Continued

Entry	Assessment	Case Goal Setting and Service Planning	Care-Plan Implementation	Review and Evaluation of Client and Program Status
criteria may be broad and procedures relatively informal. If the primary goal is "long-term care in least restrictive environment," intake must be controlled to keep case load within agency capacity to serve; referrals to alternative agencies (who can meet needs of less complex cases) must be prompt and accurate. Target groups may include institutionalized cases.	service to most vulnerable." or "long-term care in least restrictive environment," then assessment must be multidimensional and requires interdisciplinary participation or consultation. If goal is "to improve access" or "equity for underserved groups," then assessment must be incremental to avoid early barriers to worker–client relationships. If goal is "cost containment" and worker-client contact is minimal, then reassessment or other updating of client functioning is frequent.	that service utilization is enhanced beyond the "active case" phase. Program goals that emphasize "avoiding dependency" will include case goals to maximize and enhance client's capacity for self-help and involvements of family and friends, thereby using formal service providers as a back-up or last resort. Program goals aimed at "system building" and "efficient use of scarce resources" must balance case needs with system needs in formulation of care plans (the art of the possible) and must prioritize client's access to resources. Risks of liability and dilemmas of client's rights increase.	case goals include affective support and client capacity building, then case manager or counselor contact with client must be relatively frequent and case loads must be smaller. When program goals emphasize "system building," or "improving quality of services" then service delivery must be carefully monitored and case loads adjusted to permit worker time for monitoring. Some programs lodge monitoring functioning with personnel other than case managers. When program goals include "filling gaps" in the continuum of services or "increasing supply of existing services" or "long-term care in least restrictive environment," the program must have funds for the purchase of	duration of case management service for different kinds of clients. If program goals emphasize "cost containment," or "efficiency," then cost analysis must be made including costs of both case management and direct services provisions; prompt termination of less needy cases must be monitored. If program goals include "long-term care in least restrictive environment," then cases must remain active even when client is in residential care; trained case managers or their supervisors must have delegated discretion regarding appropriate time to terminate a case.

Summary
Generalization: Different goals affect entry functions. Goal achievement requires goal emphasis supported by sufficient agency resources and clear interagency communication.

Summary
Generalization: There is no one ideal assessment tool or process based on "state of the art." A program's choice of scope, frequency, and degree of standardization of client assessment should be guided by program goals as well as by agency size, qualifications of personnel, and requirements of funding source.

services or to hire personnel devoted to program development, fund raising, and class advocacy. Community leaders in governance body can help.

Summary
Generalization: Regardless of what is said in proposals or brochures, the program goals that are actually addressed may be different from stated goals. A program's actual goal priorities should be reflected in case goals and service plans. Sometimes goals are in conflict. Ambiguous program goals leave results to the accidents of personal values and skills of individual workers.

Summary
Generalization: The personnel and cost of care-plan implementation are often underestimated and follow-up is incomplete. Techniques of follow-up should reflect program goal emphasis (service system improvement, case-by-case optimization of scarce resources, or long-term comprehensive care).

Summary
Generalization: Review and evaluation of client status is an essential way to assess goal achievement and to identify degree of goal slippage. Results may suggest two courses of action: (1) correct goal slippage through staff development and revision of program design or (2) revise stated program goals on the basis of improved knowledge, new demands on the program, or recognition of what is feasible.

omous governing body. This form of organization has both advantages and disadvantages. The freestanding agency has the most autonomy. Along with greater autonomy usually come greater challenges to establish credibility and maintain a supportive environment for the organization. It can be relatively free of historical organization policies and practices that impede the case-management work. It is able to carry out its coordination functions without risk of criticism for any direct service that might be of inadequate quality or inadequate supply since it is not delivering any direct service. Similarly it need not be a threat to other service providers on whom it must depend, because it does not compete in delivering any particular service other than the case management itself. The freestanding organization, assuming that it has access to funds, is often able to provide higher salaries to its professional personnel since it does not have to be as concerned with the comparability of salaries paid to employees of any umbrella organization.

Because the freestanding case-coordination agency has all its eggs in one basket, however, it is more subject to cash-flow problems and consequent interruptions in service. As with other single-purpose agencies it is more vulnerable to the rise and fall of funding for its kind of program. Over time, though, freestanding programs have fewer constraints against opportunistically modifying their programs so that their functions follow funding.

Special Unit in a Planning Agency

Another organizational pattern is the special case-management unit within a larger local health or social-planning agency. This in many cases is an area agency on aging (AAA) with a variety of program-planning and resource-pooling functions. In other cases it is part of the public social service department that may also be charged with the ongoing planning and resource allocation for Title XX of the Social Security Act. In still other cases both the AAA and the case-management units for the elderly are lodged within an umbrella human-resources agency.

When a case-coordination unit is lodged within a larger planning and resource allocation agency it has some advantages: It is more visible and easier for users to find; it has more influence with service providers who seek funds; and it has ready access to constituencies, funds, or special expertise such as fiscal management. Its administrative costs may be more hidden in the larger organization. It may also have more immediate access to program planners who might act on service gaps and deficiencies in quality of services.

Such a unit has the disadvantage of being responsible to an administrative leader who might be closer to interorganizational and political concerns than to client-level concerns. The unit within a planning agency may experience a spillover of the conflicts with service providers that arise from the other functions of the planning agency. For example, the planning function may involve denying funds to some agencies and conducting strict monitoring procedures toward other agencies or assisting organizations of the elderly to aggressively advocate changes in programs or policies of service providers. These spillover conflicts may impede cooperation that might be needed on behalf of individual clients being served by the case manager. Some special units within planning agencies, especially when under public auspices, have had difficulty in establishing job classifications with sufficiently high salaries to attract qualified clinicians to do the case management.

In many communities the AAA initiated and designed a network of special units for case coordination within other agencies. In these instances the AAA preferred not to operate the case management itself but to delegate it to other organizations. In our national survey of current case-coordination programs for the elderly (1979), 15 percent of the case coordination programs were lodged within an area planning agency while 70 percent were receiving funds from the Older Americans Act, which are generally provided through an AAA. In contrast with this overall picture are those states in which the state unit on aging took an early and strong stand favoring case management for the frail elderly. In Pennsylvania, for example, after eight years of local option approximately 80 percent of the AAAs administered their own unit for service management rather than subcontracting to service providers. In Massachusetts many agencies were designated to carry on the functions of an AAA that had previously been established as a home care corporation, with case management and home-delivered services as its mission.

Special Unit in an Information and Referral Agency

A third kind of organizational setting is a special unit within an established information and referral (I&R) agency. There are many advantages to this kind of location. An I&R agency generally has a comprehensive awareness of the many kinds of services available in its community. It is usually viewed as nonthreatening and noncompetitive by the network of existing service providers. Its image is not stereotyped in terms of the kinds of people it serves or the kinds of service it provides. It tends to have personnel who are accustomed to eliciting from callers the essential information needed to clarify the problem and then to discuss various optional services that might be available to the client.

Such agencies have a tradition for documenting gaps in services available in the local community and then participating in ongoing planning councils to fill gaps in services. In many communities I&R agencies specializing in services to the elderly have also become the auspice for neighborhood outreach programs. There the agency engages in more-than-average home visiting not only for outreach but also for continuous counseling and assistance in securing needed services for the home-bound. Such program enrichments tend to occur when the I&R agency is lodged within a community planning council or AAA.

Many of the I&R's for the elderly established since 1973 have been severely underfunded and could not afford competent personnel. In such cases their reputations for inadequate service would be a disadvantageous base for a case-management program. Many small I&R agencies are not accustomed to the aggressive search for multiple funding sources and for the complex program and fiscal accountability procedures that funding sources for case management tend to expect. Almost every I&R gets into occasional short-term case management when it engages in several contacts with the client to clarify the problems or when there is difficulty in connecting the client with a particular agency that will assume responsibility for the case. In other words, it acts as case manager of last resort.

Special Unit in a Direct Service Agency

The largest number of case-coordination programs are operated by special units within direct service agencies such as those offering counseling (family service), homemaker or home health services, outreach, or home-delivered meals. Some of these direct service providers, such as the visiting nurse, have the advantage of accumulated experience in working with the home-bound elderly on a one-to-one basis. Others, such as family service, either have or can readily recruit the kinds of personnel needed to do case management. Their existing policies, attitudes of members of governance bodies, qualifications of personnel and case-finding techniques are usually compatible with the needs of a case-management program. However, when the case-coordination program becomes the purchaser of services and the monitor of other service providers, it may be criticized for its overlapping roles or conflict of interest. It may be criticized about the quality of its other direct service programs, for example, or accused of biases in assessing and planning services in favor of the kind it offers.

*Special Unit in an Institution or Multifunctional
Agency*

A fifth variation in organizational setting may be described as a special
unit within an institution or multifunctional agency. Examples of these
include a home for the aged that has expanded its function to serve elderly
people in their own homes or a senior multipurpose center that has a
special unit for home-based service for the vulnerable elderly who may
or may not have previously participated in the center's activities or services. A variation of this model is a special case-management unit located
within a hospital setting that serves not only those who have been dis-
charged from acute care but also people who have been referred from the
community. Such units for case management tend to benefit from the
long-standing and nonstigmatized reputations of their host agencies. There
is little evidence, however, that the personnel of such units have any
better access to the other services of host agencies than if they were
located elsewhere. Many front-line practitioners and administrators of
such units report difficulties in gaining acceptance within the larger, host
institution for the roles of case managers and the extra resources required
for a case-management program.

   Another variation of this organizational setting is the special unit for
assessment of those clients who are being recommended for residential
care with public funds. Such units are sometimes found in departments
of public social services or in health departments. The emphasis is usually
on assessment in order to divert clients from unnecessary institutionalization. The care-planning phase of case management is sometimes limited
to arranging for the instrumental services that are most essential for
maintaining the older person at home rather than dealing with the entire
range of psychosocial as well as medical needs of the client. In other
examples this special unit does assessment only in order to ensure that
alternatives to institutionalization are feasible and, if so, to make a referral
to an ongoing case-management agency that can address the multiple
needs of the impaired older person at the person's own home.

   The example of the multipurpose senior center is represented by so
many variations from community to community that it defies generalization. In some communities this term is used to describe the case-management program itself; in other communities a variety of services are
offered by the center in addition to other service providers who are
encouraged to outstation personnel. Some personnel of the center are
designated to address the needs of the home-bound elderly.

   Almost one-fourth of the agencies listed in the *1979–1980 Directory of Case Coordination Programs for the Elderly* reported that they function primarily as a senior center or multipurpose center. This trend appears to be growing as such centers are designated as "focal points" by the AAA for delivery of services in a portion of the planning and service area. In general, however, such centers are not being provided with adequate funds to staff and operate intensive and comprehensive case management programs. In such instances the quality of the program depends upon above-average skill and dedication of individual workers rather than on formal recognition of the requirements of a qualitative case management program.

Consortium or Federation

Another organizational arrangement is the consortium or federation, in which a variety of agencies (often including university departments) develop a cooperative agreement and shared governance for a case-management program that draws upon the resources of each of its members. Examples of these include the long-term-care gerontology centers sponsored by the Administration on Aging (AoA), which have as their mission not only service to individual clients but also the development of the state of the art, preparation of new professionals to undertake comprehensive programs in the future, and the conduct of research relevant to improved programming and practice.

Such consortiums have the advantage of a broad base of support and presumably access to resources of each cooperating organization that may be relevant to the case-management task. They are often allowed to operate without the traditional organizational constraints that any one of the cooperating agencies might have if the unit were placed within that agency as a host. They also tend to be viewed as more prestigious than any one of its members alone. Personnel derive some psychic rewards from the program's prestigious affiliations, and the program may encounter less resistance from service providers who view the program as more multifunctional and neutral than if it were in any one organization. On the negative side: The cooperative agreements may not be solidly based on planning; there may be ambiguities with respect to governance (everybody is responsible; therefore nobody is responsible); and the operation can become overloaded with a multiplicity of sometimes conflicting expectations.

Generally such federations or consortiums organize a demonstration program for a definite period (usually as long as the special funding lasts) with the understanding that the most valuable parts of the program will then be absorbed by one or more of the sponsoring organizations or that a new freestanding organization will be launched as a means to assure continuity and survival. It must be noted that although the programs that are sponsored by such ad hoc cooperative interagency agreements may undergo a great deal of change in becoming a sustained, continuing program (if it survives at all), frequently collegial networks and inter-organizational linkages are developed that continue to be valuable in the local system long after the demonstration ends.

Membership Associations

Finally, the organizational setting may be a membership association. At the present time this is a somewhat hypothetical model; therefore no experience has accumulated on which to judge its potential. There are many examples of occasional case advocacy by a leader or staff member of leagues of senior citizens, associations of retired professionals, labor unions, neighborhood councils, or tenants councils, but virtually no examples of formal case management programs under these auspices. A few health maintenance organizations (HMOs), in which consumers are presumably members through prepayment, are installing case-management units. New social and health maintenance organizations (SHMOs) are designed with a membership base, but this type of setting is still too new for generalized comment.

Other Variations

Besides the various kinds of organizational settings and special units for case management within certain kinds of agencies, there are many agencies that provide qualitative case management on an occasional basis or engage in considerable amounts of case management (differentiated case loads) under another name, like the geriatric unit within a community mental health center, the protective services unit of the public social services, or the home visitor of an I&R agency. Our conclusion is that the conduct of occasional case management by program staff whose primary responsibility is in another area is not a viable way for structuring a case-management program. The techniques of assessment, care planning, and follow-up require a continuous involvement in these processes and a continuous interaction with the network of services that are crucial to the clients. The time required and the emotional demands of case management with the vulnerable elderly tend to cause the person who carries two or more concurrent program responsibilities to retreat into the non–case-management aspects of the job.

Discussions of the advantages and disadvantages of these broad categories of organizational settings necessarily draw on generalizations. It must be remembered that there are a great many exceptions in each category so that an organizational setting that is totally disfunctional in the majority of communities may be the best bet in another community.

Authority Base

There are a number of ways in which case-management programs for the elderly attain the legitimacy and the authority to make demands upon the local service system on behalf of its clients. The following discussion includes four primary bases of authority common to case-coordination programs. In these bases, authority is derived from mandates through (1) public law, (2) incorporation, (3) time-limited funds, or (4) membership groups or associations.

Mandate by Public Law

Perhaps the strongest authority is that derived from a mandate stated in public law at some governmental level. For example, there are federal mandates for case management to population groups through grants-in-aid programs such as vocational rehabilitation and assistance to the developmentally disabled. For the multiply impaired elderly, however, the regulations permit rather than specifically authorize or require case management. Block grant regulations (Title XX of the Social Security Act) permit the use of funds for case management and for protective services without regard to income or assets. To the extent that the target groups and worker functions of these two programs are similar, authority for case management can be claimed by the local agency charged with the planning and administration of other Title XX services. The Older Americans Act, while calling for the provision of services on the basis of social or economic need, does not specifically require case management in each planning and service area, but, again, the use of Older Americans Act funds for this purpose is permitted.

Several state governments have passed legislation mandating some form of case management for the elderly, thus strengthening the authority of local programs. These are sometimes in the form of statutes requiring statewide coverage of adult protective services. In other states a network of multiservice centers has been established housing workers who specialize in aging services. Many states have instituted a program whereby prior to authorization of residential care a home visit and assessment must be done and, if feasible, a home-based care plan developed in lieu of residential care (this is called "mandatory prescreening"). Occasionally, case-coordination programs derive their authority from county legislation or ordinances in response to a shortage of residential-care beds or concerns about skyrocketing costs and, in a rare instance, as part of an overall strategy to develop a continuum of care within the local service network. Where authority stems from state or local government legislation, the actual case management might be operated by a governmental agency or subcontracted to a voluntary agency. In this case some of the authority accrues to the subcontractor.

An indirect source of authority may be derived from the courts. For example, in communities having public guardians or requiring follow-up services for former mental hospital patients, these agencies are facing pressures to ensure ''the least restrictive environment'' and maintain a ''whole person'' view of their clientele through the provision or arrangement of case-management services.

Mandate by Incorporation

A second kind of authority stems from a long history of programs within voluntary (private) agencies such as family service, visiting nurse, and neighborhood settlements. These are the types of agencies that developed home-care programs such as visiting nurse, homemaker services, and meals on wheels long before public legislation. They derive their authority from a board of directors within a nonprofit corporation or religious body, and from membership in a nationwide or worldwide movement on behalf of better services to people.

There is a great deal of variation from one locality to another in the degree to which these agencies meet the standards of their national accreditation body with respect to comprehensive case management. Some family services have limited their work to psychosocial counseling, with little attention to the medical and instrumental needs of clients. Many visiting nurse associations have been limited in their ability to continue with cases when the need for home nursing ceases. Most settlements and community centers in recent decades have limited their services to work with groups and have reentered the fields of home visiting and casework services only when special demonstration funds become available.

Such voluntary agencies have many advantages. They tend to have access to relatively well-trained personnel and, at the same time, have had experience in the use of paraprofessionals and volunteers. They have tended to participate in communitywide service planning and are aware of the network of agencies that may be relevant to care planning. In recent years they have gained considerable experience in expanding their services through purchase-of-service agreements with governmental agencies and have learned to deal with the complex accountability systems required by public funding. At times when human services face severe cutbacks in public funding, the voluntary agency has the advantage of a history of raising funds from private sources.

Voluntary agencies are relatively unstigmatized in the eyes of the public and among the elderly who tend to reject welfare and other governmental services. To the extent that these advantages exist in a given local voluntary agency, then, the agency's performance record lends authority to its case-management programs. Agencies that have no record of work with the elderly in general and the multiply impaired elderly in particular will have to establish a reputation through the excellence of their case management over time.

Mandate through Time-Limited Funds

The most widely known case-management programs for the elderly were initiated as a result of obtaining special demonstration funds. The development of such programs usually involves obtaining prior interagency agreements to carry out the program should the special funds be obtained. In these programs the authority radiates from the halo conferred by virtue of having been designated by a federal, state, or area agency to conduct a special program. In many cases additional authority comes from funds obtained by the agency for purchasing services from other service providers, which may include a waiver permitting Medicare or Medicaid funds to be spent for many home services without additional requirements such as previous hospitalization. Although demonstration grants are usually time-limited, as many as 60 percent of the programs begun under such circumstances were able to continue their work after these special conditions terminated. On the other hand, a number of projects have reported that sometimes crucial service providers are reluctant to join the coordination effort because they know that special funds for program expansion are time-limited.

Mandated by Membership Groups and Associations

A fourth and relatively rare base of authority comes from the membership of self-help or senior advocacy associations that call upon their own staff to act as case managers for their more vulnerable members. It is a bit more usual for association members or officers to act as case advocates or ombudsmen to ensure that needy members receive adequate attention from service providers. Some cases are so complex that they require continuous involvement that resembles case management.

Similar activities are sometimes engaged in by labor unions, professional associations, or private company's counseling programs on behalf of their retirees on an occasional, as-needed basis. Another example is in a Southern city where a senior housing cooperative arranged with the nearby university school of social work to have its students provide case-management services to home-bound residents. Where case management is conducted by a broad-based membership organization an additional authority base derives from the potential political influence of the members of the association and the association's potential access to the news media when speaking on behalf of its membership.

Finally, there are a very small number of private, proprietary (for profit) agencies who initially become involved in the case as conservator. Their authority is strictly derived from their clients (or the client's family) and is usually reinforced by a client's ability to pay for needed services.

These variations in authority base have different influences on the degree to which cooperating agencies will allow themselves to be coordinated. To the extent that case-management programs find themselves powerless to coordinate service providers, they develop tendencies to establish needed direct services within their own organizations. To the extent that agencies do have recognized authority to coordinate, they will need to structure themselves to handle responsibilities for interagency communication and program accountability.

Professional Reference Groups

A seldom discussed but nonetheless important influence upon program design and implementation is the professional reference group with which the organization is identified at the outset of the program. This initial identification may derive from the history of the host organization launching the case coordination program or from a particular person who is hired to direct or train workers for the program. This identification is further influenced by the staffing pattern (particularly which professional group is dominant within the staff) and the funding sources on which the program depends. These professional reference groups might be characterized alternatively as (1) medical/health service, (2) community mental health, (3) social welfare programs, (4) gerontological or aging network programs, and (5) others, including vocational rehabilitation and adult education. These categories are not mutually exclusive; each category has many subcategories that may be significant distinguishing characteristics (for example, governmental versus nongovernmental reference groups).

Identity patterns do not necessarily follow the lines of professional disciplines. For example, a master's level social worker might work within an agency whose identity resides in any of the five categories: a medical social worker in a hospital discharge unit, a psychiatric social worker in a community mental health center, a social case worker in family service, or a community organization and planning specialist as director of an AAA. These specialists differ with respect to the people with whom they are accustomed to working, the people whose esteem they value, and the organizations with whom they have established credibility even though there may be generic aspects to their intervention techniques and their code of ethics.

Just as individual social workers differ, so organizations are different with respect to the groups with whom they are accustomed to doing business, the groups whose esteem they value, and the groups with whom they have established some degree of credibility. Depending on their primary reference group, they have differing degrees of access, trust, and authority among various sets of organizations in their day-to-day operations. This may affect the capacity of the organization to provide comprehensive and coordinated services for its clients. Whereas some organizations will easily accept the case manager's client assessment and care plans, other organizations will be skeptical. Some organizations, more than others, will have empathy for the program's commitment to comprehensive service delivery to the multiply impaired elderly. Coordination programs using paraprofessionals or trained volunteers may find that some reference group organizations will be reticent to accept referrals or engage in cooperative activities except through another professional at a level comparable to their own.

It is the stance of the authors that no one of these domains or reference groups has preeminence in case management for the vulnerable elderly. In whichever domain the case-management function may be lodged, it will be important for the agency to develop compensatory linkages to those reference groups and sets of agencies with which ties need to be strengthened in order to do a comprehensive job in both client service and in system building.

In the next chapter we will discuss a wide variety of interorganizational linkages that might be employed. Several tactics merit special mention here as methods for enhancing relationships with new reference groups. One method is to hire a staff member who by virtue of education or experience has the credentials of merit in the eyes of the new reference groups and who is assigned to serve as liaison with those groups. A variation of this tactic is the method of employing a consultant on a short-term basis who has particular expertise and a network of relationships among the new reference groups with the precise purpose of assisting the agency staff to learn how to deal with hard-to-penetrate reference groups.

Another method is for a group to bring onto its own board of directors or technical advisory committee prestigious representatives of the new reference groups. A third prevalent method for establishing new relationships is through cooptation in the form of purchase-of-service contracts. This method usually requires more time to define and negotiate the new relationship and inevitably carries with it a moderate degree of stress if the purchase-of-service contracts are to be productive.

This discussion has focused on local reference groups, but note must also be made of reference groups which may be at the state or national level. To the extent that organizations relate to state or national bodies for certification, standard setting, technical assistance, funding streams, personnel recruitment, or program guidelines, these hierarchical relationships will also influence the design, administration, favored intervention techniques, and prevailing values of different local case management programs.

Target Group

Most planners and administrators in the United States recognize that the public is not ready to support universal service coverage to all who need services nor ready to support a continuum of care to meet the many different kinds and degrees of need in the community. Therefore U.S. program developers must look for ways to delimit the target population for a case-management program.

The criteria for delineating the target group may arise from an analysis of present use of services and their costs in relation to needs. Such analyses range from a communitywide survey to describe the neediest of the elderly to assessments of current use of nursing home and hospital beds to determine the extent to which humane and less costly substitutions of home services can be made for selected occupants. Many times, however, a local program relies on analyses performed at other places or sets its own course by the conditions for targeting or eligibility set by available funding sources.

A great influence on the organization is whether it sets out to serve a wide population within which a small percentage of clients need case management or whether it is established to specialize in clientele who need a kind of case management that is beyond the capacities of other broad-service agencies. In either case a broad target group may span a wide age range or a wide geographic catchment area or a wide spectrum of functional disabilities. A narrow target group can be wide or narrow with respect to age, geography, or need category while specific as to ethnicity, ruralness, or certification for institutional residency. In the range of delineations based on assessed functional needs there are various alternative parameters (very severely and severely impaired only versus moderately impaired or mildly impaired, at-risk persons, for example).

Table 2–2 deals with some of the program and procedural implications of broad versus focused target groups in relation to program functions at the client level. It provides a review of target groups from the perspectives of program design and administration of day-to-day operations. This narrative, in contrast, is concerned with target population as it influences basic organizational structure, governance, the organization's image in the community, and the organization's value system. These are powerful influences on how an organization positions itself and responds to the psychosocial, medical, and environmental realities within which the aged function.

Implications of Target Population for
Organizational Structure

There are a number of ways that target population bears upon the organization's authority, structure, and image. Some service providers believe that they already serve this special target group and will resist a new organization that acts as an intermediary between them and new clients. Other agencies will welcome a new intermediary who will help then deal with unfamiliar clients or ones who are particularly difficult to serve.

If the program is highly focused on the most vulnerable elderly then there may be difficulties of recruiting surrogate representatives of homebound consumers on boards of directors or advisory councils. If special target populations are widely dispersed, it may become difficult to represent all relevant groups on a board of directors, particularly if its size is limited in bylaws. This condition may make it necessary to set up an additional level of community or consumer advisory bodies or neighborhood committees in order to engage the several relevant constituencies in the governance of the agency or program. The agency's definition of the primary target population also has some influence on the program's acceptance in the community at large and in local legislative bodies.

One issue that cuts across many categories of target population is eligibility. The extent to which the organization must be concerned with strict eligibility criteria (such as income and assets) determines with which organizations it does business as well as the intake structures and procedures it needs in order to ensure compliance with those criteria.

Commonly Used and Abused Delineations of Target Population

Following are brief discussions of eight commonly used delineations of elderly target populations. Some of these illustrate the hazards of overly precise or misleading criteria. Others illustrate the need for a broad orientation and for an organizational resiliency that will permit case managers to deal with exceptions to targeting rules in an intelligent, humane way. For each of these delineations we will highlight some implications for the choice of organization to do case management or the influence that the selection of this target population may have on the organization's structure and linkages.

1. Older People with Multiple Impairments. There is a growing recognition of the interdependence of older people's susceptibilities to loss or impairment—social, economic, mental and environmental as well as physical. Although interdependencies of functional well-being pertain at all age levels, the elderly tend to be at greater risk in all these functions as their age advances. Entitlement to case management based on multiple impairments is a salient policy stance.

However, the multiple impairments criterion can have unintended side effects if it is abused (say by overenforcement) as a rationale for eligibility for either case management or for the direct services that a case-management program may control. Two contrasting illustrations follow. A client may have experienced a single traumatic loss, which can trigger subsequent losses if not properly handled, be it the death of a spouse, an acute medical problem causing temperory loss of mobility, or eviction from housing. The need for case management can be justified by the single threat and that problem can remain the sole focus of the intervention with an underlying assumption that proper resolution of the crisis will avert or at lease delay a domino effect on other latent problems. In contrast, an assessment of client impairments may show a multiplicity of disfunctions all relating to a single problem. For example, the problems of a client who reports that she has not prepared her own meals for a month, has lost all contact with relatives and friends, and feels listless (from psychotropic drugs) may all relate to an overwhelming depression. But an inexperienced worker or one who is under administrative pressure to record multiple impairments in clients may respond inappropriately with home-delivered meals, friendly visitors, and medical treatments for muscular pain, instead of approaching the overridding (and perhaps causal) problem of depression. In other, similar cases, the experienced

Table 2–2
Comparison of Broad versus Focused Target Groups in Relation to Program Functions at the Client Level

Entry	Assessment	Case Goal Setting and Service Planning	Care-Plan Implementation	Review and Evaluation of Client and Program Status
Purpose	*Purpose*	*Purpose*	*Purpose*	*Purpose*
To identify and enroll clients most appropriate for objectives and capacities of program.	To understand the client as a whole person and be aware of strengths and needs in client's situation.	To clarify expectations and agree upon an individualized plan of services and other problem-solving activities.	To arrange and ensure that services and other help are provided and utilized effectively.	To update knowledge of client and situation for possible revisions in client plan or for management of agency resources.
Guidelines	*Guidelines*	*Guidelines*	*Guidelines*	*Guidelines*
If the target group is narrowly focused, avoid broad outreach methods that will require extensive and costly prescreening.	A broad target group may be more economically and effectively assessed through incremental or successive phases.	Highly vulnerable groups such as the home-bound elderly require realistic case goal setting (for example, stabilization might be one goal).	Implementing care plans for a diverse and broad target group has an advantage in offering workers a respite from emotional drains of full attention only to the very sick.	Case reassessment, review of agency resources and policies, and case evaluation provide occasions for regrouping clients or redefining target groups.
If the target group is broad, outreach workers of other agencies in a catchment area are usually already available for case finding.	Centering on the presenting problem (with miniassessment) is often more acceptable to client expectations.	Some vulnerable target groups can be expected to continue their loss of functioning. Then case goals must be supportive and alleviating.	Plan implementation with highly vulnerable groups offer workers a specialization of skills, small case load, usually a priority access to resources for their clients.	Many high-volume programs fail to keep current about status of long-term clients and fail to sustain the differentiation necessary for case individualization, prioritizing resources and case-load management.
Client prescreening during case finding and intake is more essential for the agency whose target group is broad.	A target group that is highly vulnerable, prescreened by referring agencies, is generally ready for the comprehensive (whole person) assessment.	Locating and arranging services are the means or interventions for attaining case goals, not the goals per se.	When resources are scarce and the target group is highly vulnerable, programs may develop policies of short-term service	Agencies must periodically assess appropriateness of present clientele in light of originally planned targeting (relative penetra-
I&R service is one approach to prescreening for case coordination.	There is a distinct difference in purpose between collecting data about an	Too often the readily available resources distort		

agency target group for research and collecting information to be used for case diagnosis and service planning.

The greater the functional losses of health found in the target group served by the agency, the more is required of assessment staff in contacting doctors and other health experts and in assessing client's utilization of medicines.

When high vulnerability of the target group is related to social and affective losses, abuse, neglect, and similar problems, additional psychosocial assessment skills are needed.

Client screening at intake is minimal for an agency with a highly focused, vulnerable target group and with strong referral linkages to professional agencies.

Case-load controls are tight in agencies offering intensive services to a high-risk, narrowly focused target group.

Broad target group entry processes need funneling procedures to screen-in the appropriate cases.

An agency-defined target group will always include subtargets by program eligibility regardless if focused or broad.

Summary
Generalization: An agency's definition of its client target group(s) is of little value if its entry functions are not organized to identify and ad-

---

the service plan. "You need what we have," the client is, in essence, told.

Broad target group agencies may trim their client range at both ends, by referrals and a central focus on prevention and rehabilitation.

Service planning is always more cautious for high-cost care and scarce resources, purchased or arranged.

Time goals and structuring of time are applicable for all target groups but are emphasized more when resources are scarce.

Summary
Generalization: Assessment processes and procedures are more similar when the target groups are more homogeneous. The broader the target

---

and prompt delivery of the entire service package.

In ideal circumstances implementation of the planned service package can be incremental and can allow for sequential testing and building relationships over time.

Service utilization testing is equally important for all recipient target groups in early phases of implementation.

Case loss for a variety of reasons is more likely to occur in the initial period of implementation if services available do not meet client expectations.

Summary
Generalization: Intensive supervisory and administrative attention is needed for the agency's care-plan implementation functions, to avoid diverse and in-

Summary
Generalization: Case goals may be stated in terms of desired changes in client situation, in affect or capacities to function (rather than in terms

---

tion of the intended target groups; case loss; over-utilizers; waiting lists; equity on geographic, ethnic, and sex bases), and they must monitor case managers' tendencies to hold onto cases.

Coordination agencies with no termination or time policies may discover case files frequently are out of date regarding client status and that consequently both service delivery and program analyses are inaccurate.

The agency with a broad, heterogeneous target group has more difficulty in tracking current status of clients and in monitoring use of costly or scarce resources.

Summary
Generalization: Coordination agencies spend efforts in defining the target groups for entrance and in assessing needs, but the momentum for updating

Table 2-2 Continued

Entry	Assessment	Case Goal Setting and Service Planning	Care-Plan Implementation	Review and Evaluation of Client and Program Status
mit the appropriate clientele in a volume consistent with its capacity.	group, the greater the diversity of the diagnostic span and the greater the need for multidisciplinary expertise.	of services to be delivered). Case goal statements are not justified, however, when there is no known intervention or means of attaining the goal ends.	consistent procedures followed by different workers resulting in confusion and risk—for example, no rationale for variations in case service, no continuing feedback on changes in resource quality or quantity, irregular reporting on potential liability situations, no accurate count of inactive case population. The aim is to achieve a disciplined balance of support structure and worker ingenuity.	target group differentiation is frequently lost.

worker may indeed begin with these nonthreatening side issues in order to gain the client's trust for later mental health interventions to deal with the basic problem.

The point is that the targeting policy should not distort the worker's assessment or care planning in order to fit the client to the program's eligibility criteria. This issue becomes an interorganizational influence to the extent that other agencies are involved in case finding and in explaining the case-management program to clients, their families, and the community at large. An overly restrictive interpretation will result in important cases being missed, whereas excessive stretching of interpretations will result in misdirected referrals—false alarms. Ambiguities or sudden changes in the case management agency's criteria for clients will undermine interorganizational linkages.

2. Older People Needing Two or More Services. This criterion was used by our research project in its early phases (and subsequently dropped) as a way to differentiate case management from other forms of social casework, psychosocial counseling, or intraagency coordination of multidisciplinary treatment. As a policy for targeting it has three common hazards.

First, not all people who need multiple services also need someone to coordinate their case. Many can do the acquisition and coordination of services for themselves if they receive adequate information about their options from an information and referral program worker. Others have family members or other informal or formal caretakers whom the client relies upon for these functions. A task force of sixteen administrators concurred with a "guesstimate" that about one-half of the 10 percent of noninstitutionalized elders who need home services or multiple services do not need case managers.

The second hazard of designating multiple service use as a criterion was conveyed to us by most all administrators and practitioners who cooperated in the conduct of our study. Many older persons have multiple needs for help but either are unready to accept help from formal community service agencies or have needs that can be met by nonservice approaches or by relatives and friends without formal service delivery agencies. In these cases, it may be argued, the client should be referred for counseling or other programs that help to build and preserve the help-giving capacity of the informal support system. In many programs, when such referral is not acceptable to the client or no such resource exists in the particular community, the case manager is encouraged to assume these capacity-building tasks even when multiple services are not involved. Some programs provide partial case management to clients who are not eligible for the direct services the program can obtain. In such cases the assessment and care planning are aimed at helping the client and family to clarify the problem and to be aware of service options, and then the care-plan implementation is left to the client or his caretakers if services are needed and wanted.

The third limitation of the multiple-service criterion is best illustrated by cases in which the appropriate first step is institutionalization. Early case-management programs tended to terminate cases at the point when the client entered a skilled-nursing facility or an intermediate-care home. It was generally assumed that there was no longer a need to coordinate care since there was only one agency involved in "total" care. It is now recognized that entry into an institution may be a crucial time to intensify rather than withdraw case management so that the out-of-home episide may be short term. Case managers do not assume responsibility for the institutional care but, rather, assume crucial roles in helping family members to get respite and at the same time maintain their involvement with the patient, make preparations for some services upon discharge, and mobilize efforts to maintain the client's home intact so that it is a viable option when discharge can be considered.

The way that the case-management program treats these three issues will directly affect estimates of the size of the target population and consequently the optimal size of the case-management unit. The degree to which the program will work with clients who resist services or with families to teach them the case-management role will affect the staffing pattern, case-load size, and especially the qualifications for case managers. The extent and intensity of contact with clients who are in acute-care or long-term-care institutions may influence the choice of lead agency to ensure credibility, authority, and access to such medically oriented settings whose cooperation will be essential.

3. The "Old-Old." While most case-management programs are based on functional assessment as the key to entitlements, some programs fall back to a shortcut of chronological age as a way to target or prioritize cases. The old-old are usually defined as persons over 75 years of age. We believe that this approach to targeting is totally wrong.

The presumptive need of the old-old is based on random sample surveys that show that, *on the average,* vulnerability and chronic impairments increase with advancing age. In addition, data on in-patients at long term care facilities show disproportionately high percentages of the older group. It does not follow, however, that the case load of a case management program should limit itself to, or give priority to, the people over 75 years of age.

The programs that we studied tended to span the 60 and over age groups approximately in proportion to their numbers in the total population of elders (about 60 percent under 75 years of age; 40 percent, age

75 and over). Generally, the young-old in these programs were more severely impaired than the old-old. Many of these persons do not survive to become old-old. The young-old often needed more supports because their children were middle aged and still raising their own children, limiting their assistance to parents. The old-old often had surviving children who were retired or who at least had empty nests and therefore could attend to the needs of aged parents. It has been documented that even though minorities have a shorter life expectancy than white Anglos, the oldest survivors among minorities are in better health than their majority age-cohorts. This has been called the cross over effect. Programs focusing on the old-old also present a defacto inequity for those minority elders and to men in general, whose chances of survival to 75 years of age are below average.

This of course is not to argue for less attention to the old-old. The shortcut use of chronological age should be rejected or avoided in recognition of the many cases in which some young-old may have more urgent needs than *some* of the oldest persons of a community. This is not only a humanistic imperative but is also relevant for those programs aimed at cost containment. The most direct organizational advantage of this delineation is the relative ease with which it can be communicated to and understood by policymakers and funding sources, as well as by agencies that make referrals. We believe that this advantage is outweighed by the disadvantages of the program's participating in serious inequities.

Any discussion of chronological age must raise the underlying issue of why to restrict services to the elderly at all, whether the lower age limit is 55, 60, 65, or 75. It may be argued that services to the aged may be performed by persons with geriatric or gerontological knowledge but within programs that are for all age groups (age generic). The community's basic decision on this issue has obvious implications for the selection of appropriate agencies and for the essential interorganizational linkages and numbers of funding sources.

Historically, specialized services for the aging emerged partly in recognition that older persons were not being equitably served in age-generic programs. In addition, some modalities of service had to be modified and separate personnel trained to deal with particular needs, abilities, and preferences of the elderly. These special conditions remain salient today. Although there is clearly no uniform chronological age when old age begins, most programs begin entitlements at 60 or 65 on the basis that individualized functional assessments would be an excessively costly process for entry into such programs as nutrition, housing, transportation, or socialization.

On the other hand, in case-management programs for long-term care, in which functional assessment must be done in all cases, there is a trend to make such programs inclusive of all adults who are ill or severely impaired (beginning with 18-year-olds). As noted earlier, in programs of this kind the organization must widen its constituency base and increase the number of funding sources and interorganizational linkages. It must also have a sufficiently broad acceptance to deal with conflicting pressures from both advocates of aging and representatives of handicapped younger adults. The wider range of client situations and case goals will call for a more diverse staffing pattern than in age-segregated programs.

4. Those Needing Long-Term Care. A great deal of the momentum toward the development of case-management programs arises from efforts to reform the quality and costs of long-term care. They are part of the effort to provide care at home as an alternative to institutional care. Arranging alternative long-term care at home or in new nonmedically oriented living arrangements is a vital aspect of all case-management programs.

The organizational influences of a long-term care emphasis are many. However, there is a limitation in defining target populations primarily as those needing long-term care. Some programs will have no choice but to limit their entitlements to persons whose impairments are expected to be of long duration who might otherwise need institutional care. Other programs have, and should have, the flexibility to make case management available to an important group needing short-term intervention. Such short-term situations may include bereavement from loss of a loved one, victim of crime or adult abuse, or recovery from an accident or acute illness. Another example of what may be short term in some cases is hospice service for the terminally ill. Working with a short-term crisis may uncover long-term needs. With some clients there may be no "risk of inappropriate institutionalization" and no apparent need for long-term care, but case management may be suitable.

The organizational influences of a long-term care emphasis are many. The organization chosen to be lead agency must be credible and competent to deal with both medical and social aspects of care. Current leglislative trends require the lead agency in long-term care to have competencies in negotiating and managing huge amounts of funds for the purchase of services and for precision in eligibility determination. To the extent that the program has control over funds for medical and social service delivery, it must remain cost conscious in care planning and be structured to deal with exceptions and appeals in its rationing of services. An important organizational issue for the community at large when one program specializes in long-term care is whether separate programs should be established for the elderly who do not need long-term care but who do need case management for other reasons and, conversely, whether the same program should be expanded in scope to include all case-management clients.

5. The Underserved. Occasionally a program is organized with the objective of facilitating equitable use of existing services by subpopulations known to have relevant needs but tending to underutilize available services. The target population may be a particular ethnic minority group, rural or suburban residents, newcomers, or persons with a particular handicap such as deafness or blindness. In these programs case management can be valuable for the complex cases involving reticence of clients or ineptness or indifference of service providers as well as for the spectrum of individual situations described elsewhere.

An example of organizational implications is that many underserved populations, such as non–English-speakers, will make it necessary to have special front-line personnel who communicate well with each subpopulation and have administrators who can devise culturally sensitive program adaptations. Furthermore, in communities where pressure exists to discover and deport noncitizens who lack legal immigration status, it would be counterproductive to lodge case management for the underserved in a public agency that is obligated to report such noncitizens to the immigration service.

Not all underserved individuals or groups need case management. An efficient program to achieve equity of service access will surround the case-management component with other components such as outreach, information and referral, community organization, ombudsmen or case advocates, public information campaigns, translation services, support groups, or demonstration direct services especially designed for the needs and capacities of the target population. Only some of the individuals in such program components will need case management. Another kind of organizational and programmatic choice is whether to establish a case-management program that specializes in the target population or, instead, to advocate and assist existing case-management programs to adapt to the special characteristics of the underserved group.

6. Those Receiving Inappropriate Services. Rarely is a case-management program addressed solely to the objective of diverting clients from using inappropriate or unnecessary services, yet such diverison appears among the tasks of case managers. Most programs with the stated objectives of avoiding inappropriate institutionalization tend to direct their intervention to clients at some point *before* entering a skilled nursing facility.

Some programs, however, do enter the nursing home, hospital, or intermediate-care facility to assess the potential of in-patients for alternative, less restrictive care at home. Other agents, such as Professional Standards Review Organizations (PSROs) and eligibility workers, are assigned to validate that the client is entitled to a service by virtue of impairments but are not usually responsible for exploring less restrictive, less costly alternatives.

Case managers are usually responsible not only for seeking the least restrictive environment and the least costly set of options but also for assuring that client choice is being respected while at the same time services "do no harm" by fostering overdependency or unnecessary helplessness. Such a mission not only calls for monitoring in-patient stays but also for monitoring such services as home chores, "meals on wheels," and home health services. In cases where family members or others in the informal support network may be overdoing things for the client— with the risks of inducing overdependence in the client and burnout of the care-giver's helping capacity, the case manager may need to intervene.

Case-management programs vary greatly in the extent to which they have control over direct service resources, as noted in other sections of this book. To the extent that the program is a gatekeeper or rationer of scarce resources, the workers must make hard choices regarding which clients get how much of the available services. Thus pressure develops to withdraw services from some clients in order to redirect those services to other clients with greater need. The driving force is not one of saving clients from inappropriate or counterproductive services, since the persons from whom service is being withdrawn may have a legitimate, though lesser, need. In the sometimes unhappy process of gatekeeping, the review of service plans may lead to discovery of cases in which less restrictive or less costly services would be of greater benefit to the client (see also Chapter 3, on monitoring). These cases may involve a reassessment that results in a useful redefinition of the problem. Such cases occur, for example, when physical medical services have been overutilized and ineffective because the disabilities were from emotional rather than physical impairments or when case management or counseling is being used only for moral support and socialization, in which case friendly visiting or telephone reassurance may be substituted.

Two important organizational influences emerge. First, a case-management program that seeks to intervene between service providers and their existing clientele must have a widely accepted mission and an especially strong authority base. Second, the program that is a gatekeeper of scarce resources must be structured to deal fairly with appeals and with

possible litigation. Its conduct of assessments and care plans (and therefore its personnel) should be sufficiently competent to "stand up in
court."

7. Those without Informal Social Supports. Numerous studies have
shown that older persons who live alone and who do not have relatives
and friends to assist with personal care are most prone to use insitutional
care. Thus it is reasonable to target case management to those who lack
social support. There are two common hazards to using this criterion for
entitlement.

First, living alone is not a sufficient indicator of isolation or risk.
For many elders, living alone is related to liberation, economic well-
being, and successful coping. There is mounting evidence that many
elders who live with relatives and need help from them suffer more
depression than those in their own home who obtain help from formal
agencies and nonresident kin, friends, or neighbors.

Second, care from family members is not always helpful—whether
there is direct abuse or an excess of dependency-breeding, guilt-driven
family care. When an older person is utilizing valuable help from an
informal support network, the members of that network may need the
help of a case manager to bring an objective assessment of the situation
and to arrange for respite. In rare cases the client may be receiving
conflicting or overabundant help from too many uncoordinated informal
sources.

There are a few demonstration programs whose mission is to develop
and disseminate techniques for reinforcing the informal support system
of at-risk older persons, but, in general, case-management programs must
include some clients with, and others without, informal social supports.
The relative need and the appropriate response must be based on individual
assessments.

The chief organizational implication of this delineation is that if a
given program emphasizes only those without social supports (or only
those with social supports, as has been the case in some adult day care)
this results in the need for the community to develop a complementary
program elsewhere. In a few communities such specialization may be
feasible, but in most communities it would represent inefficient frag-
mentation.

8. The Lowest-Income Elderly or the "Near Poor." Numerous policy
analysts have argued (and found supporting evidence), that programs
exclusively for the poor sooner or later deteriorate into poor programs.
It is assumed that the middle class is more prone to exercise consumer
demands for quality in service and their participation creates a broader

political base for program support than when the poor are the only advocates for a given program. A few gerontologists' surveys also conclude that many economically and socially needy older persons refuse to use services that have a welfare stigma.

The fact remains, however, that low income is generally associated with illness, neglect, and underutilization of needed services. Equity demands that every case-management program concern itself with the low-income elderly. A number of early demonstration programs initially focused on the "near poor" on the assumption that the poorest were receiving public social services and unlimited subsidized medical care. It has since been recognized by planners that although covered by Medicaid, many poor older persons do not have appropriately coordinated care, cannot find physicians who will accept Medicaid-covered patients, and suffer long waiting lists for nursing home placement.

The fact of organizational life may be that in the 1980s many programs will be induced to serve the poorest as a result of restricted funds. Revisions in Medicaid policy and regulations, especially in waivers for home- and community-based services, facilitate the development of case management and many related services for many, but not all, poor older persons. These developments not only will benefit those who are eligible but also may indirectly help to make all physicians, families, and the public at large more aware of home-care alternatives and the potential utility of case management.

Although many long-term-care community systems and case-management agencies may give first attention to the Medicaid-eligible target group because it is important and because that is what is fundable first, the long-range targeting goal should be broader. At very least programs will seek to include the Medicare-eligible population. Even though not just the near poor but affluent older persons are covered by Medicare, some policy trends favor offering case management to this population. Medicare-waiver demonstrations by the U.S. Health Care Financing Administration not only showed social and medical benefits per se but also documented that the not-so-poor, when faced with long-term-care costs, are forced to "spend down" their own resources on institutional care and eventually become a public responsibility and eligibile for Medicaid. The case-management administrator must keep abreast of changes in Medicare policies as they may apply to both case management and direct services.

While programs may give priority to lowest income and near poor older persons, they may consider the inclusion of the affluent and middle-income population to the extent that these groups can pay their own way or are covered by private insurance. In several large urban areas such full-pay services exist, usually in combination with private guardian or conservator agencies or within a life-care retirement home or community. Members of this group sometimes need the objective assessment, goal setting, and service brokerage help of a case manager. Such inclusion will require the organization to share costs with clients, using sliding-fee scales, deductibles, coinsurance and copayments. Such cost-sharing requirements have been considered nationally even in conneciton with Medicaid-eligible clients.

The income variable in the possible range of clients is a powerful influence on organization funding and structure. The lead agency must have an acceptable reputation with all potential clients. The case-management organization must be equipped to handle cost sharing with some clients. The more that a given program is able to maintain a capacity to serve a range of income levels (even though limiting clientele via other criteria), the wider will be its linkage system and more solid will be its constituency and political support. It will also need to demonstrate to the community that it can offer the same quality of services to all clients without regard to their individual abilities to pay.

Organizational Values and Targeting Groups of
Elderly for Case Management

In this section we examine common organizational perspectives on target populations apart from the previously mentioned influences on organizational and clinical prescreening criteria. Whatever the specific administrative or technological imperatives for delineating priority clients, there remains an underlying normative stance that is based on values and philosophical commitments communicated to and through the administrator.

The value orientation or historical culture of an organization is rarely explicitly considered in the selection of a lead agency for service delivery coordination or for lodging the case-management functions. Just as this book tends to reflect the science of public administration more than the art of human kindness, so it is that in the selection of an appropriate agency the issue of which kind of agency will have the most caring attitude and the most flexible and timely responsiveness to a wide range of people in trouble is masked by considerations of more easily measured and more politically marketable variables.

Indeed many programs exist across the country that attempt to offer case management to whomever needs it—without fine-tuned delineations of target. It is difficult to recognize when this stance is merely the result of adminsitrative ambiguity. As noted in chapter 1, when programs are open to anyone, waiting lists usually develop and program impact is watered down. On the other hand, too precise and inflexible delineations of target groups may result in unreasonable exclusions of people needing help and absurd inclusions of people who meet eligibility criteria to the letter but who have little or nothing to gain from the program. To avoid these potential extremes of exclusion or inclusion it is suggested that workers be permitted considerable discretion at intake and termination of cases—assuming the case managers have sufficient knowledge and experience to exercise discretion in the spirit of the program's goals.

In the previous section we reviewed eight commonly used delineations of target population for case-management services. The possibility that some of these categories have been abused or overenforced should not deter administrators from reaching for usable delineations for purposes of setting program goals, prescreening, setting priorities, and evaluating outcomes. As discussed in chapter 1, regarding prescreening, failure to delineate target populations tends to overload the program with inappropriate referrals and cause service seekers to waste time and effort. The relationship of target group to funding is discussed in chapter 5, and to support constituencies and interorganizational relations in chapters 3 and 4. Table 2–2 summarized ways that broad versus narrowly defined target groups affect the design of the program and the organizational structure for carrying out client-level functions of entry, assessment, care planning, care-plan implementation, and case review.

Summary

The purpose of this chapter has been to review five of the major influences on coordination organizations as seen from national and historical perspectives. Most of the organizational issues discussed here and in the remaining chapters pertain to lead agencies that carry system-level coordination responsibilities as well as to the agencies that do the front-line case management. In a given community any one of the five influences may be of minor importance. Over the years the relative importance of these and other influences changes. At the outset the program planner must weigh each of these in an effort to balance organizational capacities and expectations to achieve something that may be summarized as "a good reputation."

These five influential factors alone do not explain why some programs are more productive and have more beneficial impact upon clients than others. We do know that some communities have better histories than others with respect to programs that call for interagency coordination. We also know that in a set of given circumstances, some administrators are able to achieve a better quality program or better local or national recognition (high quality and fame do not necessarily come together).

We know that many case managers are able to surmount the constraints of the organization by virtue of their technical skills and interpersonal connections, which open doors on behalf of clients. We also know that while these five distinguishing characteristics remain constant, the design of the program itself tends to be modified over time on the basis of its own experience and other pressures from the community and the hierarchy above it which causes it to "fit in" and function effectively.

While administrators of case-coordination programs are urged to make good use of increasingly available program reports and guidelines about other programs, they are also urged to be cautious in replicating features of famous programs elsewhere. In assessing other programs a number of questions should be asked: Does a particular organizational or program change promise sufficient benefits to merit the cost of making the change? Is a program famous because of its achievements and the merits of its methods or because it has prestigious and self-congratulatory administrators? Are the mission, goals, and objectives of one's own program the same as those of the famous program? While it is important for the administrator to know the entire spectrum of options available in organizational setting, program design, and practice, the particular combination that is instituted in a given locality must be custom made on the basis of the many contingencies that prevail in that community.

In spite of any disadvantages there may be in the organizational givens that an administrator may inherit, it is possible to strengthen the capacity of the organization without making basic changes in the organizational base. For example, skill and time can be devoted to the management of the agency's governing structure in terms of its composition, its relation to the host agency if any, its supplementation by technical advisory committees, and the leadership and group decision processes that are involved. In general the administrator can make a difference by assuring the best possible administration of the program, which may require bringing in an assistant or delegating responsibilities to people who have competencies complementary to those of the chief administrator. The administrator may also work to clarify ambiguous goals and reconcile or renegotiate conflicting goals held by the agency's several constituencies. An agency's administrator also needs to set up a personal peer support network in order to keep abreast of the state of the art to gain perspective and advice on solving problems peculiar to that agency. Of great importance is the selection and implementation of interorganizational linkages (described in the next chapter); in such linkages, however, as well as in the entire array of administrative mechanisms by which an agency operates, the administrator must remain aware of the processes as well as the structures of these techniques.

No one organizational model suits all purposes or all communities. This is a conclusion not only of our study but also of many previous studies of coordination organizations. Even when an organization is custom designed to suit its environment, its unique configureation of organizational characteristics (such as structure, governance, staffing pattern, funding base) will enable it to achieve some of its objectives and functions better than others. It cannot do everything equally well.

Suggested Readings

Engler, M. *The Impact of Ethnicity on Home Care Needs*. New York: New York City Area Agency on Aging, November 1980.

Holmes, D.; Teresi, J.; and M. Holmes. "Differences among Blacks and Whites in Knowledge about and Attitudes toward Long-Term Care Services." National Center for the Black Aged, *Quarterly Contact,* Fall 1981.

Kutza, E. "Allocating Long-Term-Care Services: The Policy Puzzle of Who Should Be Served." In Meltzer, J.; Farrow, F.; and Richman, H. (eds.), *Policy Options in Long-Term Care*. Chicago, Ill.: University of Chicago Press, 1980, 118–147.

Lacayo, C.G. *A National Study to Assess the Service Needs of the Hispanic Elderly*. Los Angeles: National Association for Hispanic Elderly, December 1980.

Murdock, S., and Schwartz, D. "Family Structure and the Use of Agency Services: An Examination of Patterns among Elderly Native Americans." *The Gerontologist* 18, no. 5, (1978):475–481.

Steinberg, R.M. "Impact of Minority Aging Research on Services for Minority Elderly." In Stanford, E.P. (ed.), *Minority Aging Research*. San Diego, Calif.: Campanile Press, 1979, 239–249.

Taietz, P. *Community Structure and Aging*. Ithaca, N.Y.: Cornell University, Department of Rural Sociology, November 1970.

U.S. Commission on Civil Rights. *The Age of Discrimination*. Washington, D.C.: U.S.C.C.R., December 1977.

U.S. Comptroller General. *Home Health—The Need for a National Policy to Better Provide for the Elderly*. Washington, D.C.: General Accounting Office, 1977b (Report to the Congress, HRB-78-19).

Zawadski, R.T. (ed.). *Community-Based Systems of Long-Term Care*. New York: Haworth Press, 1983.

3

Knowing, Mobilizing, and Building the Service-Delivery System

The performance and impact of a case-management program ultimately depend upon the services it can make available to its clients according to their needs. The program must be concerned with

comprehensiveness—offering sufficiently diverse service options to span the diverse needs of its clients;

continuity—coordinating the movement of clients through changing levels or types of care;

adequacy—ensuing the available supply of each kind of option; and

quality—providing services that meet performance standards that protect vulnerable clients.

Each case-management program accommodates to and then tries to influence the conditions of its local service network by developing different kinds of relationships with relevant agencies. It will need to make referrals to and receive referrals from a wide range of agencies on an as-needed basis, but it will need to have more firmly on tap a set of services most frequently needed by a frail elderly population. In unusual cases it may need to have some crucial services in-house to be used without the delays or other disadvantages of interagency referral or purchase agreements. Finally, it will need to engage in advocacy to promote the development of needed services in its community. Later in this chapter, many kinds of interorganizational linkages used to establish the relationships needed for timely and coordinated service delivery are discussed. The focus is on the processes and techniques through which case managers connect with services for their clients. Underlying these discussions are three assumptions that merit attention:

He Who Coordinates Should Not Operate.

Many program reports and evaluation studies conclude that a case-management agency should not provide direct services. This point of view arises from the following tendencies.

When there are services available within a case manager's own agency, he or she may develop a bias in favor of using those services rather than fitting the care plan to the individual client (the "You need what we have" philosophy).

When a case-management agency must monitor the quality and quantity of other agencies' service delivery, its own services must be beyond reproach or else program monitoring authority will be weakened and case advocacy will be compromised (People in glass houses . . .).

When an agency has limited resources and carries both coordinating functions and direct service functions, the direct service demands for time and resources prevail over the needs of the case-management program (Daily routine displaces planning).

At present, the majority of case-management programs for the elderly are located in agencies that also deliver direct service, and in those settings effective case management is taking place. It is urged that case management be lodged within a special unit of the agency, not only to avoid the problems mentioned but also to enhance the development of staff expertise and administrative supports for the coordination functions. Therefore, in the ensuing discussion of linkages it is assumed that case management is not merely the adjunct of delivery of a particular service.

There Is No Point in Coordinating Incompetent and Irrelevant Services.

This assumption was based on conclusions drawn from the literature, but did not hold up during the course of the study. It is generally agreed that community planning agencies should devote primary attention to the development of basic direct services for the elderly. But, for the following reasons, administrators and front-line practitioners in case management without exception consider it worthwhile to establish a case-management program even in those communities where these basic services are not fully in place:

When but a few baseline services exist, they often fail to serve the elderly most at risk, who then have few alternatives to institutionalization. The case-management program helps to obtain more appropriate utilization of what does exist, including institutions.

An effective case-management program assists in documenting service gaps and in developing new, needed services; thus case management can be viewed as a *catalyst* for filling service gaps and upgrading the quality of existing services rather than as a digression from the development of the most needed services.

Some of the chronically impaired elderly either do not need formal services or do need assistance with understanding their needs and overcoming their own resistance to accepting help before they can utilize services. Others need moral support for mobilizing their own capacities for self-help and for reinforcing their natural support systems (relatives and friends). Therefore, some clients obtain assistance from a case manager in a planning and action process that in the short range may not call for coordinating formal services.

These and the other functions of case management described in chapter 7 add up to a *revised assumption:* Case management *is a service* that assists clients to engage in a problem-solving process of identifying needs, exploring optional solutions, and mobilizing informal as well as formal supports to achieve the highest level of independence. Although most case management is aimed at maintaining at-risk elderly persons in their own homes through the coordination of in-home and community-based services, it also is relevant for many of those who are in acute-care or extended-care facilities and foster homes.

Case management, then, is seen as a service and is appropriate even when two or more formal services do not need to be coordinated. This conclusion reinforces the conviction of many administrators that the case manager should have the prerequisite clinical skills. At the same time it does not diminish the importance of the worker and the agency having better-than-average knowledge of community services.

No One Model Fits All Communities.

Many issues concerning the need of case-management programs to fit their particular community environments are discussed in other chapters. A variation on this theme concerns the selection, phasing-in, and time required to establish interorganizational linkages to obtain the full spectrum of service options for clients.

Some communities have a good record in achieving interagency teamwork for special target groups whether it be to combat juvenile delinquency, fight poverty, or deal with developmental disabilities. Those that do are usually easier environments for initiating case-management programs for the frail elderly.

Communities in which interagency projects have been resisted, regarded as controversial, or dropped when special funds terminated are more difficult, though not impossible environments. The difficult communities call for more time to develop programs and require more careful involvement at the earliest stages of all who will be affected by the new program. Difficult communities require a process of well-planned, patient sequencing of interorganizational linkages so that the least demanding, most quickly established, and least threatening linkages are introduced first. Leaders will need to begin with an emphasis on the *processes* of building a program before moving into a highly task-oriented management style (see chapter 4 regarding the program development process). Therefore program models or techniques that have been developed elsewhere must be adapted to fit a new community and must be phased in.

We will now review some of the activities that enable a program to become aware of the existing supply of services in its community, to mobilize the existing services for its clients, and to help to reform and augment the delivery system so that it can better meet the needs of the elderly.

Developing and Maintaining a Resource Inventory

A comprehensive and accurate inventory of existing services is an essential tool for care planning by case managers. The development of an inventory is not merely an accumulation of data to be organized into a printed directory, a resource card file, or a computerized data bank. It requires an ongoing process of updating, verifying, and expanding of data, and periodic assessment of whether the form and content facilitate case management.

One of the difficulties in searching out available services within a community is the lack of widely understood terms or accepted definitions of services. Different communities describe the same service by different terms and any of these names may denote different services in different communities. For example, *homemaker, housekeeper, chore service, home maintenance*, or *home health aide* may all refer to the same service. Another example is *respite services*, which may not be listed anywhere. Various services are used for the purpose of respite (day care, friendly visiting, or nursing homes) without being named respite services. Thus the initial development of a resource inventory requires precise and consistent labels with service definitions that reflect the service arrangements of the particular community. (See also chapter 8.)

Who develops and maintains these inventories varies with the size of the program. In very small programs case managers usually carry this responsibility. In larger programs one worker or a supervisor might be responsible, while very large programs, particularly in populous service areas, are likely to have a specialized paid position for the job. Whatever the case, it is important that workers provide relevant information about changes as they become aware of them during the conduct of their referral tasks. Interagency task forces can also be organized, not only to identify new resources but also to help develop policies and criteria regarding which services are legitimate for referral and which services do not meet acceptable standards. Once it is clear who carries primary responsibility for the resource inventory, sufficient time must be allotted to keep it up to date.

An important aspect of inventory development and maintenance is the establishment of good working relationships with other organizations in the community. The manner in which these tasks are performed will affect, positively or negatively, the many other case management tasks to be done. The number and characteristics of resources included in the inventory will vary greatly with the size of a particular community and the relative complexity of its service system. For example, small towns and rural areas usually have a strong focus on informal support from churches and civic groups.

One of the first relationships to cultivate is with existing information and referral (I&R) programs. Administrators should be willing to ask for their help rather than duplicate what they already have accomplished. I&Rs usually know not only what exists but also what is missing or in short supply for given target populations. Even when the case-management program is part of one of the I&R, it is valuable to contact all of the other I&Rs so that they know about the case management program. This would include specialized I&Rs for the elderly; hotlines for suicide prevention, mental health, developmental disabilities, voluntary health agencies (cancer, heart, arthritis); and central registries for residential care or housing. Other agencies might include religious, ethnic, or occupational organizations that engage in mutual aid and case advocacy. These contacts will enable the development of a resource inventory that ideally would contain detailed information about available services including the extent of home-delivered services, eligibility criteria, and the waiting list situation. In addition, these contacts provide an opportunity to let others know about the case-management program and its potential ability to help their clients. Most administrators will be fully cognizant of these simple steps, but numerous sophisticated agencies have started with wasteful and competitive surveys to develop a resource inventory.

After the initial resource inventory is in place, it is important to use staff meetings to review discrepancies between what agencies say they do and the actual experiences of clients and case managers. Some programs attempt to routinize this feedback through reporting forms, but written reports do not fill the need for colleagues to discuss the dilemmas of whether or not to use a service that is substandard, hard to deal with, or discriminatory on the basis of age or ethnicity. This is especially true when the "good" agencies become overloaded with hard-to-serve clients referred by the case-management program. The ways in which case managers attempt to improve the quality of existing services will be discussed later in this chapter under monitoring.

Mobilizing Existing Resources

The most recurrent lesson of the past is the great importance of involving in the planning of the coordinated service program all those agencies and organizations whose cooperation is essential to implementation. Staff time must be devoted to building interpersonal networks with agencies at both the administrative and service-delivery levels.

There may be a limit to the number of formal coordinative relationships a new program can carry. Whether or not there is an optimum number, the administrator of a new program needs to decide which agencies require the most attention. Then formal linkages must be phased in, commensurate with the agency's capacity and the interagency climate in which the case management program was launched.

Usually some sorting out of priorities for interagency activities and agreements is necessary based on such criteria as which services are most crucial to clients; which leaders or organizations have the biggest stake in the outcomes or survival of the program; and which sectors of the locality can be most effective facilitators or barriers to the program's acceptance by other agencies, community leaders, governmental decision makers, and, of course, the elderly and their families.

The following discussion of techniques for mobilizing resources is divided into two categories: formal linkage mechanisms and participation methods. They are not mutually exclusive. Formal linkages must be reinforced by interpersonal relationships and participatory exchanges. Informal cooperation may be the prelude to formal agreements and procedures. All of these techniques are shown in Table 3–1 in relation to client-level functions.

Formal Linkage Mechanisms

Formal linkage mechanisms are agreed-upon and recognized means of interaction designed to achieve common goals. They cover a variety of

Table 3-1

Intraorganizational and Interorganizational Design Components in Support of Program Functions at the Client Level

Entry	Assessment	Case Goal Setting and Service Planning	Care-Plan Implementation	Review and Evaluation of Client and Program Status
Purpose To identify and enroll clients most appropriate for objectives and capacities of program.	*Purpose* To understand the client as a whole person and be aware of strengths and needs in client's situation.	*Purpose* To clarify expectations and agree upon an individualized plan of services and other problem-solving activities.	*Purpose* To arrange and ensure that services and other help are provided and utilized effectively.	*Purpose* To update knowledge of client and situation for possible revisions in client plan or for management of agency resources.
Guidelines Be sure that all personnel understand the entry functions and all staff roles. Use *staff meetings, procedures manuals, and orientation sessions.*	*Guidelines* Design the extent to which client assessment is done by case manager alone or with assistance of	*Guidelines* Develop own *resources inventory* or negotiate use of files of the I&R agency.	*Guidelines* Clarify extent to which case managers versus other personnel within agency perform support and follow-up functions:	*Guidelines* Supervisors and front-line workers are a primary source of feedback on accomplishments and frustrations and of suggestions for remedies. *Staff retreats* are sometimes needed for prioritizing problems, for initiating important changes in goals, design, or procedures, and for maintaining good staff morale.
Ensure that entering telephone calls are effectively and courteously handled thru *training* in telephone use.	interdisciplinary assessment *team* within program;	All workers need periodic *information updates* on changes in key services.	search for or *create new services;*	Sampling case records is an economical method for assessing program progress and problems.
Develop some *I&R* to refer inappropriate applicants elsewhere and to handle emergency cases.	*Loaned staff* specialists from other departments or agencies;	*Care plan* process and documentation should specify the desired outcomes, or case goals; what is to be done by the client; what is to be done by members of the informal support network; what is to be done by the *case manager*; what is to be done by other workers within agency (*case aides, specialists* such as	*monitor service providers;* arrange for *reimbursement* for services; Monitor client acceptance, utilization, and satisfaction re service plan; troubleshoot bureaucratic barriers;	Large-volume agencies need an *information management specialist* to or-
Broad outreach methods are usually to be avoided unless intake capacity is great; these include *neighborhood outreach, news-*	*purchased assessment* from other agencies; purchased *consultation;* specialized staff units such as for medical screening, housing assessment, substance			

Table 3–1 Continued

Entry	Assessment	Case Goal Setting and Service Planning	Care-Plan Implementation	Review and Evaluation of Client and Program Status
letters, speakers bureau, press releases.	abuse treatment, psychiatric evaluation;	the nurse practitioner, volunteers, and group workers); what services are to be obtained (or continued) from other agencies (in what sequence, for what duration, and what method of payment, if any).	provide counseling or education to client or significant others;	ganize data and prepare informative reports for both internal and external uses. Director needs to facilitate information exchange with other agencies.
Targeted case finding is enhanced by interagency referral agreements, staff visits, and "open house" orientation meetings for key referral agencies; outstationing staff to selected sites; written referral instructions that specify service area, eligibility criteria, and prescreening indicators.	formal diagnostic reports requested from private practitioners and other agencies.	Care plans also should specify what other changes or services would be desirable but are not feasible at present time (reasons); what should trigger the initiation of new steps in the plan, reassessment, a new plan, or termination of this case.	provide case consultation to other agencies;	Service gaps and barriers need systematic follow-up by administrators. Some program use resource procurement or community development staff to conduct advocacy and program development tasks, but top-level staff must link to local planning bodies such as AAA and HSA, state agencies in aging, human services, etc., national standard-setting bodies, senior action groups, and local legislators.
	If case manager follows client from assessment through plan implementation, establish policy and procedures for assigning prescreened clients to workers who have differentiated case loads based on such criteria as location of client residence, type of presenting problem, gender, religious preference (if multiple entry), and medical versus social complexity. Clarify whether toughest cases will go to particular experienced workers or be distributed equitably to all for balance.		authorize service provision when coordinator controls the funds;	
Negotiate local regulations or agreements requiring channeling to your program of high-risk clients for social-medical diagnosis and plan when identified by law enforcement agencies, public guardian, utility companies, psychiatric emergency teams, hospital emergency wards, board and care homes, and agencies that authorize payments for institutionalization.		Most programs have a case review, by supervisor or interdisciplinary team at this point, others have case review after intake or assessment. Case reviews help a program to assure quality control in its own practice, to prioritize cases so that neediest get sufficient attention and resources, to develop differentiated case loads	initiate or participate in case conference committees.	
Some programs need special committees and information campaigns targeted	Select the assessment guide or tool and process that is most conducive to a good client–worker relationship and suitable to re-		Interorganizational linkages that enhance case plan implementation, as well as service coordination in general, include purchase-of-service contracts, referral agreements, case conference committees, joint training, colocation centers, and outstationing. Linkages that need longer development time are client-tracking systems, joint administrative supports, joint program planning, and shared core services such as transportation, escort, or jointly funded staff specialists.	Some ways that programs maintain communications with inactive cases (to keep aware of accomplishments and to be alerted to new problems) include telephone reassurance, written greetings for

to private practitioners such as doctors, nurses, lawyers, and clergy in order to assist case finding.

Summary
Generalization: A successful reach to the target group, a smooth, dignified entry process for each appropriate client, and an avoidance of false starts with inappropriate applicants depend upon wise choices regarding which functions are performed by which personnel within the agency, and which functions are requested of outside agencies. In addition to clear criteria and procedures, efficient entry design requires continuous communication links (internal and external) to keep intake aligned with program capacity.

spond. Avoid *recording* assessment information that is rarely used by anyone. Clarify policies as to when partial or incremental assessment methods may be used.

Summary
Generalization: There is no one best assessment method. Assessment practices should be consistent with the goals and capacities of the program and in balance with skill levels and resources devoted to intake, care planning and care-plan implementation.

for the best possible fit between needs of client and skills of the particular worker assigned to case, and to buttress *staff morale* through collegial discussion and support.

Summary
Generalization: Service plans become distorted or incomplete when too little time is devoted to this phase (as compared with lengthy assessment) or when insufficient attention or skill is devoted to taking into account client values, preferences, capacities for self-help and dependency needs. Service plans suffer also when there are pressures to fit clients to the easily available services instead of fitting services to clients; when clients become distrustful or hostile due to bad experiences during intake and assessment; and, when workers are not kept informed of new resources or have had bad experiences with elitist or overly bureaucratic service providers.

If the coordination agency also provides direct services it must avoid bias in service plans and the quality of its services must be above reproach if it is to engage in *advocacy* and monitoring of other service providers.

Summary
Generalization: Care-plan implementation requires role clarity among staff, functional differentiation among agencies, time budgeted for follow-up, and continuous supportive *interpersonal communication.* Control over funds for service providers helps but does not guarantee coordination.

birthdays or holidays, newsletters, annual assistance with tax forms, or routine follow-up inquiry with continuing service providers.

Summary
Generalization: Effective agency administration requires a constant flow of information, and times for reflection and planning of change at all personnel levels of the organization.

activities, include different levels of staff, and involve governance as well as services. These mechanisms are the heart of a coordinated service system. Sixteen formal linking mechanisms are described on the following pages.

Referral Agreements. These may be one-way or two-way referrals, describing which kinds of clients will be referred *to* the case-management program by another agency and which clients will be referred *by* the case-management program to the outside service provider. It is useful to exchange written instructions specifying screening criteria and referral procedures for distribution to all service personnel of both agencies. Some agreements specify expectations that each agency will report periodically to the other regarding the progress of referred clients.

Mandatory Prescreening. In this arrangement a direct service provider (such as a nursing home) or the agency that authorizes expenditures of public funds for specific clients or patients (such as the medical assistance agency) is required to refer clients for case assessment and care planning *before* the older person is institutionalized. The purpose is to make sure that appropriate alternatives to institutionalization have been explored with the client and his family. This requirement for prescreening might be negotiated by the case-management agency or mandated by a higher governmental authority. It goes beyond the preadmission review (PAR) of Professional Standards Review Organizations (PSRO), which validates that the patient is eligible for acute care or long-term institutional care by virtue of functional disabilities or needs for medical treatment. Generally the PAR is completed after admission and does not explore in-home care plans as a potentially preferred and less costly substitute. The same limitation is found in many physician referrals of patients to long-term-care facilities without full consideration of available alternatives. In a system with mandatory prescreening the case manager's assessment may intercept the physician's referral.

Several community care organizations or channeling agencies for the elderly have negotiated this linkage with respect to nursing-home admissions and the potential exists for similar mandatory referral arrangements (subject to client consent) with law-enforcement agencies, public guardians, utility companies, psychiatric emergency teams, hospital emergency wards, board-and-care homes, and others who deal with the eldery in crisis. By early 1982 the U.S. Health Care Financing Administration reported that twenty-eight state governments had initiated mandatory prescreening policies for Medicaid patients, but implementation continues to require vigilance and assertiveness on the part of local case-management agencies.

Purchase-of-Service Agreements. Purchase of service is generally considered to be the most powerful way to ensure that the case manager's clients have access to particular services. The case-management agency commits providers to deliver services through block grants, individual purchase orders, or capitation agreements. These variations of funding are described in chapter 5.

Control over the funds of providers does indeed strengthen the responsible agency's ability to coordinate service delivery for its clients, but the administrator must then provide the agency with staff (or borrow staff from elsewhere) competent to formulate and negotiate the fiscal as well as program specifics of purchase contracts. The implementation and monitoring of purchase agreements generally produce interagency stress, so the administrator must stay close to the negotiation process and be ready to troubleshoot sources of friction throughout the life of the program. The responsible agency must be clear whether purchased services are being monitored primarily for compliance or as a vehicle of technical assistance to improve the caliber of available services. (See also the description of monitoring later in this chapter.)

The administrator or supervisor should be aware of the tendencies of case managers to overutilize purchased services rather than search for alternatives that may be more suited to their client's needs but that are harder to access. At the same time administrators must avoid pressuring workers to expend the available purchased services within a funding period, when those workers may be creatively finding alternative services more suitable to client needs or the same service on the basis of eligibility without resort to purchase.

Colocation. A frequently used mechanism for interagency coordination occurs when two or more agencies share an office or program facility and represent the joint effort as a multiservice or multipurpose center. To avoid confusion with centers that are operated by one multifunctional agency, the interagency mechanism is appropriately described as colocation. The rationale for using colocation as a linking mechanism is that when agencies are in close proximity there are several advantages:

It is convenient for ambulatory clients who may need more than one service. Not only do clients save time, but also their familiarity with the location of one service enhances access to another service.

The multipurpose center is more visible to new clients, to the community at large, and to elected officials.

Interagency staff relationships develop that enhance coordinated ser-

vice delivery to clients as well as foster interagency meetings and
interpersonal peer relationships.

Cost savings may result from the use of common reception, waiting
room, conference rooms and restrooms, and shared telephone system
and other equipment, as well as from reduced travel costs;

It is one of the easier linkages to initiate when it presents no threat
to the autonomy of participating agencies and provides proximity to
concentrations of their client target populations.

Grant-getting abilities of each agency are enhanced when it can show
potential funding agencies that it is participating in a visible coordination effort.

Evaluation of colocation or multipurpose centers sponsored by community action, services integration and aging programs have shown several common, but not inevitable, disadvantages to colocation:

Colocation alone can create the illusion of coordination. Formal coordination does not happen if there is no central authority (with a
central budget) to manage the center and to organize planned coordinative activities such as cross-agency orientation and training, good
client screening at reception, formulation and promotion of shared
program goals, and maintenance of shared space and equipment.

Agency representatives experience conflicting loyalties between the
center and their home office.

Workers who are distant from supervision of the parent agency are
subject to two hazards: They may lose their place in career opportunities, or they may begin to neglect performance standards.

Poor staff morale in one agency can be contagious to all.

The difficulties of finding a suitable facility to house many agencies
may lead the planners to accept a site that is less accessible to clients
than the individual sites of participating agencies, thereby impeding
rather than facilitating client accessibility. Especially in rural areas
it may improve access to have different agencies scattered through
the service area so long as each agency provides a link to all other
agencies through referral and outstationing.

Outstationing. The locating of a worker (or workers) from one agency
at the facility of another agency is called *outstationing*. It can be scheduled
by appointment or on a regular part-time or full-time basis. Outstationed

personnel provide the services of their own agency and remain under the direction of and accountable to their own supervisors. Although outstationing generally improves access for clients, its coordinative merit varies with the extent to which outstationed staff work with clients of the host agency or merely use the site for easier access by a different target population. The coordinative value of outstationing can be enhanced by having visiting workers participate in staff meetings, case conferences, and public presentations.

Loaned Staff or Jointly Funded Staff. Loaned staff members work under the direction of the host (borrower) agency and are temporarily accountable to the host's administrators. This linkage is often used when a special kind of expertise is needed for a limited time or intermittently. Staff loans usually flow from well-established agencies to the newer case-management agency. Sometimes staff loans are initially motivated by the need for nonfederal share (local matching funds) in a federally funded program as well as the desire of established agencies to ensure that their interests are being taken into account in the activities of the new agency. Occasionally a case-management agency may lend staff to another agency to assist with training, preparation of a grant proposal, or to launch a gap-filling service in which it has a stake.

Loaned staff members not only supplement the staff size of the borrowing agency but also can greatly enhance each agency's knowledge of the other and serve as liaisons in teamwork activities. Loaned staff, as noted in chapter 2, can also enhance the organization's credibility with new reference groups, especially in bridging medical and social services. As in the case of colocation, long-term loans can create difficulty for staff members whose loyalties become strained or who lose their place in the career ladder of the permanent agency. A fruitful variation of this linkage is the use of a *jointly funded staff member* who divides time between two agencies, assisting in the routine work of each while facilitating coordination between the staffs of both agencies. The joint funding usually intensifies the determination of both agencies to benefit from the collaboration.

Assessment or Care-Plan Review Team. This linkage is a formal case review in which reviewers from outside the case-management agency have decision-making authority. This is in contrast to case conference, which is for interagency consultation and voluntary joint planning, and different too from reviews of a random sample of cases for purposes of supervision, monitoring, or program evaluation. The primary purpose of this linkage is to provide checks and balances to the frustrating dilemmas of rationing services when there are many more client needs than resources to meet the needs. For example, in one county in the Southwest an interagency team is authorized to decide which priority clients may have a continuation of home services beyond the normal time limit or may have a more intensive level of service than program policy generally permits. In an Eastern city, a nurse and social-worker team of the AAA reviews the assessments and care plans of paraprofessional case managers in subcontracted senior centers before purchased services may be used.

In most programs dilemmas of rationing services (and ensuring equity between clients of workers with varying skills and assertiveness) is an intraagency responsibility of clinical supervisors or resource procurement officials. One of the advantages of an interagency mechanism for rationing is that there develops a larger constituency for advocating the development of a more adequate supply of services for the frail elderly. It not only helps the case-management agency to ensure that its rationing decisions are as wise as possible, but it also enhances the program's image of fairness with clients and agencies.

Information Systems. As an interagency linking mechanism for purposes of client service, a shared information system provides either a common resources file or a common client-tracking process. In both cases, there are difficulties in motivating all participating agencies and workers to keep the information up to date. As described more fully in chapter 8, the design and implementation of a shared information system requires much time and patience until it begins to pay off.

In a research-oriented context, in which the information system must be developed at the earliest stages, it is essential to involve during the planning stage all those who must provide information. Such systems do not fail because of technological problems but, rather, because of human factors. On the other hand, if there are not immediate requirements for research or accountability across agencies, it is wise for the planner or administrator to attempt a shared information system only after other coordination experiences have been achieved with other linkages that are easier to install and that provide quicker payoff, such as a case conference committee or referral agreements.

Interlocking Governing Bodies. This linkage is a formal one when the case-management agency has on its board of directors any number of members who are appointed by another agency to represent it. The case-management agency may also have the power to appoint its representative on another organization's board. This may be a stronger interagency linkage than informal overlap of board or committee members that exists when one individual is active in the governance of two organizations. Formal interlocking governance, however, has some risk of being excessively cumbersome when representatives must delay decisions until they sound out their sponsor. On the other hand, when informal overlap is the result of a specific organization's nomination (rather than appointment) of board candidates for another agency, there is some risk that the individual lay leader will abandon the originating organization in favor of the more interesting or prestigious coordinating agency. In the process the leader's value as an interorganizational link may be diminished. When prestigious organizations have formal representatives on the board, it enhances the prestige of the case-management agency in exchange for the opportunity of the prestigious organizations to have someone in a decision-making position who will guard its special interests.

Joint Program Supports. Whether or not agencies are colocated, they may decide to pool their resources to establish core program services that they all need (like outreach, I&R, and transportation). The decision to pool resources and coordinate use of a common support program is often precipitated by funding agencies who wish to reduce costs and eliminate duplication. Each kind of shared core service has its unique logistical problems in assuring equitable distribution among cooperating agencies and in arriving at methods whereby each cooperator gets a fair share of recognition with clients and the public.

Administrative Support Services. Most examples of shared administrative supports occur when a large, established agency is providing help to a newer, smaller coordination agency. In other cases, when the coordination agency subcontracts to agencies that have acceptable services to provide but that do not meet basic standards of administration, especially fiscal management, it may retain and control the administrative supports. In the first instance the support may be a contribution to in-kind matching nonfederal share or reimbursed from the user's budget. Examples of administrative support services include payroll processing, central purchasing, fiscal technical assistance or supervision, computer services for information management, and equipment or facilities maintenance.

Appeals Committees. Some people are denied service as a result of demands that outstrip supply. Other appeals cases arise when an individual worker makes a mistake in judgment. In either case it is essential for all agencies that have a gatekeeping function to approve or deny public benefits to have an appeals mechanism. Although most governmental agencies have statutory requirements for appeals procedures, both public and voluntary agencies can involve personnel of outside agencies in the appeals process. Such participation not only adds to the breadth of the perspective through which appeals issues are viewed but also spreads appreciation of the dilemmas that the gatekeeping agency faces in responding to requests for services.

Program Review Team. This is a formal linkage that is intermittent rather than continuous. An interagency review team can assess program progress without elaborate evaluation machinery. Such teams of experts are usually asked to assess attainment of performance goals and to make recommendations for improved structure or policy. When relationships between cooperating agencies have become strained, it is useful to include out-of-town counterparts of the conflicting parties to bring a fresh perspective, build trust in the recommendations, and possibly serve as mediators of the conflicts. Program reviews of this type are usually compressed into a few days and use interviews, site observation, program records, and group debriefings. They supplement rather than replace research-based techniques for evaluation of performance or outcomes.

Technical Assistance and Membership in Competency-Building Associations. Administrators, like all other people, prefer to give advice than to ask others for advice. Outstanding administrators are skillful in identifying others who have special areas of expertise and are not reluctant to ask for help when they need it. Usually members of the agency from which help has been received feel an increased stake in the survival and success of those whom they have helped. Even though there is much exchanging of advice or information among colleagues on an informal basis, the technical assistance process requires a formal contract or memorandum of understanding regarding the goals, methods, timetable, and expected commitments of both parties. When the case-management agency provides technical assistance to a service provider agency it is good diplomacy to allow the provider agency to receive the recognition for the positive changes it makes.

A relatively small but pesky dilemma arises for administrators with respect to how much money the budget can provide for organizational memberships in competency-building associations and for participation of the staff in annual conferences or training events. Similar dilemmas may arise regarding release of staff time for participation in their respective local professional organizations. Innovative organizations tend to be those with multiple links through diverse staff affiliations.

Interagency Central Intake/Standardized Intake Forms. Two popular program coordination concepts that defy successful implementation are those of central intake and standardized intake forms. Program administrators should be careful *not* to take the advice of program documents that describe what that program intended to do or even what they did during the first year in coordinated intake. Even when interagency centralized or standardized intake gets off to a good start, it crumbles away as a result of its sheer complexity and doubts that emerge about whether the benefits outweigh the costly efforts required to make it work.

No common intake form yet invented can answer all the questions that diverse agencies need to know about a client for their particular service or can satisfy the changing requirements of their diverse funding sources. It would take many acts of Congress to eliminate the regulatory and statutory constraints to consolidation. Several local programs have developed a "common data set" that permits the case-management agency to maintain essential facts about each client. A common data set is feasible and can be cost effective when kept to a minimum and when it allows each agency to obtain additional information as needed for its particular program.

Most service clients do not need coordination of services. Interagency central intake imposes too many extra time demands on both clients and agency personnel when only a small percentage of clients will need to utilize more than one service. While conceptually these intake linkages have similarities to case management, the latter is reserved ony for that prescreened and small percentage of the elderly (perhaps 5 percent) who need professional assistance in assessment, care planning, and follow-up.

A term that is beginning to appear in professional and legislative language is "single point entry." Different meanings are inputed to the term, and therefore it is not used here. Some sources use the term to designate a system in which all clients must come through one designated agency door (central intake). Other sources use the term with the intent of describing multiple entries, any of which will permit clients to access the entire continuum of care.

Monitoring. A final formal linkage mechanism is monitoring. Because of its complex purposes and the diverse activities required to carry it out, special attention is devoted to its discussion.

Monitoring is a mechanism for accountability and for technical assistance. It is a form of surveillance and support in which the coordination agency engages the providers of service. The degree of authority and intensity with which the case manager handles monitoring functions varies with different agencies and their contexts.

Authority for monitoring is strongest in those programs where the coordination agency is paying the provider. However, it does not hold that all one needs is the power of the purse strings to influence the quality of the service provided. Sometimes the understanding and expertise of the monitor in helping the provider to solve problems is a more effective force for change.

The power to withdraw funds from an errant provider agency is rarely used, because this would also deprive clients of the service, especially in communities where no alternative providers are available. Furthermore some providers have a larger, more committed constituency or more status at higher levels of the hierarchy than the case-management agency. This constituency-based power can compromise the power of the purse strings, placing a heavy responsibility on the agency to prove its case when threatening withdrawal of funds. Nevertheless, in this arrangement the legitimacy of monitoring the services for which one pays is seldom challenged.

A second formal linkage for monitoring occurs when the case-management agency is mandated to monitor a service provider on behalf of a funding source, but without serving as a vehicle for the actual dollars. One example of this is when a county government provides revenue-sharing funds directly to a nongovernmental provider but wishes to have the program monitored by an appropriate county agency. Another example is when the Title XX agency contracts with providers in aging and requests the coordination agency (usually the AAA) to coordinate and monitor the segment of the Title XX plan that involves services to the elderly. Some of the community care organizations that are used for mandatory pre-screening also have an implied or expressed mandate to monitor the services over which they have checkpoint or veto powers. Formal program surveillance is relatively limited since the case-management agency is not directly accountable for the proper expenditure of funds. Case-by-case troubleshooting is improved by this arrangement, however.

A third kind of linkage for monitoring is less formal in that it does not appear in a statute, regulation, contract, or written agreement. This is the monitoring of agencies to which clients have been referred in the traditional way, without purchase or without a legal mandate to monitor. While many programs and front-line practitioners do not do as much follow-up of referrals as they deem desirable, it is a commonly acceptable practice, consistent with professional ethics, that a worker "check" on how well a referral worked for the client both with the client and with the agency to which the referral was made. Case managers working with the frail elderly can legitimately do this kind of follow-up to referrals. The legitimacy derives from mutual concerns for the interests of the client rather than one agency's authority over another. If there are problems in the success of the referral, the case manager may become involved in intensive monitoring either to assist tactfully in solving problems or in gathering information for a complaint, appeal, withdrawal of the client, or deletion of the provider from the resource inventory (see also discussion of follow-up in chapter 1).

Monitoring Roles. The case-management program and its caseworkers have a variety of roles in monitoring. Five roles will be described with examples of the techniques that may be employed in fulfilling them:

1. Validating that the provider agency is delivering the quantity and quality of service that it has promised is monitoring for compliance. Tasks may include the review of written reports with summary data on utilization and expenditures, the examination of sample case files, study of requested written progress reports on individual clients, observation at the service site, and interviews with staff and clients.

2. Providing moral support and technical assistance to the provider in solving programwide as well as case-specific problems is another role. The monitor may use some of the same activities mentioned for the first role plus consultation conferences and staff meetings. In this role it is essential that the monitor have a counterpart—a staff member in the provider agency who has day-by-day responsibility to solve problems within the agency. This role sometimes calls for the monitor to help the provider obtain specialized technical assistance from other personnel in the case-management agency or from other cooperating sources.

One of the most effective tools for helping providers to improve their practices is for the monitor to arrange for interagency meetings of those with similar services so that the cluster of agencies can help one another to arrive at solutions to problems. In the short run there is some risk that agency frustrations will lead to gripe sessions about the case-management agency. In the long run, however, monitors may discover how their own agencies may be contributing to the problems or standing in the way of the solution. At the same time interagency meetings may develop peer pressure for its members to improve and then may give recognition and positive reinforcement to those who make effective changes. Similar assistance may sometimes be needed from the provider's national standard-setting body or state licensing agency.

3. A third monitoring role is addressed to the client. Through telephone and in-person contacts the monitor verifies that the client has taken the necessary steps to utilize the service appropriately and that it is being delivered. If problems exist that have to do with the client's attitudes or behavior rather than those of the service provider, then the monitor seeks to assist the client through counseling, obtains counseling from another source, or works with the client to revise the care plan to better suit the client's preference. In the process the monitor (usually the case manager)

can clarify whether the reluctance to use the service stems from misunderstandings, conflicting opinions in the family, mistakes by the service provider in its initial contacts with the client, or a faulty assessment and care plan on the part of the case manager.

4. Teaching clients to monitor their own care givers is a fourth role. It is increasingly common for case managers to meet with family members and friends individually and in natural support network meetings at which the clients are invited to ''let the case manager know'' if service delivery is not satisfactory. A more formal method of engaging the client in monitoring used by one community care organization merits further experimentation. In that program clients were given a monthly calendar on which the worker recorded the scheduled in-home services. Clients were asked to mail back the calendar each month with comments as to whether satisfactory services were received as scheduled.

5. Evaluating the effectiveness of service delivery in particular cases is the fifth monitoring role. Formal program evaluation is discussed elsewhere in this volume. Here we refer to the art rather than the science of evaluation. The preceding four monitoring roles are concerned with whether the intended services were received in the intended manner. They represent monitoring of performance not of impact. The care planner's assumptions are that if the intended services are delivered well, the achievement of the case goals is enhanced.

In some cases the case manager becomes aware that the services are not having their appropriate effect or that they are producing unintended, undesirable side effects. For example, the client may be becoming overly dependent in order to enjoy the company of visiting aides or the family may be experiencing excessive depression due to increasing care demands as the homemaker is being phased out. This kind of clinical monitoring can lead to reassessment or modifications in service plans. For example, the monitor may conclude that it would be more nurturing and less stressful for the son to prepare the food (rather than use meals on wheels) instead of assisting in toileting and changing dressings (which can instead be done by a home-health aide). Since this kind of monitoring is based on discretionary judgment, it is helpful to consult with supervisors or convene a case conference of relevant care givers to confirm the worker's perceptions.

Additional Interagency Participation Methods

Mobilizing the wide range of resources necessary for comprehensive services to clients and for program survival not only depends on formal interagency linkages but also on many kinds of exchange methods. The

investment of time of case-management agency personnel in these exchanges serves both instrumental and promotional purposes. The purposes
are instrumental in that they connect the program with individuals and
organizations that have what it needs—services, information, expertise,
influence, legitimacy, or material resources. They are promotional in that
they broaden the base of ownership or stake in the case-management
program. ''What people are not in on, they are down on'' is a basic
principle of community organization.

To the extent that a case-management program is a change agent
within the local human services network, it is important that it have
communications channels for knowing in advance where opposition may
develop and whether there may be any unanticipated negative side effects
to its activities. Other shared activities develop interpersonal relationships
that facilitate later formal activities of client referral and interagency
agreements at the policy or administrative level.

Committees and Task Forces. Case-management administrators must
allocate time to staff the program's interagency committees properly, and
to staff task forces and advisory councils for planning and implementation.
Interagency case conference committees are especially useful for case
problem solving, for drawing attention to gaps in services, and for recommending changes in policies and practices.

Shared Staff Development Activities. A relatively easy way to accelerate
interagency teamwork is to organize joint training events. Variations are
to invite outside agency personnel to help conduct in-service training or
to provide informal consultation.

External Memberships. In addition to formal organizational memberships in competency-building associations, the individual participation
of staff members in planning councils, professional, and civic organizations, and in collegial friendship circles (''invisible colleges'') can
broaden appreciation of the case-management program and keep it in
touch with important practice, organizational, and political developments.

Volunteers. Some case-management programs organize their own corps
of volunteers. Others obtain volunteers through voluntary action centers,
volunteers bureaus, and/or RSVPs (Retired Senior Volunteer Programs).
There are numerous good handbooks on recruitment, training, and supervision of volunteers, so that work can be productive for the agency,
satisfying to the volunteers, and supportive to the program as a whole.
It is recommended that case-management programs make a special effort
to recruit retired program-related professionals who can help the program

to interact with specialized agencies, including those from which they retired.

Special Events. Among the special events by which a program can orient or update its partners and constituencies are open houses, small group briefings (ad hoc), and annual meetings, which can include a recognition banquet. Public hearings provide opportunities not only for the case management program to speak for itself, but also for inviting cooperating agencies to give testimony. Opinion polls and periodic evaluation studies can be used to give the program feedback and to communicate to respondents that their opinions are valued and that the agency is open to improving its programs.

A kind of special event used by many experienced executives is the one-to-one visit or breakfast, lunch, or dinner meeting with important individuals. Such off-the-record exchanges may involve not only the program director but also other staff members who are relevant to the topics to be discussed. Administrators need to be aware of the limits of personal diplomacy, recognizing when a person-to-person commitment must be advanced to a formal interagency agreement so that the cooperation does not hinge on participation of a single individual.

Some Guidelines Concerning Interorganizational Relationships

The preceding pages have detailed a variety of formal and informal linkages that must be selected in harmony with the specific environment of each case-management program and developed gradually. From our collection of many conclusions and recommendations concerning interorganizational relationships, the following four guidelines cut across all linkage strategies:

1. Time is an important factor in the development of a coordinated system. Program effectiveness, legitimacy, and good working relationships cannot be legislated but require a process of getting acquainted, planning, and working together over a period of time.
2. Interagency teamwork entails moderate stress. No stress usually indicates that there is no change. Excessive stress drains energies needed for goal achievement.
3. In attempting to get other organizations to change, service coordinators must be aware of responsibilities and accountability that those organizations may have to their individual parent bodies and constituencies and that may be in conflict with the goals or tasks of the

interagency cooperative effort. The coordination program must have rewards to offer that are commensurate with the costs of change.

4. Although a case-management program is in a constant state of evolution, its behavior must be as predictable as possible. When programmatic or procedural changes are desired that will affect the operations of other agencies (as well as of personnel within the program) every possible effort should be made to inform all levels about the pending changes and what the changes are expected to accomplish.

Helping to Reform and Augment the System

While the primary task of the case-management program is to maximize utilization of the existing human service system for the benefit of its multiproblem clients, many of its activities have a cumulative effect that benefits a much larger group of service users. The system change role is strengthened when personnel at all levels are conscious of it, understand the direction and purpose, and encouraged to devote time to it.

First of all, there is the case-by-case advocacy role in which most case managers are involved. By tracking instances in which another agency had to be persuaded to reconsider a decision, waive its policy in order to accept a referral, or modify its practices to serve a client in a suitable manner, the program can document the need for converting the case-by-case exceptions into a basic change of policy. In rare instances the program will need to ''go public'' and undertake a ''class action'' appeal on behalf of all clients of that agency. Also, if on a case-by-case basis the program has had to improvise solutions to client problems because there is a gap in community services, the program will help to establish a new service. For example, the Society for the Prevention of Cruelty to Animals or the city pound might be persuaded to provide free or low-cost pet care for elders who face short hospital stays. A fund might be established for emergency financial aid to fill the gap until formal income assistance is approved. Or a new corporation might be organized to provide needed home health services.

If the program does not have purchase-of-service funds, it may assist other agencies to apply for new funds to meet the needs of special problem clients. Conversely, when a service provider fails to cooperate, the case management agency may appeal to the provider's funding source to require compliance or redirect its funds to a more cooperative provider.

In the case-management agency's reports are opportunities to draw attention to barriers and solutions as well as to applaud outstanding contributions or changes made by service providers. Facts and opinions alone do not produce change, however. They do arm individuals who are motivated to be agents of change. Facts and opinions must be communicated by such means as testimony in public hearings (local, state, and federal); written responses to proposed regulations and annual plans; participation (of staff and board members) in planning committees; and newsletters and press releases. Such advocacy sometimes is in the name of the agency itself; at other times it is undertaken through the outside organizations in which personnel or board members participate.

One final caveat with respect to activities aimed at reforming and augmenting the system: Many directors of innovative programs have been swept into a whirlwind of local and national meetings to herald the good intentions and accomplishments to date of their own programs. While a wide-reaching good reputation of the director and program does help mobilize resources and can elevate staff morale, there can also be diminishing returns if the director is excessively diverted from providing steady, effective management to the program itself. Nobody loves a self-congratulatory or self-aggrandizing director whose own program is not getting the administrator's attention in solving problems that inevitably emerge. A confused or disgruntled staff that feels it is being neglected by the leader can quickly undo the interorganizational linkages which have been established. In order to coordinate others a program should first have internal coordination and a manifest commitment to its clients.

Suggested Readings

Holmes, M.B., and Holmes, D. *Handbook of Human Services for Older Persons*. New York: Human Sciences Press, 1979.

Quinn, J. "Triage: Coordinated Home Care for the Elderly." *Nursing Outlook* 23 (September 1975):570–573.

Reynolds, W.S. "Case Conference, Need, and Plan." *Proceedings of the National Conference of Social Work* 46 (June 1919):336–339.

Steinberg, R.M. "Case Service Coordination: Senior Center Issues." In Jacobs, B., and Flaum, R.P. (eds.), *Senior Centers: Helping Communities Serve Older Persons*. Washington, D.C.: National Council on the Aging, 1982.

Taietz, P., and Milton, S. "Rural–Urban Differences in the Structure of Services for the Elderly in Upstate New York Counties." *Journal of Gerontology* 34, no. 3 (May 1979):429–437.

Tobin, S.S.; Davidson, S.M.; and Sack, A. *Effective Social Services for Older Americans*. Detroit, Mich.: Univ. of Michigan, Wayne State Univ. Institute of Gerontology, 1976.

U.S. Comptroller General, *The Well-Being of Older People in Cleveland*. Washington, D.C.: General Accounting Office, 1977a.

4 Process in Developing and Maintaining Coordination Programs

The preceding chapters have focused on three levels of coordination programs—the client pathway, the agency or organizational level, and the environmental or interorganizational level. The program developer or administrator is faced not only with the numerous choices to be made at these levels but also with the questions of how to organize, mobilize, seek involvement, shape agreements, and keep the pieces coordinated. This is the process involved in developing and maintaining coordination programs. Process skills and strategies differ for each level. That is, clinical process skills at the client–worker level differ from the broader scale repertoire required of the administrator at the agency or interagency levels. Seldom is one person equally competent as a program organizer, an agency manager, and a case practitioner.

We shall proceed by setting forth a process planning model that covers the phases or stages of a general sequence used in launching a new program. Some of the considerations in selecting process skills and techniques at different levels will be discussed. The chapter concludes with a set of guidelines and a list of key concepts for administrative and supervisory personnel.

A Process Planning Model

At this point we are concerned with *induced* processes, a sequence of community and agency interventions introduced by professional agency staff as well as supportive community leadership (both individuals and organizations). This professionally planned process is in contrast to demographic and environmental changes taking place in communities and neighborhoods that are nondirected.

Table 4–1 outlines the process steps in program development as they apply to case-management organizations. The purpose in offering this chart is to provide an understanding of the general pathway of a planning process. The steps outlined in eight phases follow a pattern frequently used by planners to guide a decision-making or a problem-solving process. The explanations labeled *Description* and the *Examples of Issues and Methods* are drawn from our research findings and experience.

The phases described in table 4–1 are not distinct, separate steps.

Table 4-1
The Process Steps in Program Development

Process Phase	Description	Examples of Issues and Methods
1. Developing Goals	Goals are usually broad value-determined expressions of belief about what ought to be. Goals communicate aims or intentions and point in a direction to go, while objectives (phase 3) specify how to get there. Consensus on goals is easier to reach than is consensus on program objectives.	Some commonly expressed goals for case management include: to improve the quality of life of the elderly; to prevent inappropriate institutionalization; to contain the cost of long term care; to develop a comprehensive, coordinated continuum of care; to promote quality and efficiency in the delivery of services; to facilitate the appropriate use of services by those who have been underserved.
2. Assessing Community Needs	A needs assessment documents undesirable community conditions and degrees of malfunctioning within a specified population. The findings serve to justify the proposed program in later phases of formulating objectives and mobilizing human and material resources. Some assessments include an inventory of existing services and an analysis of the discrepancies between needs and resources or gaps in the continuum of services. When undertaken as a "feasibility study" for a particular program idea, assessment will include opinions of leaders who will affect acceptance of the idea and its sponsor.	Methods for obtaining documentation of needs include: interview survey of a sample of the target population; survey or task forces involving informed leaders and agency personnel; analysis of secondary data from census or service records; distillations of findings and recommendations from previous field studies by universities, planning bodies, research firms, and service providers; preparation of case studies of typical or most difficult problem situations; public hearings.

3. Formulating Program Objectives

Objectives specify the means that will be used to attain the goals. They may be operationalized in terms of action steps or measurable expected levels of achievement. Objectives may be aimed at changes in client conditions, improvements in the community service system, enhancement of legislation or policy, or redistributions of costs or benefits. Other objectives (or subobjectives) may be addressed to organizational needs such as resources, client quotas, productivity, or efficiency.

Examples of objectives in case management programs include:

to provide comprehensive assessments for all older people who are about to enter a nursing home;

to develop a computer-based client tracking system covering persons in community-based or institutional long-term care;

to provide case-manager service to the home-bound;

to identify and enroll chronically impaired persons who are not receiving the services they need;

to organize and maintain an interagency case conference committee for the coordination of home-delivered services;

to obtain Medicaid waivers to permit flexible use of funds for care plans and services.

4. Examining Alternative Actions

The consideration of alternative program designs must involve the leaders and agencies who will be expected to help to implement the plans. The planning process must focus on all three action levels—the community service system, agency operations and linkages, and the client–worker level. Best professional practices and successful program models from other localities must be adapted, not adopted, to avoid later rejections of transplants.

Considerations of alternatives may include the possible and the apparently impossible.

A dilemma exists in posing designs which, on the one hand lack innovativeness and fail to evoke enthusiasm, and on the other may be overelegant and promise too much too soon.

Usually valuable local sources of information and expertise remain untapped because these sources may not be in the traditional network of the sponsoring agency. Conversely, well-timed and well-selected visits from or to outside consultants and technical assistance resource centers can assist in breaking away from out-dated local patterns by offering examples of new program ideas currently being implemented in similar communities.

Table 4–1 Continued

Process Phase	Description	Examples of Issues and Methods
5. Estimating Consequences of Alternative Actions	This phase calls for consideration of the positive and negative effects in a given community before a choice is made. Incremental implementation strategies permit low-cost, low-disgrace adjustments in program design if undesirable side effects or political rebounds occur. Initial design choices can be tested and modified within existing programs or in small-scale pilot programs.	Among the many considerations during this phase are: the domains, power bases, sensitivities to threat among other agencies; prevailing community values and opinion centers that affect acceptance of goals or methods; population subgroups that may have been under-represented in the planning process so far; preferences and service utilization patterns of the intended beneficiaries of the program; implications of design choices for foreseeable sources of stable funding; the suitability of fit between the program and the proposed administering agency or its governing body.
6. Making Choices	A key to a productive process in this phase is the differentiation of who needs to make which decision at which point in time. A close second in importance is the prompt and clear communication of decisions made to all parties who are affected. Unavoidable limitations in time or optimum decision-group size may prevent inclusion of all who wish to influence every decision, but layering and sequencing of decisions among appropriate-as-possible groups will enhance credibility and ultimate acceptance.	Design choices that must involve governance bodies or a coalition of representatives of several boards include those concerned with program goals, selection of administering agency, sources of funding, and population to be served. Choices delegated to groups of agency executives include interorganizational linkages, strategies for targeting and case finding, information system objectives, and location of the case-management functions. Decisions that may be deferred to the program director and staff include assessment methods, training plans, and termination policies.

7. Implementing the Design; Making Modifications

During the implementation phase the personnel, structures, activities, and communication channels are set in place. Rules and procedures are clarified and disseminated so that organizational behavior is predictable and accountable at the client–worker, agency, and service system levels. At the same time, implementation calls for constant feedback and reconsideration of the initial program design, taking advantage of the competence and creativity of staff, the reactions of clients, and the experiences of cooperating organizations. Changes must be formalized and communicated promptly to avoid program drift or slippage. There must be coordination within the agency before there can be inter-agency coordination. While implementation requires the executive to become increasingly task-centered, a process orientation must be maintained to motivate productivity and conserve partnerships.

Neighborhood or senior groups may need to be involved in decisions such as site, eligibility, and volunteer roles as well as in some of the foregoing decisions.

Implementation tasks at the *worker/client level* include:

developing procedures and materials related to client-level functions such as entry, assessment, care planning and follow-up;

promulgating of prescreening and intake criteria and of termination policies;

distributing responsibilities for client-pathway functions among types of front-line personnel;

establishing norms for case-load size, differentiation of case-load composition, and priority-setting among cases.

Implementation tasks at the *administrative level* include:

setting in place patterns of supervision, staff orientation, and training, personnel policies, work schedules, and staff meetings;

arranging office sites and modes of transportation for office and home visits;

ensuring courteous and efficient handling of callers by telephone or in reception room;

installing support functions such as information management, fiscal management, resources mobilization, public relations, and specialized consultation.

Implementation tasks at the *system level* include

formalizing working agreements and contracts with providers;

Table 4–1 Continued

Process Phase	Description	Examples of Issues and Methods
		organizing linkages such as case conference committees, shared outreach, transportation, or interlocking governance;
		participating in planning and action bodies to fill gaps in services;
		searching for additional or more stable funding.
8. Evaluation of Performance and Outcomes	There is a wide range of evaluation approaches and seldom is any one method sufficient for evaluating a complex coordination program. Informal feedback, routine data analysis, one-shot scientific studies and expert review panels each have value. Operational objectives provide a framework for performance evaluation; goals provide a framework for evaluation of impact. Evaluation designs must take into account deviations made from the initial plan based on operating experience. Anticipatory involvement of staff and careful explanation to clients and partner agencies regarding evaluation purposes, methods, and consequences are essential.	Guidelines regarding evaluation include: Evaluation of program impact is not feasible in the initial year due to start-up problems and delays in bringing the program model to full stride and efficiency. Early evaluations should provide prompt feedback for administration and practice, focusing on the degree to which the design is in place at all levels and functioning as intended. Administrators, board members, and funding sources should be aware of staff time and other costs of research tasks. Investments in evaluation should be kept commensurate with intended uses. When evaluating costs or impact of case management, account for activities beyond client service such as research and service system development. No one type of organization can attain all goals and objectives with equally high levels of achievement. Therefore, the administrator should ensure that a balance of attention is given to the several aims of the program in proportion to their relative importance. Narrow-focus third-party evaluations can be balanced with internally developed evaluative activities.

The tasks of developing, planning, and implementing a case-coordination program do not occur in a rigid continuum. There will be some looping back in the process sequence because some phase of preparation was neglected. There are regressions because some unexpected contingency must be incorporated at some point. Planning decisions should not be brought to closure too abruptly. When several ideas are under consideration, the stage is set for innovation and creativity. The main idea is to avoid tunnel vision in designing a new program. Open options allow for adaptations suitable for local use and compatability. The "givens" and the constraints are not the same for all communities, but each will have a set of its own barriers. Program planners may find it necessary to accept some of the "givens" in the intial phases that later can be changed or circumvented.

The organizing process makes the greatest demands on community organization skills. The leadership talents of the administrative group continue to be important as implementation proceeds. If the program design is working well and the initial goals and objectives hold up, the program can develop according to plan. But if there are warning signals of distress, then another process cycle of problem solving begins. A checkup for problems is made and corrective action should be taken.

The Launching Phase

The eight-step model of a program planning process is presented as if each of the phases were of equal duration and significance. We have already called attention to the fact that planners do not rationally complete one step; then, having completed that step, proceed to the next one. Rather, the model should be considered as a set of eight components that serve as a checklist for testing whether all the bases, from program goal determination through evaluation, have been covered, with provisions for feedback and corrections.

The launching phase of the program planning process is the most complicated one. Process difficulties are created because of the interdependence and interaction of a number of events that may take place simultaneously, such as the following:

determining program goals and some specific objectives that are readily acceptable (such as adaptations for cultural differences or rural environments);

negotiating for funding that affects agency authority and client target groups;

securing federal waivers or state legislation that shapes program goals and authority;

interpreting the program idea and the planning progress to relevant community groups and leaders who may resist what they do not understand;

revising initial program goals to realistic expectations as the launching process continues;

mobilizing additional leadership and agencies as the potential scope of the program increases (or in reverse if the scope decreases);

modifying the total design, target groups, and size of operations because of increased credibility or community support and as additional funds become available (or the reverse);

redesigning program agency structure because of unexpected "turf" problems affecting goals, client target groups, and allocation of funds; and

adjusting to predetermined research demonstration goals, funds, sanction, authority, and other prescribed design features. It is easier to sell client needs and services than it is to sell the research demonstration requirements.

Conforming to requirements of funding sources regarding target population or scope of program can shorten the launching because fewer local decisions seem possible (defining objectives, delineating target group, averting turf disputes, agreeing on program design, and implementing the staffing pattern). On the other hand, trying to conform to an overload of bureaucratic "givens" can conflict with the community's priorities of interest or action.

Although the client pathway should be the principal frame of reference throughout the program development process, most of the activities during the launching period center on the organizational level rather than the client level. There are several reasons why the specifics of client–worker planning trails behind the other two levels in the program launching process. First, there is no stability for program operations until the foundations for the agency are in place and the program is sufficiently accepted by the community of agencies. Moreover, the new program budget generally provides first for executive positions, which starts the time lag in employing program specialists or service delivery personnel. Finally, the involvement of essential service agencies and leadership always takes much more time than expected. As a consequence the harassed executive may be unprepared for this time investment in securing acceptable agreements from provider agencies.

There are many versions of what a case manager is supposed to be. This conflict does not surface early in the planning; thus planning for the client–worker pathway may be delayed. When the program design calls for an innovative staffing pattern there is seldom a testing period in the early launching process. Sufficient time must be allowed to clarify the innovation and to operationalize it before the program gets into high gear.

The administrator must ensure that program functions at the client level are planned and launched in a balanced manner. Too often the launching of the service delivery plan begins with months of work on the development of a comprehensive assessment tool. When overemphasized, it can control the shape of the client pathway and practice options. It can monopolize the time available for case practice training. Too much emphasis on the tool often detracts from the concept of assessment as a continuous process as well as from the other phases in the client pathway.

As a conclusion to this discussion on the unevenness of the launching phases over the three levels, we should add that blunders at the interorganizational level have serious and swift consequences for all levels of the program. It takes a longer time for the poor choices and subsequent mistakes to rise to surface from the client–worker level.

Process Implications in Some Critical Areas

The launching phase presented in the preceding section emphasized the interrelationships of decisions being made in the start-up phase—formation of goals, definition of the target group, obtaining funding, and establishing authority (control). The organizing-mobilizing stages are heavily process laden, but as the program is launched there is less emphasis on the process of program development. Even though the agency administrator must become increasingly managerial and task oriented, the program will continue to make use of process skills for maintenance, growth, and continual adaptation to community environments. Those areas we consider most important for program developers and implementers are (1) the politics of planning, (2) precipitating events, (3) public education and marketing, (4) prediction of barriers, and (5) leadership.

The Politics of Planning

The term *politics* is used in a broad, general sense, although partisan politics may create a background for some unexpected influences. The following list offers some guidelines and examples.

Project your own leadership and working style as early as possible. Some consistency in expected behaviors from the administrator creates a climate for more trusting responses.

Show evidence of flexibility, negotiating skills, and an interest in listening.

Leave an escape hatch open on early promises. When changes and modifications are necessary, suggestions on alternatives may sound better coming from other respected leaders.

Know the local political situation, some of the conflicts, and centers of power. Neutrality is often the best stance for the agency executive. Partisan intermediaries are often part of a strategy, however.

Make early contacts with relevant local government officials and related government agencies. Recognize the contacts that must be made by your going to *their* offices.

Identify the issues that may arise in the design and implementation of the program for which the help of community leaders will be needed. Each community influencer has his own domain of power.

Assess the social consciousness level of the community with respect to services for the elderly, including housing, food stamps, and social programs in general. Sound out the potential of the prevailing value system to accept the goals and methods of the proposed program.

Be informed about the medical community segment and the history of its relationships with other professions and programs.

Explore the modes of rewards, exchanges, and trade-offs acceptable among local leaders and agencies.

Review the community history of joint planning or coordination projects in the human service area.

Find out about successful local programs in the human service field. Get some case histories on executive survivors in newly created agencies as well as finding out "where the bodies are buried."

Develop shared program leadership as soon as possible. Mobilizing community resources is never a one-person job.

Precipitating Events

This topic has generated a number of axioms, such as "Go with the flow," Ride with the tide," "Make hay while the sun shines." In the same way the prelude to the initiation of a new program or the remodeling of an established program has been hastened by some community event or crisis related to the purposes of the new program. Sometimes a slow start or a proposed change that has been put on the back burner picks up momentum. A number of circumstances can precipitate or add impetus to action:

Follow up on news events or feature stories communicated by the media concerning the plight of individuals or groups of elderly such as victims of fire, eviction, or abuse. Enlist the interest of a self-help group of family members following a state action to close down several nursing homes with no preparation for relocation.

Keep in touch with emerging changes in public policy. New mandates or drastic budget cuts can create a crisis climate that calls for action.

Watch for opportunities created by the release of citizens' needs studies, or assessment surveys by universities, planning agencies, or advocacy organizations, and demands for action by community leaders. The timing of a program start-up is often a response to rising concern about needed programs.

Follow some of the professional fund raising techniques. The first announcement of a grant award or a private start-up donation starts an immediate spurt of optimism that attracts the next money for program development. Emphasize the good news.

Link legislative events, a crisis event, and other precipitating circumstances together with an initiation of a new program or change of function in an existing agency. The cumulative effect of a series of events can be a boost to the impetus for program development.

Keep tuned to opportunities such as the formation of a coalition, for instance when three major hospitals join together for a federated home care service for the elderly.

Public Education and Marketing

Case coordination is not an easy product to interpret and sell. The role of a case manager is difficult to explain, even to the client receiving the help. It is much simpler to sell the idea of scarce resources, efficiency, and linkages between service agencies providing for coordination of services at the client level. Results are available from several coordination programs showing greater efficiency as compared with noncoordinated services.

Case management must be interpreted as a service in itself. The client pathway in a simplified form illustrates the functions provided along the client route. Unless case management is clearly interpreted, the message given may be received as just another layer of administration.

Too often the agency executive does not keep close enough to the client level to know firsthand the product of the agency. Boards of directors hear about policy and budget issues but seldom hear directly from a caseworker—about what *was done* for particular clients. (Minimize the case process story and stick to the client situation and what got done.)

Although community surveys of needs of the elderly are similar across the country, each community wants its own. A survey with community participation, trained volunteer interviewers, and with citizen reports from the different segments of the community offers an unusual public education opportunity. This survey approach also offers credibility and a step in social consciousness-raising because community people were there in the field and know the story firsthand. Self-surveys have their own purposes even when they do not conform to traditional scientific survey methods. Nonetheless any survey designers must ensure there is no systematic bias against inclusion of the needs of the frail and home-bound elderly, often a difficult group to locate.

Planners need recent demographic information, good inventories of available services and waiting lists, and other specific information. Being ready to show you have mastery of the best tools of the trade makes for good public relations. The marketing of case coordination should focus on both the client and efficiency.

An administrative policy of program education should include the closest audience group, the clients. Clients and their families should know how the services got to them and how it was made possible. Many times it has been found that clients do not know the name of the coordination agency, or where it is located. In some instances clients do not understand the connection between the lady who made the home-visit assessment and the chore lady who comes twice a week.

Aim promotion activities at particular target audiences as well. For example, adult children of frail elderly are often more receptive to case-coordination programs for vulnerable elderly than are the active elderly in senior citizen centers. Community professionals have been found to be the most interested groups for promotion of help for vulnerable elderly.

The cost and benefits of the many approaches for organizing support groups must be assessed. Mobilizing volunteers may absorb a great deal of time and money. Utilizing volunteers as service workers requires strong supervision and support; however, they broaden the constituency of the program. Similarly, fund-raising auxiliaries require staff support but extend both the fiscal base and community awareness.

One tough public information job is getting the appropriate message to other agencies. Explaining what case managers do is never easy. Explaining more precisely what the coordination agency does brings better client referrals and dissipates potential doubts about competitiveness.

Be cautious about overselling promises to reduce nursing home populations. For every frail elderly person "prevented" from institutionalization there is another frail person uncovered by outreach activities who should have been placed in a nursing home. For the same reason nursing home interests need not regard case management as a threat to full occupancy.

Prediction of Barriers

Early recognition of barriers and problems is as often based on hunches and listening with the "third ear" as it is on competence and knowledge about the field. The start-up of a program is often buoyant, but the enthusiasm may hide some problems that were present all along but have not yet surfaced.

Unexpected delays in receiving start-up payments from bureaucratic funding sources can create a serious crisis. This necessitates a bank loan, which leads to problems in getting approval for interest payments as a budget item.

Unexpected delays in matching the new program staff positions with comparable governmental or United Way position classifications can delay recruitment. Allocation of staff time, especially on the part of the directors of experimental coordination programs becomes a daily process of rearrangement. And as one director of a beginning innovative demonstration said, "No one told me to expect such a barrage of interested callers or audiences wanting an explanation of what we are doing. I am so busy talking to the press, on a T.V. panel, receiving visitors, etc., to explain the new program we are conducting, that I have no time left to do what I say I am doing."

Repeatedly, the accounts of case-coordination projects have emphasized the inordinate amount of time required during the start-up period to work through acceptable provider agency agreements and contracts. Negotiation is another time-consuming process. The time required for obtaining waivers or getting an interpretation of new or questionable regulations is also usually longer than expected, and negotiations are complex at both state and federal levels.

A final common problem is that funding levels in the next several years will have little room for inflationary adjustments for salaries, supplies, transportation, and utilities.

Leadership

The importance of leadership is a theme that weaves throughout all the guidelines for decision making and choices of alternatives in program design, development, and implementation. Different kinds of situations require different kinds of leadership, each with its own set of dimensions and characteristics.

In a coordination agency or program leadership usually refers to the qualities of the executive. It also includes staff associates, the board or governance group, and others who share the leadership role. There is seldom a successful social program in a community where the leadership flows from only one person. Nonetheless, it is generally expected that the executive will provide the overall leadership and possess the required skills.

The leadership found desirable in our project research, as well as other sources, calls for a range of talents seldom found outside of Superman or Wonder Woman. To quote a few of these special traits, the leader must be an advocate, a community organizer, a rebel, a strongly dedicated person able to inspire and spread enthusiasm, and be a good public speaker. This set of traits includes another series of qualities: the executive needs administrative, management, public relations, technological, and program knowledge and skills, with appropriate educational background and experience. Also expected are an impressive appearance, clothing that is compatible with community norms, and a touch of charisma.

Many executives profit from the institutional leadership and credibility of a community group, a coalition or an established agency that helped to launch the program. But even executives with this initial advantage must soon establish their own credibility and leadership role.

Weak leadership and leadership failures are easier to communicate than a definition of strong leadership. Every community has its own inventory of case histories in leadership failures of agency executives. Lessons from the past are worth reviewing.

In some human service agencies the executives may come and go, but the agency as a social institution is the carrier of the community trust, prestige, and leadership. Continuing strength and dedication in the governance body, stability in competent staff, and constituency support make this possible.

Case-management agencies have three built-in obstacles for which administrative leadership must compensate: (1) Interdisciplinary staffed programs are more difficult "to lead" and integrate. (2) Survival supports must begin early, for continuity and stabilization of funding as the basis for institutionalizing a program. (3) Case-management programs are complex to interpret to the public although some of the concrete activities are understandable—for example, purchase of unavailable services, providing assessments for nursing home admissions, monitoring over- and underutilization, promptly responding to complaints (or referrals) regarding abused, neglected, or disturbed elderly persons.

Not every one of the foregoing examples of a special area for process attention is pure process alone. It is difficult to separate style and manner from what is being done to accomplish a task or objective. Process is an integral part of the means. After these skills of relationship become part of the behavior of a professional, there can be conscious choices of how tasks get done. At the same time personality, flexibility, personal sensitivity, and insights become an important part of the picture. The next and final section of this chapter will summarize some of the key process concepts as they are used in developing and maintaining a case-coordination program.

Some Tested Process Concepts

We have identified some of the most common concepts that apply to the organizational and interorganizational levels. Some key concepts are defined in principles or rules of operations. Others are at the level of "Keep this idea in mind and it may be useful to you."

Timing means knowing or getting the feeling that this point in the process is the best time to act. Timing is most important in predicting delays and preparing in advance for time slippage. The effective administrator sets agency plans, products, and objectives within a time frame yet remains ready to advance or delay planned steps in order to adjust to the most opportune time.

The notion of *pace* is concerned with the rate or the gait in pushing to get things done. Pacing must take into account the interpretation of feedback and correction for the next planned steps. Repetition or extension of a step may be indicated. An administrator must be aware of variations in the pace of planning at different stages and contexts. The start-up on negotiations for service contracts may begin at a run but slow down to a crawl during negotiation of contract specifics of a legal, fiscal, or evaluative nature. Some communities move like the tortoise in taking on a new program; others progress harelike, in big jumps.

Sequencing as a concept in leadership and administration can be compared to arranging the action steps in the best order for reaching an objective. For example, before data on service statistics can be collected, units to be counted must be defined. Another illustration of sequencing is the wise administrator who gets agency staff and constituency into a favorable state of acceptance and support before organizing the outside provider agencies. (Motto: "There must be coordination within before there can be coordination with others.") Similarly, some program objectives may need to be attained before others can be attempted.

There may be standardized tests for reading readiness in education but there are no precise instruments for testing the *readiness* of health and welfare agencies and community leadership to join together in a coordination program. Past history, trial and error, judgement, experience, intuition and carefully-sought good advice are some of the clues which tell us that there is readiness to act.

Following the leader is an idea that has served as a guide to those who are finding their way in leadership roles or attempting to influence a committee. The simple rule is that the leader should not run too far ahead of the followers. The administrator-leader must continually assess the gap, revise expectations, and provide bridging experiences. The opposite can happen: The isolated leader can find that he or she is ten paces behind the followers.

Problem solving in communities and in organizations requires recurrent analysis of the *force field*—the forces that facilitate or impede a proposed solution or objective. The identification of these forces and the assessment of their direction and strength provides the backdrop for strategic planning of actions that may reinforce the positive influences and neutralize the negative. Not all such forces can be dealt with at any one time, and the influences change over time. Therefore the game of force-field analysis must be played and replayed in order to select priorities based on importance, timing, and relative feasibility.

Credibility has its own worth and aims. It is usually linked with trust and others who have earned trust. A community also expects expertness and competence in the program field. Competence and credibility not only must be earned and learned but it must be communicated to the agency environment and the agency staff.

Negotiation is a working concept that is an essential technique at all levels in developing the service system, in building consensus within the agency, and in implementing service plans for particular clients and their respective families. There can be no negotiation unless there is room for trade-offs, rewards, and alternative choices.

It is essential that an organizer be able to cope with a broad *span of action*, often as many as ten or twelve developing streams of progress at any time. The compulsive type who must finish one job before starting another would quickly be submerged in launching a new program. As the program stabilizes, the administrator may be able to reduce the internal span of control, but in a case-management program, the administrator's span of action continues to be broad.

Exchange of rewards and trade-offs is part of the process of coordination. Goodwill and love of helping others who are needy are seldom enough to motivate cooperation. Coordination always calls for losing something in autonomy, agency recognition, or certain freedoms. The exchange process can also include the basic carrot-and-stick idea, but this approach must be well-couched in acceptable language and packaging. Mutual benefits in exchange are most acceptable. Agencies seldom come asking to be coordinated.

A *talent for conceptualization* is essential. Administrators need a talent to generalize, to put things together of a similar order so that agency functions and activities can be categorized and grouped. A capacity to conceptualize will help the administrator to orchestrate a multiplicity of component parts into an integrated effort. This is in contrast to fumbling with a burdensome number of unconnected program details.

Tolerance of ambiguity is a quality that supports the administrator's ability to cope with the stress of uncertainties that inevitably occur while initiating a new program or making critical changes. It is a flexibility without loss of enthusiasm or discipline with respect to goals. Tolerance for ambiguity is usually accompanied by a sense of humor and satisfaction in meeting challenges of multiple choices.

Summary

A successful case-management program needs more than a technically good design. The processes of shaping and launching that design can make or break the program. The planner or administrator is the key person in guiding the program development process. He or she asks the right questions, knows when to listen, patiently establishes relationships, grasps the sensitive issues, handles a mixed agenda of work at any one time, organizes participation, keeps communication lines open, keeps tuned to group as well as individual changes or suspicions, maintains an enthusiastic stance, tolerates ambiguity when necessary, brings related past experiences in other communities, communicates competence, can handle hostility, recognizes anxiety and is able to share the leadership spotlight. Most important for improving process skills in community work is a capacity to get, take, and make positive use of criticism as well as respond appropriately to unexpected resistance or barriers. In spite of the incredible demands of skill involved in program development, managing the process components can be the most interesting and satisfying part of the job.

Suggested Readings

American Health Planning Assn. (AHPA). *A Guide for Planning Long-Term-Care Health Services for the Elderly*. Washington, D.C.: AHPA, 1982 (Silver Springs, Md.: AHPA, 1975 [HEW-05-74-283 and HEW-05-74-299]).

Callahan, J.J., Jr. "Delivery of Services to Persons with Long-Term-Care Needs." In Meltzer, J.; Farrow, F.; and Richman, H., *Policy Options in Long-Term Care*. Chicago, Ill.: University of Chicago Press, 1980, 148–181.

Carter, G.W. "Community Organization and Social Planning." In Freidlander, W., (ed.), *Concepts and Methods of Social Work*. 2nd ed. Englewood Cliffs, N.J.: Prentice-Hall, 1976, 158–215.

Coward, R. "Planning Community Services for the Rural Elderly: Implications from Research." *The Gerontologist* 19, no. 3 (June 1979):275–282.

Demone, H.W., Jr. *Stimulating Human Services Reform*. Washington, D.C.: Department of Health, Education, and Welfare, June 1978 (Project SHARE, Human Services Monograph Series Number 8, DHEW Pub. No. OS-76-130).

Kahn, A.J. *Theory and Practice of Social Planning*. New York: Russell Sage Foundation, 1969.

Mathematica Policy Research. *The Planning and Implementation of Channeling: Early Experiences of the National Long-Term Care Demonstration*. Washington, D.C.: MPR, 15 April 1983.

Pfeiffer, E. (ed.). *Alternatives to Institutional Care for Older Americans: Practice and Planning*. Durham, N.C.: Center for the Study of Aging and Human Development, Duke University, 1973.

Rothman, J. *Planning and Organizing for Social Change: Action Principles from Social Science Research*. New York: Columbia University Press, 1974.

Seidl, F.W.; Applebaum, R.; Austin, C.; and Mahoney, K. *Delivering In-Home Services to the Aged and Disabled*. Lexington, Mass.: Lexington Books, 1983.

Steinberg, R.M. "Functional Components and Organizational Issues in Rural Service Systems for the Aged." In Watkins, D.A., and Crawford, C.O. (eds.), *Rural Gerontology Research in the Northeast*. Ithaca, N.Y.: Northeast Regional Center for Rural Development, Cornell University, 1978.

Weiner, M.E. *Application of Organizational and Systems Theory to Human Services Reform*. Washington, D.C.: Department of Health, Education, and Welfare, April 1978 (Project SHARE, Human Services Monograph Series No. 6, DHEW Pub. No. OS-76-130).

5 Funding, Grants Administration, and Costs

The cultivation of adequate and continuous funding sources is a major occupation of case-management program administrators. While the constant search and the inevitable tasks associated with accounting for funds divert time and talent that could otherwise be invested in other program service functions, they are essential to the survival of the program.

The motto of social-program planners and administrators is ''Function follows funding.'' Case-management programs for the vulnerable elderly call for a particularly wide range of functions. Therefore a diversity of funding sources is needed in order to span the variety of potential client groups, to respond to the full spectrum of needs for services, and to carry service-system development roles. It should be noted that programs operating with diverse sources of funds with separate rules and procedures for the use of and accountability to each require highly competent, well-informed fiscal personnel. Although mixed funding broadens the financial base, it can create budgeting and cash flow problems.

Mobilizing Material Resources

Current case-management programs have obtained funding from a variety of sources on both short term and long term. For example, the 330 respondents to this projects' national survey report that their major funding sources for 1979 were

Older Americans Act, Title III (70%)

Title XX, Social Security Act (45%)

Local government (43%) including revenue sharing (10%)

Comprehensive Employment and Training Act (CETA) (40%)

State funds (38%)

United Way (20%)

Other private sources (20%), including local foundations and service clubs

By 1981 increasing numbers of programs were obtaining time-limited demonstration grants, not only from state governments, but also from federal sources such as AoA, HCFA, and the National Institutes of Mental Health, and from foundations such as Robert Wood Johnson Foundation. It should be noted that while time-limited flexibile funding may help a program to get off the ground without typical concerns about comingling of funds, conflicting eligibility rules, and multiple accountability systems, it will eventually need to seek long-term, usually categorical, sources of funds if the program is to provide service beyond the start-up or demonstration phase. Federal trends toward block grants to states may result in fewer dollars but also fewer of the regulatory constraints of categorical funds. By 1982 competition for reduced funds at the state-level emerged as an issue of major concern.

Longer-range impacts on funding availability and stability are the result of important developments in both the private and public sectors. Some private health insurance programs are broadening their coverage to include more kinds of home-based health care when it is used as a substitute for acute care or extended care in institutional facilities. Some of the most dramatic and rapid changes are occurring in the public arena, where state legislatures and the U.S. Congress have been developing legislation that makes comprehensive assessment or prescreening mandatory before public funds can be used for nursing home care. Some legislation proposed provides for designation and funding of local community care organizations to do assessment and follow-up case management and cost monitoring. Other new laws permit use of medical assistance funds such as Medicare and Medicaid for case management itself as well as for case-planned combinations of home care, day treatment services (social as well as medical), and respite without requirements of previous hospitalization.

Each year the opportunities for funding case management and related services to the elderly change. Lists of funding sources and their program priorities become out of date quickly. There are great differences from state to state. In order to keep informed, the planner and administrator must build a personal support network of colleagues, beginning with personnel at area agencies on aging, state units on aging, health systems agencies, community planning councils, and public social services that deal with Title XX. It may also be advantageous to recruit paid or volunteer specialists in resource development.

In addition to contacts with the public funding network, it is most important for the administrator to become knowledgeable about nongovernmental sources. In many cases, local sources are available for specific cost items on a case-by-case basis from

ethnic beneficial organizations;

service clubs;

voluntary health agencies (such as the American Heart Association) and special group agencies (for the blind, the deaf, and others);

small local foundations/corporations/individual donors;

public housing authorities;

labor unions and corporation philanthropic programs;

churches, denominational offices, ecumenical groups;

private insurances;

senior clubs and associations of retired professionals;

individual or family donors

for such items as rent or utility subsidies; transportation and escort; friendly visitors and other volunteers; furniture, canes, wheelchairs, and so on; emergency shelter; special medical supplies; and dentures, eyeglasses, and hearing aids. Another means for increasing resources is through sliding-fee scales (client copayment or contributions) and third-party payments (Title XVIII, XIX, XX, insurances, and so on). A program with sliding-fee scales not only maximizes resources but avoids fragmented, duplicative programs that segregate people according to income.

In-kind contributions for program needs may sometimes be obtained from agencies, organizations and businesses for such items as loaned staff or free consultation; free or low-cost office space or use of vehicles; and publications (brochures, directories) especially from banks, newspapers, or public relations departments of large firms. Mobilizing funds and in-kind resources from a diversity of sources not only helps the budget but also widens the network of organizations which know about the program and have a stake in its success and survival. One of the important tools for improving access to funds is the inclusion on governing boards and advisory committees of persons who have direct access to funding sources and other persons whose involvement (as individuals or as representatives of constituencies) enhances the organization's prestige with funders.

In their efforts to seek resources, program administrators must be cautious in their claims that they will save money for the community through case management. There are likely to be some short-term *increases* in costs for the following reasons:

Outreach identifies and serves clients who were previously not served at all and who may need in-home or institutional care.

Previously known clients are served who need to catch up on previously neglected medical and social problems. Hence costs during initial phases of case may be higher.

Serving clients more comprehensively than in the past—that is, offering more services per client—costs more.

Investing more case-manager effort to deal with reluctant clients or those with complex interrelated needs may at some points exceed institutional costs even though long-term costs per case may be diminished.

Taking responsibility for highly vulnerable clients may require more administrative, clinical, and legal checks and balances than in single-purpose service provision, resulting in higher administrative costs.

Especially when making presentations to legislators and other audiences who expect cost savings, keep in mind that demographics: the growing numbers of elderly who are living longer (and often "spending down" their personal savings) will tend to increase total expenditures with or without a case-management program. Several programs have indeed demonstrated that case management can result in greater efficiency in the use of resources, and that care of the elderly at home is cost effective when compared with matched cases that are receiving institutional care.

Purchase of Services

A case-management agency's ability to mobilize services for its clients is enhanced to the degree that the responsible agency has control over the funds of service providers. Mechanisms for controlling funds include purchase-of-service contracts; a role in approving funding requests from service providers; overlapping memberships in governing bodies; or other rewards to exchange. (Such rewards include taking "tough clients;" assisting with grantsmanship; providing public recognition of the worth of the provider's services; and arranging for administrtive supports or complementary services that given providers need.) Of the various mechanisms of control, purchase of services is considered the strongest for the deployment of funds for specific purposes. Services may be purchased from a public or private nonprofit agency, from a proprietory organization, or from an individual. Descriptions of three forms of purchase contracts follow.

Program Grants

With this form the responsible agency or its funding sponsor makes a grant to another service provider specifying the number of clients or number of units of service (in hours) that will be delivered on behalf of the programs' clients. It becomes the case manager's responsiblity to decide which clients receive what quantities of service and to ensure that the total amount stays within the limits of the contract. This form of purchase is the easiest one for service agencies to enter since it anticipates the total volume of work and permits the retaining of personnel suitable for that anticipated volume. It also usually involves less paperwork for the responsible agency than separate purchase orders or contracts on a client-by-client basis.

Individual Purchase Orders

With this form the case-management agency purchases specific services for individual clients as needed. It permits more flexibility in choosing the most suitable provider and varying the volume of services purchased but requires more preparatory steps and more monitoring than the program grant approach. It is sometimes used to purchase proprietary services when the available supply of such services from nonprofit agencies is overloaded or falls below an acceptable standard of quality or cost. Another application, especially in rural areas, is to purchase from individual vendors anything from home repairs to in-home psychiatric treatment where community agencies are not established to deliver the needed service. This form of purchase, again, specifies the units of service, the amount per week, the duration for each client and, of course, the cost per unit of service. When purchases are made from individual vendors or proprietary firms, there must be better-than-average monitoring since there is no ongoing community governance or accountability as is the case with nonprofit voluntary or governmental agencies.

Capitation

The third variation in purchase arrangements is relatively new for community-based care though it has many precedents in institutional care and in health maintenance organizations (HMOs). Capitation contracts are those in which the purchasers agree to pay a uniform amount per capita per month in return for comprehensive services, which may vary in volume or duration over time for each beneficiary according to need. It usually covers a number of clients concurrently and in sufficient numbers so that those who have above-average needs for high-cost care are balanced by others who have below-average care costs.

In principle the provider takes the risk that overall costs will not exceed the estimated average per capita, which was the basis for the contract. For the purchaser the expectation is that the service provider will be motivated to engage in preventative and rehabilitative services in a timely manner in contrast to incentives of traditional reimbursement patterns, which pay more and pay longer when the client becomes or remains ill.

One variation of capitation is the purchase of high-quality adult day care that orchestrates individual and group interventions in accord with the needs of individual clients as they change over time. Individual or block contracts that specify each unit of service become cumbersome and deter diagnostically determined creativity in the provider's approaches to different clients receiving day care. Some of the demonstration channeling agencies, funded and launched by the Department of Health and Human Services in 1980, will be experimenting with capitation approaches. A few new social and health maintenance organizations (SHMOs) for the elderly are attempting to apply this method for organizing and funding a broad continuum of care within a single agency.

Purchase of services offers an effective means to expand the provision of services to clients. At the same time it offers an effective means of controlling funds, which in turn gives the responsible agency considerable influence with service providers. Influence is further enhanced when funding is stable. Uncertainties of funding, cash flow delays, or inadequate funds can result in a breakdown of interagency coordination efforts. But even with control of funds and relatively stable funding, effective coordination requires considerable diplomacy and interpersonal reinforcement on the part of staff.

Building a coordinated service system is part of the business of case management. Control over funds through the use of mechanisms such as purchase of services enables the responsible agency to facilitate participation. As one case-management administrator put it, "The best reward for agency participation and coordination is the exchange of money for services."

Budgeting

Many references exist regarding standard principles of line-item and functional budgeting. More important, every agency needs to have access to people experienced in budgeting. However, program personnel must be involved in the process so that service to clients is not inadvertently impeded by budgeting choices. Case management calls for some particular budget considerations.

While a budget is assumed to be devoted as directly as possible to working with clients, it must also allow for such indirect costs as

program evaluation;

staff time for recording and reporting;

staff time for interagency relations and meetings;

staff time for communicating with collaterals relevant to particular clients;

staff orientation, training, supervision, and respite;

staff meetings;

staff turnover;

telephone costs (can be significant in some service areas and should not be deterred—adequate use of telephone can save other costs of staff time and travel);

costs of steering persons to other agencies who are inappropriately referred to the program;

costs of consultation and technical assistance.

In assigning costs of operations to various funding sources or program functions, consideration must be given to such technical issues as

service definitions (Is *homemaker* the same from Agency A as from Agency B?);

units of service specifications;

eligibility rules of each funding source;

whether or not to consider costs to clients and families;

method for logging staff time going to different functions or different cases;

the start-up costs of a new or revised program should not be included in evaluations of the long-term costs or efficiency of a given program model;

delays in the first year in staff recruitment and training, case finding, and cash flow from funding sources.

Costs per Client

Many approaches exist for calculating costs per client. In some analyses attention is devoted exclusively to the cost of the case management itself. In other analyses the costs of case management plus the costs of the packages of formal services that have been arranged through the case-management program are examined. Other cost analyses include *all* formal services and subsidies being received by the client whether or not they were obtained through the program. Still other approaches attempt to include the actual out-of-pocket costs to the client or to the client's family and friends or the "market value" of informal services being obtained from the family and friends.

The broader, most inclusive, approaches to cost calculation become important in attempts to show the costs of keeping frail people in their own homes as compared with the costs of institutional care as well as the cost trade-offs of different service packages within a given program. This project's bibliographies list studies that illustrate these different approaches to cost accounting.

The discussion here will explore the simplest of these approaches—the costs of case management itself. This cost is an essential base for the other approaches and is usually the initial concern of the program designer and administrator.

In its simplest form, cost per client is a matter of taking the entire case-management budget, including administration and indirect costs, and dividing it by the number of clients being served over the same fiscal year. The resulting cost figures may be of use to a program to document its own increasing efficiency as it emerges from its start-up problems, as its staff gains experience and competence, and as it clarifies its focus and goals and procedures over time. Such cost figures, however, are of very little use in comparing one's own program with others in other localities. The gross cost figure will mask enormous differences in programs with respect to

frailty of the target groups;

geographic dispersion and ethnic diversity of the target group;

intensity of case management service (including relative promptness and continuity);

scope of case management practice (comprehensiveness);

local community resources available to clients (medical, psychological, housing); client resources for copayment;

acceptance of the agency; age, reputation and power of the program;

commitment of the program to system building and class action; for improvement of national policy or professional practice;

differences in definitions as to who is an ''active case'';

prevailing value orientations among clients that facilitate or impede effective utilization of services

A Machiavellian Guide to Reducing Costs per Client

The calculation of costs per client, as well as breakdown of costs by the various functions within the agency, is a useful tool in administrative problem solving, but it is too frequently abused or overused because it is expressed as a precise dollar amount. It is a step toward problem clarification and no more. In order to illustrate how misleading such cost figures can be and how they can be manipulated, as well as to illustrate legitimate variables to consider in constructing a formula for a useful cost analysis, we present the following *tongue-in-cheek* guidelines:

1. Account separately for the costs of activities that benefit persons beyond your own clientele.
    a. Separately log activities devoted to identifying service gaps and participating in community planning to establish new resources.
    b. Separately log time devoted to consultation and public speaking that helps other agencies and the community at large to understand the needs and resources of the elderly.
    c. Separately log time devoted to preparation and presentation of reports and testimony aimed at improving legislation, policy, or regulations that affect more people than your target group within your service area. Also separately log time devoted to disseminating information about the program to sponsors or administrators from other communities, to universities, and to government officials.
    d. Separately log time spent in planning and advocacy for future years of the program so that this effort is not attached to the costs of this years' clients.
2. Isolate the costs of searching and accounting for funds and costs of program evaluation.
    a. Log administrator's time going into preparing fund applications, periodic reports to sponsors, and troubleshooting cash flow problems;
    b. Log costs of xeroxing proposals, funding reports, and purchase-of-service contracts.

    c. Log the client assessment time spent to obtain data for evaluators or management information systems that do not also serve the clinical purposes of the case manager in helping the client.

    d. Log the time that goes into logging staff activities for purposes of cost analysis.

3.   Manipulate your target group and functions

    a. Screen in more clients who are "easy cases"—who have fewer needs and who require less effort from the program.

    b. Never terminate clients—so that relatively inactive (and even deceased) persons can be included in the head counts or case loads. Include your waiting list in your head count, if you can get away with it.

    c. Have case managers limit their focus to the most crucial needs of clients or the most available kind of services so that they don't spend time on such "frills" as creating new services to fill gaps; assisting clients' families and friends to respond to clients' needs; providing support to clients and service providers to facilitate effective service delivery; identifying and responding to clients as a whole person including mental health needs, physical comfort, morale, and so on; or on expansive goals such as rehabilitation and development of client capacities.

    d. Limit time devoted to quality control and program improvement, such as case reviews, case conferences, supervisory or specialist consultations, personnel training, and data analysis.

4.   Other

    a. Encourage staff turnover so that new employees can be hired at lower steps on the pay scale.

    b. Discourage expensive teamwork between staff members.

While the foregoing list is facetious, serious attention must be paid to the consequences of at least one point—screening in many "easy cases" that might well be served by other direct service agencies. Inclusion of easy cases may have some positive effects on a staff, which becomes emotionally drained if required to work only on complex, tough cases. Another effect may be to gain a more positive image in the community, showing that not only the most down-and-out people use the program. More of the community at large will know someone who has been helped by the program in some little way and will support the program when public support is needed. On the other hand, these easy cases pull away staff effort that may be needed for the tough cases—and the costs per *appropriate* client become higher when the program is evaluated on the basis of cost in relation to need and is located in a community in which other single-purpose programs exist to respond to persons whose needs are not so complex.

Relationships of Funding to Client-Level Functions

Table 5–1 illustrates funding and grants administration issues that influence program capacity and policies. These in turn impinge on the five broad categories of functions at the client level.

Clearly the amount and sources of funds influence *entry,* especially the number of clients who can be served at any one time and which subgroups of elderly are the targets. Case finding may be broad when a program is located within an agency with multiple sources of funds for case management or other kinds of programs with diverse target groups, but additional internal steering must take place to locate the initial appropriate category for each client. It is important that a multifaceted program not fall victim to "hardening of the categories," where clients receive services only on the basis of eligibility rather than need or where there is no flexibility to charge given clients' services to different funding sources as their status changes over time.

An important cost factor related to the *assessment* process is the instrument used. Many state and federal funders are currently attempting to install a standardized assessment tool among all their grantees in order to make comparison studies of program effectiveness. The administrator may need to yield to these requirements and, indeed, may professionally desire to be part of such comparative studies. However, the full standardized assessment does not need to be utilized for all clients when only some of the clients pertain to that funding source. The development of assessment tools that accommodate research requirements inevitably adds to the cost of the assessment process and may compromise both the diagnostic process and the worker–client relationship. For those experimental cases that are contributing to the development of new social policy and improved practice, these compromises may well be worth the costs, but the program need not extend those compromises to all its work if it is multiply funded. While there are some disadvantages to using different assessment approaches for different clients, the use of alternative miniassessments and incremental assessments can provide a comparison for levels of client and worker satisfaction, costs per client, and comprehensiveness of service plans.

In the third column of Table 5–1, eight common issues in *care*

Table 5–1
Issues in Funding and Grants Administration in Relation to Program Functions at the Client Level

Entry	Assessment	Case Goal Setting and Service Planning	Care-Plan Implementation	Review and Evaluation of Client and Program Status
Purpose To identify and enroll clients most appropriate for objectives and capacities of program.	*Purpose* To understand the client as a whole person and be aware of strengths and needs in client's situation.	*Purpose* To clarify expectations and agree upon an individualized plan of services and other problem-solving activities.	*Purpose* To arrange and ensure that services and other help are provided and utilized effectively.	*Purpose* To update knowledge of client and situation for possible revisions in client plan or for management of agency resources.
Guidelines Funding sources influence eligibility criteria (income, needs, catchment area).	*Guidelines* Funding sources may require reports of specific client characteristics.	*Guidelines* Funds may limit staff expertise necessary to extend beyond instrumental needs of clients (affective or capacity building).	*Guidelines* Agency budget may not include enough funds to purchase services—or staff time for advocacy, follow-up and/or monitoring.	*Guidelines* Regulations may specify short-term services or termination of the case upon institutionalization.
Funds limit total number of clients who can be served at any one time.	Third-party payments may require specific kinds of need documentation or doctor diagnosis.	Inherent conflict exists between making service plans comprehensive and making them cost containing.	Interagency linkages have costs in staff time but may benefit many clients over time.	Calculate costs of retaining least active cases.
Funds limit resources for case-finding activities.	Local match for some funds may be in-kind. Loaned staff to assist with assessments.	Funds may limit availability of sufficient supervision of casework.	Find out about other agencies whose funders require coordination with your kind of program or increased service to elderly.	Staff overload requires either more staff hiring or stricter termination policies.
Administrators must expend much effort in search for funds. One strategy is to find new funds for additional target populations or subgroups of existing target group (rural, the blind).	Some kinds of medical and psychiatric assessment may be reimbursable or basis for funding requests.	Some third-party payments have a limit of duration or cost.	Forward funding enhances flexibility to vary levels of client costs according to fluctuations in needs and reduces stresses of cash flow.	Some clients may have to be reclassified for different funding sources in accord with eligibility or status.
In-kind contributions may include decentralized locations for personnel and intake.	In-house assessment specialists can result in cost savings; may have negative or positive impact on interagency relations and reimbursability.	Purchase of service and cost accounting require standardized definitions of units of service.		Cost per client may be higher during start up period of program and for first catch-up needs of new clients.
Sliding-fee scale for clients is essential for		In purchase of service, the more drastic the		Functional budgeting is time consuming, but periodic and selective use of

most surviving programs; funding sources may require or prohibit client fees. Be sure clients know cost factors, if any, at entry.

Intake personnel must be familiar with available options to client for third-party payments or other comprehensive or categorical programs for which client may be eligible (blind, Medicaid, veterans, Native Americans).

Funding sources may require standardized next steps (comprehensive assessment, means test).

Summary
Generalization: Issues of sources of funds, funding requirements and restrictions, cash flow, continuity of funding, time limits of funding, time limits of demonstration monies and similar money problems begin their impact on clients at entry and continue to case closing.

Monitor costs of doing a standardized assessment for all clients; develop differentiated assessment approaches for different kinds of cases.

Client assessments are sometimes purchased or provided in-kind through agency agreements.

Summary
Generalization: Regardless of the good reasons for additional assessment information required for research, policy conformity, or funding documentation, there is a cost. There are social costs for the client, consequences for worker time and clinical effectiveness, as well as the price paid from the agency budget.

---

change required of other agencies, the higher the cost expected.

Special in-house funds for emergency financial aid are usually needed.

Funds to purchase services on a client-by-client basis give better access and control to the coordinator than do contracts funding service providers for an estimated number of service units. It is hard for service providers to plan readiness to deliver uncertain amount of services, however.

Summary
Generalization: Agency goals, funding source goals and a client's own expected goals may not be in congruence. The test of which goals are emphasized is found in the resource allocations.

CETA and other worker programs may be a source for special support workers (transportation, shopping, telephone reassurance) but not a desirable source of primary case managers because of required turnover.

Seek special private fund sources for appliances, furniture, other costs not allowed by federal or state funds.

Provision of direct service increases costs of case management unless accounted for separately.

Summary
Generalization: Among the most serious impediments to service implementation are the disruptions caused by funding discontinuity, variations in budget cycles, delayed payments, and changes in rules regarding allowable duration of services.

---

functional cost analysis can be a useful managerial tool.

Document ways that funding delays or inadequate funds interfere with goal achievement.

When client needs exceed agency resources or when a program is on short-term funds, the search for ongoing funds is a constant activity of director.

Summary
Generalization: The most powerful influence on the quality and continuity of client service, on the survival of the agency and on the mental health of the administrator is the security of stable sources of funds.

planning are listed. In addition to these, an important influence upon service planning is the relative amount of control that the responsible agency has over service provision funds. Different degrees of control for different kinds of service will depend on whether the service is easily available from another unit within the same agency; whether the agency has funds to purchase services directly from other providers; whether the agency has some leverage over the allocation of funds to other service providers through program or case review; and whether there have been prior written interagency agreements committing needed services. Such control mechanisms facilitate the case manager's job when those particular services are needed. An unintended side effect can be that in their service plans, workers may overutilize the services that are most available and, conversely, avoid recommending those services that are in short supply and over which there is no special access or control. In some cases this can lead to providing a more costly service than is necessary or to providing less relevant low-cost services when a costlier but harder-to-obtain service is needed.

Case goals, of course, are influenced by program goals, as described in table 2–1. Program goals are often guided by the interests of the funding source.

In *care-plan implementation,* the most often discussed issue related to funding is whether there are purchase-of-service funds to assure service delivery. Less recognized is the fact that the more control the responsible agency has as a funding intermediary, the more its activities must include orchestrating the assignment of costs to appropriate sponsors and handling the paperwork associated with billings and fiscal accountability. At the same time, these fiscal responsibilities provide case-management staff with legitimacy for monitoring the delivery of services from other agencies.

Care-plan implementation often calls for the staff to exercise considerable creativity in utilizing resources from other than the principal funding source. This is especially true for such occasional needs as emergency financial aid, appliances, furniture, or for paraprofessional workers who can extend the reach and impact of the case manager.

The *review of client or program status* is important for humanistic as as well as fiscal reasons. Such reviews primarily serve the purpose of tracking the well-being of clients and keeping work demands on staff to a reasonable level. At the same time they serve several fiscal and administrative purposes such as: assessing costs per client (or different types of clients), reviewing equity or balance in the allocation of program resources, documenting operational and fiscal barriers, and, of course, accounting for the proper use of resources.

Summary

This chapter does not cover everything that every administrator should know about mobilizing resources and fiscal management. We have highlighted only the matters that most frequently emerge as priority concerns of administrators and evaluators of case-management programs. The 1980s could be a time of rich program documentation and congressional and state action to reduce some of the present problems in categorical funding. At the same time the competitive scramble for reduced governmental block funds may turn the attention of program directors to a broader implementation of resource development, with increased involvement of the private sector. Although the goal of stable funding for case management for the vulnerable elderly remains distant, present patchwork funding is maintaining many programs that provide this group of the elderly with the least restrictive environment and a high quality of crisis resolution and individualized long-term care.

Suggested Readings

Federal Council on the Aging. *Public Policy and the Frail Elderly*. Washington, D.C.: FCA, December 1978 (DHEW Publication No. OHDS 79-20959).

Gottesman, L.E.; Ishizaki, B.; and MacBride, S.M. "Service Management: Plan and Models." *The Gerontologist* 19, no. 4 (August 1979):379–385.

Hodgson, J.H., and Quinn, J.L. "The Impact of the Triage Health-Care Delivery System on Client Morale, Independent Living, and the Cost of Care." *The Gerontologist* 20, no. 3 (June 1980):364–371.

Meltzer, J.; Farrow, F.; and Richman, H. (eds.). *Policy Options in Long-Term Care*. Chicago, Ill.: University of Chicago Press, 1980, 78–117.

Monk, A. "Family Supports in Old Age." *Social Work* 24, no. 6 (November 1979):533–538.

Skellie, F.A., and Coan, R.E. "Community-Based Long-Term Care and Mortality: Preliminary Experimental Findings." *The Gerontologist* 20, no. 3 (June 1980):372–379.

Stassen, M., and Holohan, J. *Long-Term-Care Demonstration Projects: A Review of Recent Evaluations*. Washington, D.C.: Urban Institute, 1980.

U.S. Comptroller General. *Entering a Nursing Home: Costly Implications for Medicaid and the Elderly*. Washington, D.C.: General Accounting Office, 1979b (PAD-80-12).

6

Case-Manager Personnel and Support Staff

Deciding who should run the agency and deliver services to the targeted groups is a crucial step in developing the agency design. After the agency has tentatively carved out some goals, determined target groups and funding sources, and settled some issues of authority and control, then decisions about staffing must be made.

The start of personnel selection for all coordination agencies is influenced by some of the initial organizational forces discussed in chapters 2 and 4. In chapter 7 on case-manager practice, as well as in chapter 1, on the client pathway, there are discussions about what case managers do and how they do it. This chapter is focused on decisions for case-manager selection, assignment of worker functions, kinds of case managers, and kinds of support staff.

Some coordination program units begin with transfers of available clinical staff already a part of the agency. Some start fresh with a new personnel recruiting list. Others have a mixture of seasoned professional workers or experienced workers such as social workers or nurses who are then augmented by additional recruitment. Information and referral (I&R) workers are frequently recruited from existing programs because of their intimate knowledge of community resources. Some programs become possible only because a staff of CETA workers or community service aides formerly in an outreach program became transferrable or because new paraprofessional temporary "job slots" become available. (The latter pattern has had its problems with short-term limitations and expenditures of time for training and supervision.)

Although the origins of the case-manager staff differ widely, some aggressive administrators have demonstrated the possibilities for progressive staff upgrading. In at least three coordination programs the initial use of underqualified staff was changed by the addition of professionals within two years. Therefore, although staffing origins are often considered a given in the start-up of many new programs, either the personal conviction of the administrator or experience gained in the start-up usually results in upgrading staff requirements as well as offering better salaries. The best organizational design, the most advanced technical tools, and sufficiency of resources will make for a program whose quality can be no better than the quality of agency personnel.

Generalizations about the "best" type of case manager are impossible

because of the great variety of objectives and organizational configurations now in existence. Personnel who may be described as case managers
are found in such diverse settings as

> long-term-care coordination agencies, which may be known as central
> registries, community care organizations (CCOs), alternative health
> programs, or channeling agencies;

> I&R services, some of which are neighborhood based and include
> outreach, while others are centralized and computerized at a local or
> state level;

> multipurpose centers, home health agencies, home care corporations,
> and most recently, social and health maintenance organizations
> (SHMOs), which combine direct service with case coordination;

> direct services agencies such as family service, protective services,
> community mental health centers, and homes for the aged, which
> engage in case management as an adjunct to direct service.

Programs also vary in the degree to which a one-to-one relationship
between worker and client is essential. Numerous programs have har-
nessed telephonic and other electronic technology for client tracking,
early warning systems for crises, and matching of client needs with
available resources for case planning and monitoring. But the human
factors (vis-à-vis both the worker and client) are never replaced by technology, and in fact the new technology tends to require more highly
qualified and sensitive personnel to develop usable inputs and to interpret
outputs to advantage.

Case Managers Differ in Title

Our project used the generic term "case coordinator" in order to avoid
stereotyped responses to traditional names for those who are engaged in
a case-coordination job. This generic term facilitated our consideration
of a wide variety of programs regardless of the title given to the front-
line practitioner. By the end of the research phase it was clear that "case
manager" was the most prevalent term; therefore we are utilizing this
title extensively in this book.

There are many variations in titles. In some programs an official
effort is made to avoid the term *case manager,* or titles used by workers
before expansion of functions to case management persist. Examples are
service manager, facilitator, information and assistance worker, advocate,

service broker, caseworker, or case aide. Titles that emphasize one of the case manager's roles even though other functions may be included are counselor, assessment team, human services planner, or resource coordinator.

Further variation is introduced by the official or unofficial use of professional identities: social worker, nurse, rehabilitation specialist, gerontologist, or senior companion. In a few programs it is the practice to avoid distinctions of discipline or status by highlighting the program name: the worker from SCAN, the ACCESS worker, the TRIMS home-visitor.

Typically programs use a variety of names: one for the official job classification, another with the client, and yet other titles in dealing with particular agencies or the mass media. The prevalence of the term *case manager* was found not only in the professional literature but also in our national survey of 333 case-coordination programs for the frail elderly (see chapter 9).

Case Managers Differ in Professional Orientation

The most prevalent professional orientation reported by case-management programs was social work. The second most frequently mentioned orientation was nursing. In both cases the national survey was inconclusive with respect to the level of educational attainment associated with those professional names.

In our in-depth examination of six cities and 140 cases: almost 30 percent of the cases were served by workers with less than a four-year college degree; only 15 percent of the cases were served by workers with at least a master's degree; the majority (55 percent) were served by workers with the four-year undergraduate degree, one-third of whom had some postgraduate education.

The national survey revealed that less than one-half of the programs utilized volunteers, but in all but 11 percent of such programs at least part-time professionals were involved. In one intensive but short-lived demonstration of the potential use of volunteers as case managers, the workers were recruited, screened, trained, supervised, and evaluated by a very experienced multidisciplinary leadership team.

Many programs incorporate a combination of professional orientations and skill levels, either by intent or by accommodation to the limited availability of qualified personnel. Other programs have a predominance of one kind of worker orientation but supplement the staff mixture with one or more persons of a complementary discipline in order to bring a more comprehensive perspective to selected cases or to the program as a whole.

Although there is no one best program model or one best kind of case manager, we do have a recommendation for staffing a kind of program that is gaining in prevalence. If a program is aimed at spanning the long-term medical and social needs of the very frail elderly, we believe that there should be both master's level social workers and nurses with public health or community nursing backgrounds. These professionals should be supplemented with paraprofessional case aides who receive pre-service and in-service training and continuous supervision. (See table 6–1 and this chapter's section on skill levels for differentiation of functions.)

As a general principle, we believe that nonprofessional volunteers are unsuitable as case managers. Trained volunteers can be significant resources in specific tasks such as outreach, friendly visiting, telephone reassurance, escort, peer counseling, and ombudsmanlike service monitoring. Retired professionals in all the helping disciplines can be rich resources for a program, but as part-time volunteers they are not best used as managers of specific cases. As with most generalizations, exceptions can be well planned with a particular volunteer.

There are several considerations in selecting the professional orientation of case managers. Every profession has its own body of knowledge, methods, value system, and professional organizations that safeguard its members' standards, and interests. Standard-setting and certification roles of professional associations or licensing bodies are safeguards to both the employer and to the client group. But there is no such profession for case managers. The skills of the background profession are adaptable to different agency settings, but each profession brings its own emphasis. There is a similar range of practice differences within a profession as graduates move into different positions. No matter from which disciplines, this adaptation to the agency's coordination service job must be made. Administrators and supervisors must be able to interpret this required adaptation. For example, the family service agency counselor cannot continue to practice in the same way.

Completion of a professional education and being screened into a professional membership association may represent only entry qualifications. Successful job experience is another yardstick for assessing competence and salary levels.

Most coordination agencies have multidisciplinary staff or access to specialists from other professions. At the administrative level or the supervisory level, one or another discipline influences the stance of the agency. Most frequently it is social work, followed by nursing. Choice of a professional perspective serves to integrate diverse kinds of staff. The basis for choice is influenced by funding source, waivers, target group and the principal segment of the community providing the sanction for the agency program. (See also chapter 2 on reference groups.)

The choice of professional perspective directly affects the kind of agency induction given new workers, the job classifications used, and the content of on-the-job supervision and training as well as access to funds for continued staff development.

Case-coordination agencies with no professionals are practically nonexistent. Paraprofessionals have been advancing as a necessary adjunct in personnel recruitment for agency staffing such as in dentistry, law, education, medicine, social work, nursing, and nearly all other human services professions. The ratio of paraprofessionals to professionals must be tailored to program contexts. Employing paraprofessionals is not only a way to conserve professional time but also can bring needed skills of language, maturity, and community know-how that many professionals may lack.

Case Managers Differ in Intensity of Direct Contact with Clients

The best known and most prevalent kind of case manager is one who maintains continuous face-to-face contact with the client and significant others. Many programs exist, however, that limit the degree of direct client contact as a result of funding constraints, interorganizational jurisdictional disputes, scarcities of qualified personnel, or unique interpretations of case manager as a manager rather than clinician.

A common but not necessarily recommended adaptation is to focus the case manager on the client assessment phase. After assessment and possibly after case planning the case is assigned to another kind of worker to assist in implementing service delivery. The case manager may remain available to the intake and follow-up workers as consultant or supervisor. Our hesitation with this accommodation is that the assessment, care planning, and care-plan implementation are in the case of the frail elderly not separable phases. The incremental, cumulative nature of assessment, which sharpens as the worker–client relationship deepens, and the trial, error, and replanning of services in relation to the client's changing conditions and preferences tend to require continuous face-to-face contact throughout the active phases of the case.

Another variation is to use the most skilled manager for prescreening. By this method less complex cases are assigned to appropriate aides or service providers, who maintain direct contact with the client. More complex cases are assigned to other case managers, if any, or are continued by the original prescreening case manager.

In a few well-respected demonstration programs that have a primary interest in cost containment the case manager virtually never sees the client face-to-face. In this model the case manager may send an aide to conduct a prescreening in-home visit or visit to a residential acute-care setting. Then a subcontract agency is assigned to conduct the comprehensive client assessment and preliminary service plan. The case manager later arrives at a service plan by telephone with the client, a significant other, or with the service provider that is to be lead agency for the case. Reassessments and service plan changes are similarly negotiated by telephone or correspondence. The counseling aspects of case management are clearly treated as a direct service that is obtained by contract. A variation of this model is the resource coordinator who is the consultant and gatekeeper of services for cases that are being carried by multipurpose senior center workers, information and assistance workers, or direct-service workers in a variety of provider agencies, including multipurpose centers.

Case Managers Differ by Sets of Functions

As previously noted, not all case managers perform the entire continuum of functions listed in the tables—entry, assessment, care planning, care-plan implementation, and evaluation. Thus case managers may be differentiated by the stretch of their functions across the entire client pathway. The pathway functions not assumed by the case manager are then carried either by other personnel within the program or by outside agencies that have working agreements with the program.

Another way of differentiating case-manager functions is in relation to the skill levels of case managers. One program may have two competency levels of case managers with corresponding differences in the functions performed. Thus clients may be channeled (by screening) to two kinds of case management, based on the level of complexity or vulnerability of the client. Table 6–1 illustrates client-level functions in relation to competence levels of case managers. For example, looking at the Entry column in the chart showing the client-level pathway and the five columns of functions, we note two skill levels suggested for outreach programs. If the job to be done is supervision of the outreach program, training of volunteers or neighborhood residents for home visits or to evaluate the benefits of the program, a higher level of staff is needed. If the job to be done is a routine home visit for each new client as a prescribed agency follow-up, a lower-level competence is all that is needed. Occasionally, we would want a worker with more competence

Table 6–1
Comparison of Skill Levels in Relation to Program Functions at the Client Level

Entry	Assessment	Case Goal Setting and Service Planning	Care-Plan Implementation	Review and Evaluation of Client and Program Status
Purpose	*Purpose*	*Purpose*	*Purpose*	*Purpose*
To identify and enroll clients most appropriate for objectives and capacities of program.	To understand the client as a whole person and be aware of strengths and needs in client's situation.	To clarify expectations and agree upon an individualized plan of services and other problem-solving activities.	To arrange and ensure that services and other help are provided and utilized effectively.	To update knowledge of client and situation for possible revisions in client plan or for management of agency resources.
Guidelines	*Guidelines*	*Guidelines*	*Guidelines*	*Guidelines*
Lower skill level outreach: Friendly visiting, knocking on doors in the neighborhood; meeting with members of the senior center; peer identification of potential clients.

Higher skill level outreach: Calling at the client's home to evaluate reported emergency, a client at risk; offering immediate help as indicated; providing quick access for continued service.

Lower skill level intake: Prescreening clients by following a prescribed agency outline; making tentative decisions to be checked by supervisor or caseworker; steering applicant at reception for | Lower skill level: Following training instructions and administering a tested assessment tool; developing rapport with client for the assessment session; gathering some additional information if instructed.

Higher skill level: Administering assessment form with options for some selectivity; seeking information directly from other experts, such as the client's doctor; reviewing client medications; assessing client functioning in her environment; identifying architectural barriers; testing and facilitating client participation; establishing a set of relationships with and for clients; assessing personality traits | Lower skill level: Allowing client to discuss expectations and goals; explaining service arrangement possibilities; seeking agreement on possible resources (instrumental help from family); individualizing client plan and agency assistance; writing tentative goals and plan.

Higher skill level: Interpreting assessment results to client as appropriate; encouraging client reactions, considering preferences, and mobilizing informal help system; explaining to client about service possibilities and client's role in arranging service; exploring client's noninstrumental | Lower skill level: Applying knowledge and experience about community resources; seeking help and supervision when resources are difficult to obtain; arranging for the resource; delivery timing; keeping client informed, modifying as necessary; recording services delivered, setting follow-up schedule.

Higher skill level: Using knowledge of resources, personal and agency linkages with provider agencies, client utilization potential, skills in choosing alternative resources; offering support, consultation (if appropriate) to provider agency re service standards, expectations; | Lower skill level: Understanding and adjusting mismatches of client service and utilization; identifying excessive expenditures of worker time on particular cases; accepting inevitable infirmities of certain clients, including death; using supervision in termination planning, changing case status to less or more active attention; keeping supervisor aware of caseload management issues and problems; reviewing practice performance as basis for on-the-job training.

Higher skill level: Initiating own case priorities if there are no agency-defined criteria; recognizing |

Table 6–1 Continued

Entry	Assessment	Case Goal Setting and Service Planning	Care-Plan Implementation	Review and Evaluation of Client and Program Status
worker attention or to the intended agency. Higher skill level intake: Prescreening clients as an initial intake and assessment step; offering prediagnostic interview; conducting an intake interview using own decision as to next entry steps; making decision as to scheduling assessment; arranging referrals elsewhere; making judgment as to type of assessment to follow; encouraging the reluctant, in-need client.	and past experiences in resource utilization. Lower skill level: Keeping in close contact with supervisor regarding client acceptance of agency help and worker's interpretation of assessment. Higher skill level: Using own judgment as to expert resources to use in assessment; bringing only selective issues to supervisor such as liability problems, purchasing supplementary diagnostic service within cost limitations.	needs and present interest in personal goals; setting an additional focus on capacity-building goals as appropriate; establishing worker–client sequence or priorities as to next steps; suggesting (giving techniques or modeling) things client can do to increase or maintain self-help in own case management; keeping summary recording, tentative client plan/agenda in writing (or follow agency policy); planning for more operationalized client objectives and possible intervention methods or tactics for achieving case objectives.	giving consideration to priority use of scarce or costly resources (which clients get the limited resources); estimating the worker time investment for a particular case as it will affect case-load management; setting tentative time goals for selected case objectives; planning implementation of capacity-building goals for the client and his family; identifying criteria for workers' self-evaluation.	balance between overall agency intake and continued case load and sharing agency responsibilities for this; developing self-help methods for the client and the client's family to participate in coordinating services; assessing progress with client on earlier goals, modifying for present status or recycling full assessment; maintaining policy or initiating policy review of agency termination procedures, including active case definitions; proposing case evaluation criteria and service system evaluation criteria for the worker level.
Summary *Generalization:* The entry process can be divided into a number of different functions/tasks. Restructuring job functions allows best use of different levels of staff (or specializations) but some situations may require continuity in	*Summary* *Generalization:* The lower the level of skill the more reliance there must be on procedures, formalized supports, supervision, and continued on-the-job training, less reliance on worker's self-evaluation. Agency controls must be	*Summary* *Generalization:* Case goals will change as the client's situation changes or health status changes or program eligibility, or as the informal support system or the community-services resources system vary. Changes also occur	*Summary* *Generalization:* Achievements in care-plan implementation become the reality test for assessing staff skill levels. Workers should formulate client goals and objectives for which there is an expected (or potential)	*Summary* *Generalization:* The pile-up of cases, increased worker burnout, benign neglect of continued service clients and other negative pressures result from insufficient attention to the impact of the open door entry of elderly cases

worker-client relationships throughout the client pathway.

tighter when skills are lower, when clients are at risk and when agency is likely to be exposed to liability issues and high expenditures.

with changes in worker experience and skill level. Goal setting and service planning are not perceived as a simplistic step that occurs in between intake and plan implementation. These functions are more or less focused in this phase but are never confined to one point in the case process.

means of intervention. This means deciding what tactics or approaches will be used.

destined to grow older and more infirm and the impact of the narrow door exit out of the system. Failure to balance case exit policies, to enhance workers' skills, or to increase case staff will create an unmanageable caseload problem.

if, for example, the home visit were made in response to a crisis situation reported to the agency by a police officer who was called in by neighbors.

As previously mentioned, job structuring can be used to sort out the tasks by performance level. This is particularly applicable to the high-volume agency with several levels of staff, such as front desk receptionist, intake application worker, professional social caseworker, supervisor. In some crisis situations or specialized cases such as that of an abused frail person continuity of the regular worker relationship may be considered more important to sustain than to send out a higher-level worker. Increased supervision rather than a switch in workers would be recommended.

Nearly all jobs in the human service field are graded and scaled by professional practice criteria heavily based on the level and amount of independent decision making. The principal assumption is that more education or experience is needed and, consequently, a higher salary or fee is expected when the job requirements demand considerable reliance on personal discretion by the employee. Jobs that require routine, repetitive behaviors from the employee, the use of prescribed supports (standardized interview, matching transportation needs with a set schedule, checking on client and reporting to a supervisor, and so on) may not warrant higher costs of professional salaries.

Another consideration is the degree of risk involved in exposing staff to problem situations or an unexpected crisis they are not equipped to handle. To what extent is the worker in an exposed position to do harm to the patient, personally to obligate agency expenditures, to create conflicts, or engender poor public relations with other associated agencies or community leadership? These types of risks cannot be handled with cookbook decisions. It is important to explain to a board of directors or a fiscal officer about risks in liability or financial risks when salaries offered for case managers will not attract staff with the competence needed. It is more difficult, however, to illustrate or describe to laymen the needs for higher- or lower-level worker performance and different pay scales when the tasks or functions appear to be similar.

When it comes to assessment functions, volunteers and paraprofessionals generally follow an agency's standard assessment form. The skilled worker is given more leeway in adding questions or approaching the assessment in increments, following the client's priorities and preferences. Lower-skilled workers need more support, standardized procedures, and routine supervision. (Note the generalization comments at the bottom of the assessment columns of table 6–1.) Also, skilled workers are more likely to conceptualize assessment as a continuing process, not just completing the assessment form.

In the column on case goal setting and planning, skill differences are noted. For example, the skilled worker should be more competent to implement capacity building in clients or behavior-change objectives. Lower-skilled workers should focus on improving the client's environment and on tangible service objectives rather than dealing with complicated personality problems. Care plans for changing family attitudes or alleviating a severe depressive state of the client are certainly not realistic for the untrained, inexperienced worker. However, lower-level workers are often experienced in locating services that are open to all who meet the defined eligibility. In cases where admission is based on clinical judgment, properly screened referrals from skilled workers able to judge the client situation in relation to an agency's present criteria for admission are much preferred to referrals by paraprofessionals or inexperienced workers. Sometimes prestigious agencies will not respond to a referral from a nonprofessional or volunteer. Such professionalized (or elitist) agencies complain about inappropriate referrals because they consume costly time to redirect clients to a more appropriate resource.

As a final comment on table 6–1, the criterion of more or less discretion (independent decision making) is reflected in the distinction between the higher and lower skill levels. The increased reliance on supervision is stressed in the review and evaluation column as well as an obligation for on-the-job training for workers of less competence. Another important distinction is emphasized in the generalization at the bottom of the column: the more highly skilled worker should be able to identify some of the agencywide problems that contribute to overload and burnout. It is noticeable that skilled clinical workers are also quite ingenious in approaching their administrators for changes in agency policies and procedures. Administrators and supervisors can lose contact with front-line situations unless there is not only reporting back about a problem, but also some suggestions as to causes and remedies. Increased professional clinical skill should be braced by increased understanding and concern about the agency, its policies and program changes.

One of the most important decisions of program design is the level of personnel recruited. It may appear that there are no choices offered when a program is to be based on available CETA workers for a certain time limit. But choices still remain with respect to training, supervision, target groups, and the professional orientation to be used as the framework for practice.

Education and experience must be written into job descriptions along with typical skills and tasks to be performed. These must conform to comparable jobs in the agency setting in similar agencies and to communitywide pay scales or a county merit system.

The comparison of skill levels in table 6–1 can be used as an explanatory tool in personnel planning and decision making. The chart can also serve as a basis for discussion leading to planning choices of skill levels across the client pathway. We can agree on the importance of performance levels as a key issue for differentiating staff. There is less agreement as to the best set of qualifications for identifying and recruiting the skill level that agencies ought to have. Whatever the choice, the alternatives and consequences must be considered.

This section has outlined ways that case managers vary according to the sets of functions they carry. These sets are influenced by the overall program design and by the skill levels of personnel. The relative benefits between these variations cannot be judged without taking into account the entire staffing mixture of the program and the configuration of program leadership and support staff.

Case Managers Operate with Different Configurations of Support Staff

The capacity of case managers to do their jobs is clearly related to the supports provided by their respective agencies. Perhaps the most difficult situations are when an agency has only one case manager and no other staff to assist in the case-coordination functions. There is no respite. There is no opportunity to reflect on one's work. There is no peer stimulation to escape burnout.

Single-worker case-management programs are sometimes unavoidable, especially in rural areas or in programs targeted to a particular ethnic group. In these programs it is essential that workers have opportunities to meet or conference with similar isolated peer workers in other agencies even though their time to break away from the job is limited.

Most programs, however, do place case managers within a context of other types of workers who are important to the case managers' effectiveness. The following list of support staff is oriented to the point of view of case managers.

The *receptionist* can be anyone receiving telephone calls and handling the files, dictation, or procedural forms. Case managers report that if the receptionist or switchboard operator is overworked, the back-up responsibility falls on them. Case managers want to participate in orientation and training of the support office personnel. Office personnel need to be informed of their importance in helping the case manager to maintain good communications and rapport with clients and agencies.

Following are some perceptions of what case managers want from their *supervisors:*

to be kept informed about program and policy changes that affect their work;

to receive information through some regular channel;

to be given practical examples of policy implementation, not just abstractions;

both formal and informal supervision through staff meetings and individualized sessions;

to discuss problem cases, which is helpful to the workers and also helps to keep the supervisor in contact with their jobs;

the supervisor's support on some of the tough decisions where boundaries of authority are uncertain;

books or journals on gerontology available in a reading room.

In addition, case managers have indicated that when there is a choice in seeking a supervisor for help, they prefer to go to those who are carrying some cases or know firsthand about their jobs and the clients to be served. Where supervisory support is lacking, case managers report low morale and severe frustration. Case managers seek peer support when supervision is not available. Some suggest getting a "second opinion"—where peers make a team and jointly appraise a situation. They strongly believe that time is saved, the quality of their performance is improved and they are more satisfied about their work when there is available supervision.

Case managers report considerable contact with *fiscal officers*. Fiscal staff, claims and business managers, and contracting officers are important to case managers in the conduct of their work. Complaints from case managers about fiscal staff are usually related to required paperwork and delays in processing payments to caregivers.

Only a few agencies were large enough to warrant employing a *resource developer*, but the job was considered important. Sometimes consultants are brought into the agency to update resource files. Some case managers become recognized for their superior resource knowledge in certain areas, and an informal specialization results. Sometimes the supervisors or director will open new resources from provider agencies or obtain funds for purchase of service. Resource development and communication about changing provider agency services may be handled in several ways, but it remains one of the most important props for the case manager and should not drift into the job function of every case manager. Personnel who organize mutual aid groups, solicit contributions from civic and religious organizations, recruit volunteers, or create new services may be known as *community workers*.

Legal and psychiatric consultation from *specialists* or *consultants* is available to many coordination agencies although it may be the supervisor rather than each case manager who has the direct contact with the specialists. Physicians, nurse practitioners, and pharmacists may be scheduled for consultant sessions to review case records or to see the client.

Program specialists vary greatly among agencies according to the direct service programs within the overall organization, which may employ psychologists, occupational and physical therapists, or homemakers. Case managers report frequent contacts with these program specialists.

Since few agencies assign *case aides* to case managers as assistants, this kind of supportive help was not frequently mentioned in our survey. When paraprofessional or case aides are assigned to prescreening functions or to monitoring of clients, they are considered a part of the case-management team.

Researchers, evaluators, and *system analysts* may be among support personnel handling program statistics or computerized systems for billing client services, and so on. Sometimes case managers are directly involved in research or evaluation activities. Most case managers view these specialists as necessary for the agency, especially when participating in a demonstration or pilot program. They are likely to classify all data gathering as paperwork. In a small agency or unit, case managers are aware of agency research and evaluation objectives. Case managers become discouraged when they are expected to report case data but seldom receive feedback on the results or use of their reports.

Case managers sometimes carry supervisory responsibilities for *students* placed in agencies by local universities and colleges. Students can serve quite effectively as support staff to case managers.

This list of support staff for case managers is more limited than a list that would describe the agency-community network used by case managers in the conduct of their jobs. Developing and sustaining a personal network beyond the agency setting is an important component in the work of an effective case manager.

Case-Load Differentiation and Case Teams

A final consideration in delineating kinds of case managers has to do with the particular kinds of clients with which they work. Some agencies or interagency systems permit the screening or channeling of particular kinds of clients to workers with particular skills or subsets of functions.

Obvious examples of differentiation by target population are clients who are not English-speaking, those with speech or hearing impairments, those struggling with substance abuse or those with tendencies to suicide. Clients are often assigned to workers based on geographic area, type of residence, or the relative degree of acute illness. Subtler variables in case assignment are taken into account in some programs: personality type, sexual behavior, or mode of social deviance such as substance abuse.

Cases are frequently differentiated as complex or simple cases. In some programs this permits complex cases to be assigned to the most highly skilled workers. In other programs, where workers are considered to be of equal competence, the simple/complex designation is used to balance or equitably distribute the work load. There are, of course, crossovers to be expected: Simple cases become complex and vice versa.

To the extent that case managers deal with complex cases or cases with specialized needs, the general model of following a client through the entire pathway may be modified on a case-by-case basis to permit the transfer of some functions to another worker.

Many programs report that they work in case-management teams. On closer observation it appears to us that team case management rarely occurs. When everyone is responsible, then no one is responsible. Many programs have begun with a team concept of case management but have modified it over time to a pattern in which different members of the staff team take primary responsibility for particular cases, especially after the assessment phase. Other team members remain on tap to perform adjunct functions as needed.

Summary

In this chapter on case managers and staffing patterns of coordination agencies a broad range of choices has been presented. Our conclusions for designing staffing patterns may be summarized in seven guidelines:

1. Case managers must be clinically oriented, be skilled in establishing and sustaining personal relationships, like and respect older people, be able to coordinate medical, social, and instrumental needs and services, participate in assessment and carry through with implementation. Various kinds of human service workers are employed as case managers, but social workers and public health nurses are most frequently employed because of their community and clinical backgrounds.
2. Case management work is not a distinct profession and is not likely to become one.
3. Case management includes a coordination strategy and an individualized case service that can be adopted effectively for long-term-care interagency programs on one hand to a large, complex, multifunction agency on the other.

4. There are many kinds of case managers. A core of general functions and tasks is similar for all case managers but there are sets of specific job requirements that are unique to each agency setting.
5. Maximization of scarce professional skills in combination with the help of paraprofessional and volunteer staff appear to be the central consideration in designing staffing patterns.
6. Staff turnover is high among case-manager personnel, salaries are comparably low, and the career ladder is limited. Program demonstrations, research projects, and experimental programs attract usually good personnel. Overload, resource shortages, mixed unstable financing, and the absence of improvement or cure in many clients adds to a cumulative burnout among the staff. Turnover can be expected.
7. Support staff is limited except in the larger agencies. The clerk-secretary person gets highest priority from case-manager staff. Qualified supervision and training is ranked a high second by practitioners.

Creative deployment of staff and a sound managerial practice of structuring and restructuring jobs tasks and functions not only open up better alternatives for different kinds of case managers but also facilitate a flexible, responsive delivery system.

Suggested Readings

John, D. "Managing the Human Service System: What Have We Learned from Services Integration?" *Human Services Monograph Series* 4 (August 1977) (Project SHARE, P.O. Box 2309, Rockville, MD 20852).

Libow, L., and Sherman, F. *The Core of Geriatric Medicine: A Guide for Students and Practitioners*. St. Louis, Mo.: The C.V. Mosby Co., 1980.

Morris, R., and Lescohier, I. "Service Integration: Real versus Illusory Solutions to Welfare Dilemmas." In Sarri, R., and Hasenfeld, Y. (eds.), *The Management of Human Services*. New York: Columbia Press, 1978.

Oglesby, W.B., Jr. *Referral in Pastoral Counseling*. Englewood Cliffs, N.J.: Prentice-Hall, 1968.

Rao, D.B. "The Team Approach to Integrated Care of the Elderly." *Geriatrics* 32, no. 2 (February 1977):88–96.

White, M., and Grisham, M. *The Structure and Processes of Case Management in California's Multipurpose Senior Services Project*. Berkeley, Calif.: UNEX, University of California, 1982.

7

Case-Manager Practice

The tasks and activities included in case management and the actions taken by case managers on behalf of their clients are varied and complex. Case management is rarely achieved by case managers alone. Administrators, supervisors, other professional staff, support staff, and personnel connected with other agencies all affect the quality of the case manager's work. This chapter is designed to identify and to clarify the components of case-management interventions and selected issues that may aid administrators, supervisors, and case managers in understanding their own and one another's roles in serving the elderly through a case-management approach.

Case-Management-Practice Concerns of the Administrator

While the administrator (or the board) does not have to know everything about the clinical interventions used in the coordination work with the clients, enough information must be in hand to recognize the consequences of policy actions and to promote decisions that will develop and improve the worker–client level of service. What the administrator decides to do and what procedures are implemented will have a direct effect on how the case managers carry out their job. The types of case-management concerns listed here require administrative consideration and decision.

The Impact of the Case-Finding Strategy

The case-finding strategy selected by the agency will affect the case manager's time. For example, if other agencies' referrals supply the right cases in a proper flow, then case managers will have more time for other activities. On the other hand, if the coordination agency decides to use its case managers for case-finding, the investment of time for outreach may have to be compensated for by recruiting, training, and overseeing volunteers or paraprofessionals to assist the case manager at other points in the client pathway.

Administrators should note that the term *outreach* connotes different meanings to the general public. Some agency programs are called outreach programs for the aged although their programs include all of the case-management sequence of activities, from case finding to assessment, case planning, and service delivery. Outreach in our terms means the entry phase of the case manager's service.

Case-Manager Time Available

Administrators, supervisors, and sponsors frequently make demands on workers with no consideration as to the impact on time left for client–worker activities. One way of examining how much worker time is available for client contacts or interactions is to sketch a bar chart of several worker patterns in the agency according to the distribution of time expended among at least three categories of activities: case-specific activities, administrative activities; and other (illness, vacation, personal). If 10 percent of the worker's time is spent on personal uses, 50 percent on work time that cannot be charged to any one case, then only 40 percent can be allocated to specific client cases in the worker's case load.

Activities that are case specific represent the services done with, for, and on behalf of the specific client or patient. This category includes direct contact with the client, developing relevant information on the client's situation, mental and physical status, needs, and preferences as well as external factors including social supports, environment, housing, and whatever else is required to begin the helping process. The case-specific work functions also include developing the best possible relationship with the client's social support unit, developing a tentative plan for the client, getting appropriate approval for authorizing the service(s), maintaining a continuing relationship with the client, keeping communication lines open regarding the client's utilization of and satisfaction with the service-providing agencies, and negotiating any needed service changes or improvements. It may or may not include some direct service.

Administrative activities that are not case specific are sometimes underestimated as a major drain on the time and skills of a case manager. Such activity includes participating in agency reporting systems and research, adapting to major changes in policy or procedures, cultivating interagency cooperation, updating information on service standards, and speaking or writing for the public, as well as engaging in regular staff meetings, supervisory conferences, or training. Some workers serve as speakers, organizers, resource developers, or student supervisors. These nonclinical assignments quickly take away from case service when time is reallocated by supervisors or administrators. The impact on case load expectations for agency practitioners is dramatic.

The personal use of time is variable and may include such essentials as vacation, sick leave, personal necessity, and participation in professional organizations. When estimating the total number of clients within the program's capacity and the number of cases that will constitute the case load of workers, the administrator must realistically take into account that not all work time goes into case-specific activities.

Differentiating Case Loads

This topic is discussed in chapter 6. It is also relevant to this section because the administrator's decisions about case load size have a direct effect on case-management practice. Furthermore, if there is no decision or policy about case-load, this puts a burden on the worker for all of the case prioritizing. The result can be a pile-up of cases contributing to the worker's burnout.

A weak termination policy can add to this dilemma. A case-load number of fifty or sixty per worker may not be of great help as an agencywide case-load standard unless there is a classification and distribution of cases according to the amount of work they require. This may also be known as a system of weighting of cases. For example, one worker with fifty cases that are in the implementation phase and some that are inactive or require only intermittent monitoring has a case load equivalent to another worker's fifteen new cases, which require intensive activity during assessment, care planning, and crisis resolution.

Staffing Mix

When case-management personnel are classified at the same position level and all have case loads of similar composition, their case-manager activities (intervention repertoires) are much alike. When decisions are made to introduce paraprofessionals or case aides, the entire staffing pattern must be reorganized with respect to functions performed and techniques or activities used. When paraprofessionals and professionals appear to be serving the same client group and utilizing similar intervention techniques, there can be problems between workers and confusion for the supervisors. The use of paraprofessionals, volunteers, and case aides also has some cost implications. The additional supervision that will be required may equal the cost savings gained by using lower-paid staff. The use of volunteers can be even more costly. Many volunteers leave during the summer and in some cases, a program unit has to be dropped or covered by other staff. Case aides also tend to have a high turnover rate, often because job expectations are not clearly defined. In spite of these hazards in mixed staffing, the well-planned and differentiated use of volunteers and paraprofessionals can enhance and extend the benefits derived by agency and clients from the case manager's time and expertise. These kinds of issues must be treated when considering staff mix.

Models of Practice

It is hardly necessary for the board or executive to be deeply familiar with the prevailing models of clinical practice. There are numerous discussions and debates about the distinctions between medical and social models of care programs and case-coordination programs. Increasingly, medical models are including social components and paying more attention to patient participation, preferences, and beliefs. Similarly, the so-called social model used in helping the elderly must include health care. This unfreezing of interdisciplinary boundaries stems from increasing recognition that with an elderly, frail population the physical, mental, and social conditions are interrelated and require multidisciplinary approaches in practice.

There are numerous variations in social practice models—a problem-solving process model is predominant. Task-oriented casework and behavior-modification approaches may use a contract strategy, formal or informal. Clinical psychologists have added the social environment to some of their models; thus the differences between helping professions become less distinct as traditional practice approaches are modified to fit the situations of the older clients.

In adapting any of these practice approaches, the administrator must keep in mind that a case manager is not a therapist, but a clinician who only occasionally offers direct service and whose job is to facilitate the coordination processes. The agency must distinguish between case-manager practice and other kinds of intervention such as social or medical treatment models, rehabilitation, or psychological therapy.

We have spoken of the advantages of bringing professionals into case-coordination agencies and their capacity for adaptation to a coordination setting. Administration must be alert to the exceptions where the treatment-oriented nurse or social caseworker does not properly incorporate the case-manager tasks. Supervisors and trainers must guide the practitioners on the case-coordination track, minimizing direct service as part of the case manager's job. For example, being a therapist is not the same as being a case manager for the elderly.

Advocacy

Advocacy on behalf of clients involves different strategies and techniques than collaborative linkages directed at the service system or at the social policy level. In some programs case advocacy means obtaining help for clients through pleading, cajoling, seducing, or convincing; sometimes it may call for aggressive confrontation or threats to the unresponsive bureaucrat. But administrators must ensure that case managers are very clear about what interventions or tactics to use and how to avoid undisciplined overreacting and stirring up more trouble than good. Case managers may need to develop new skills in case advocacy. Some advocacy activities that affect many clients and that have serious implications for interagency relations or community policy should be handled at the administrator and board level. Workers must understand the limits of personal confrontation tactics in securing needed help for their clients and assertively put forth the merits of the case. They must be able to distinguish types of advocacy appropriate at the case level and know when to refer situations to the administrator for class action. The administrator must clarify and disseminate policies on advocacy and provide for prompt decision making when exceptional cases arise.

Service System Development and Maintenance

The administrator will find that case management requires a wide range of interagency activities at the worker level. Within the staff there may be case managers who are competent in community work and interorganizational development. Quite a few organize meetings for similar groups of service providers to discuss service standards or particular clients where there are problems. In some agencies the case managers do the follow-up on all purchased service for their own clients. In others, one person—a supervisor or contract officer—may be assigned this responsibility for all purchased services.

It is important for administrators to understand that some case managers cannot handle the strain of swinging from clinical work to interorganization or community work. The intervention techniques may be beyond the grasp of the "very clinical type." It becomes a matter of administrative decision as to how these interorganizational functions are allocated among staff and recognizing that case loads need to be adjusted.

Agency Investment in Supervision and Training

Even programs that have been able to recruit and hire highly skilled case managers need to continue supervision and training because of the variability and intensity of the job. Many administrators have dealt with budget constraints by setting salaries very low without recognizing the concommitant costs for additional supervision and training of less-qualified case managers. It is not only low salaries that deter qualified workers from seeking case-management jobs but also the general reputation of case-management programs. They are seen as temporarily funded, with paraprofessionals dominant in proportion to professionals, and, of limited transferability to a career ladder in traditional professions.

When a program's case managers are paraprofessional or volunteer, the administrator must be certain to provide for adequate numbers of supervisors and sufficient released worker time for supervisory conferences and other staff development activities. Every supervisor must have the skills of a senior worker and be a leader in practice and service improvement. The more the administrator understands about the job content of case-manager practice, the better the staffing decisions.

Case-Management Concerns of the Supervisor

Case-manager supervision is fairly new and is virtually unmentioned in the literature of service coordination. This brief section is offered as a pioneer step in giving some attention to supervision as an important component in the development and maintenance of the agency program.

Case-management programs often require supervisors to carry two or more concurrent roles. In some programs, the supervisor may carry a token case load either to retain cases that are too complex for other workers or in order to keep in touch with front-line practice realities. In other programs the supervisor is either director or deputy director charged with myriad administrative tasks that may compete with time available for supervision.

Another variation in emphasis that affects the supervisor's work with case managers is the degree to which resource control and accountability are dominant. Since the administrative aspects of supervision cannot be generalized here, this section for supervisors by design emphasizes the staff development aspects of supervision, especially (1) overseeing activities, (2) some dimensions in case-manager intervention levels, and (3) support activities for improving case-manager practice.

Overseeing Activities

The term *oversee* has been used because the supervisor does not always have line authority over all agency operations that directly affect the morale and productivity of the practitioners. Nevertheless the supervisor must facilitate the work of the front-line staff. The supervisor's responsibilities include a number of activities.

Agency induction of new workers is usually a supervisory responsibility. The start-up of a new agency will emhasize a more formal and well-prepared induction and training program. In time replacements get less attention. The supervisor is the one person who must see that the new worker receives sufficient training to begin work.

The supervisor sets the framework for practitioner practice, emphasizing some techniques and tasks over others. A staff made up of primarily the same discipline helps to firm up a practice model best suited for the agency. An interdisciplinary staff will continually need integrating help by the supervisor, who keeps in close touch with the best blend of disciplines.

The supervisor must know the personal strengths and weaknesses as well as areas of professional competence of each case manager. With an interdisciplinary staff, there are opportunities for the supervisor to utilize the special expertise of staff for shared learning. For example, the nurse supervisor may rely on the social caseworker practioner as the consulting expert on family conflict matters. Appropriate use of staff expertise is as important as identifying gaps and need for staff development.

Allocation of scarce resources, purchase of services, and setting priorities in use of high-cost services must be done by the supervisor or person at the next administrative level. Peer groups usually cannot oversee each other.

The front office and stenographic support may be under another administrator; but the practice supervisor will oversee these operations in terms of their effectiveness in providing the back-up for the case managers.

Types of everyday events that require the supervisor's attention include dealing with overidentification on the part of indigenous workers in outreach programs, a worker's overinvolvement in an interesting client situation, or a potential burnout of an overworked practitioner.

Another scanning technique is the use of case reviews. Areas for review include policy conformity, freeing up of services, cost containment, implementation of case plans, identification of unmet needs and inferences for client improvement and satisfaction. To keep case file reviews manageable, a sample of active cases should be drawn every few months to test agency policy conformity on closings and case time investment.

Supervisors at the middle-management level are in the best position as the conduits for information between the board, the administrators, the service system network, and, of course, the front-line staff in the field. The supervisor stands at the hub of the intelligence center (in the middle-sized organization). This central placement means that the supervisor has responsibilities for identifying what is important to channel to the management level, what is within the supervisor's domain for action and what should be channeled to workers for their information.

Practitioners have made a point of wanting their supervisors to be familiar with clients and to know what it is like "out there" in the struggles to get the right services needed by their clients. They want policy and procedures to be explained with concrete examples. They ask for better understandings about the boundaries of their discretion to make decisions on their own. They want to know how to make headway with a difficult, hostile client. Their requests are pragmatic and related to specific cases. Yet the person at the supervisor level, like the teacher or trainer, must begin to generalize, to view classes of cases, and to use conceptual ideas. Concepts and theory pieces are economical to use. As workers become more competent, they, too, will find that a few useful concepts are a lighter load to carry around than a hundred familiar case situations.

The next section presents an illustration of using some selected dimensions that can help to identify levels of client complexity or worker levels of competence. These dimensions cut across groups of cases. Practitioners easily learn to generalize about clients and their situations, but it is more difficult for them to identify and generalize about difficulties within the service system or within their own limitations.

Some Dimensions in Case-Manager Practice

The two components most frequently used in differentiating case loads are time and talent required. Some case-manager interventions are at a simple, beginner's level, like friendly visiting and follow-up procedures. Others are quite sophisticated, requiring considerable knowledge, experience, and skill, such as preparing the client and family for the older person's relocation. Below are illustrations of six dimensions related to case-management practice that may serve the administrator as handles for sorting out work requiring more or less practitioner competence.

1. Potential for Adverse Client Effects. The first principle in clinical practice is "Do no harm." In some client situations dangers are inherent if poor judgment is exercised by the practitioner. The greater the danger or risk to the client the greater the level of practitioner expertise required. Conversely, instrumental help such as locating a lost check or securing transportation to the nutrition center is not likely to harm a client, even if poorly handled. When a client's rights are threatened and there is family conflict regarding a pending institutional placement, a high level of competence on the part of the worker is required. Aged clients who have suffered a series of losses are more vulnerable to adverse effects from the next loss if the agency should take away the companion service or propose an unwanted relocation. Insensitivity to client vulnerability and strain can cause such damage that the client would be better off with no service.

2. Span of Coordination Efforts. This dimension includes the span in number of services the case manager is getting in place to be utilized by the client. Span is also increased by the number of family members, medical specialists, or others who are an active part of the client's personal network. Span also includes the (geographic) distance to be covered in keeping personal contacts with the client and coordinating the service providers. Too many active persons involved in the client network adds to the demands on workers and is not necessarily a blessing.

3. Degree of Complexity Caused by Multiproblem Situations. Aged persons receiving case-management service will likely have some type of chronic medical condition along with social or economic problems. Problem situations need not be overwhelming if coping skills are within the client's or client's family's resources. In complex situations the client may have a galaxy of problems and needs, especially if he is completely alone and is in a neglected state. Different problems have different degrees of seriousness.

The competent worker confronting a complicated situation reassesses the client's status. The possible from the impossible must be sorted out, incremental steps of doing the important things first must be decided in plan implementation, case goals must be realistic, time distribution and resources budgeted. Inexperienced workers have difficulty in ordering priorities when a client's situation presents an overwhelming array of needs and problems.

4. Degree of Worker Expertise Expected for Professional Agency Referrals. Several obstacles face case managers in the search and procurement of services for their clients. When the client's need for service is a matter of entitlement or the resources are readily obtained, then the practitioner follows the resource file and the channels of familiar agencies. Some scarce resources such as affordable housing can be located by an alert volunteer with persistant footwork. But other scarce resources such as homemaker service, companion service, protective service, or psychiatric or neurological treatment are procured only by meeting the criteria or diagnostic procedures of the provider source. The client who has an inexperienced paraprofessional as his case manager often has a willing but unsophisticated advocate, unable to present his client's case on a peer level. Practitioners with less credibility recognize the "brush off" received from professionals in certain provider agencies or institutions. Too often it takes peer-level negotiation for resources where discretionary opinion enters into admission of a client for service.

In addition to skills needed for obtaining certain scarce resources or in negotiating a service controlled by discretionary professional opinion, more expertise is needed for creating a new service. For example, putting together a home service package for a hospital discharge patient often requires a service component that is not available to the client, such as physical therapy or speech retraining. The skilled worker more often has the conceptual and organizational techniques for creating a new mode of service delivery to solve newly confronted problems.

5. The Degree of Benefit/Risk Conflict in the Client Situation. The greater the degree of independent judgment needed for decisions regarding clients at risk, the more competence needed for protection of the client as well as the agency. A long list of touchy case situations can be cited where the rules in the manual are of little help: the client who is receiving scarce, costly resources but is misusing the opportunity others need; the aged person in family care who is used and abused by a mixed-up family; or the numerous cases reported by neighbors or police where the aged person lives in unsafe, unsanitary, unhealthy conditions but prefers it to other alternatives offered. One of the most subtle benefit-versus-risk conflicts emerges when the family and the doctor press for institutionalization and the case manager becomes sensitive to the negative emotional reaction of the aged parent.

Supervisors and administrators may never have reports from their paraprofessional staff on these conflict situations because paraprofessionals are not encouraged to report problems and moreover, not being aware of the expertise needed for these complex situations, would not want to report their failures.

6. The Degree of New Interorganizational Linkages Involved. Agencies' policies differ regarding the delegation of responsibility for negotiating new agreements with existing service-provider agencies or for seeking new interorganizational alignments. Services available by entitlement present no interorganizational issues if the service is sufficent for all those who qualify. When client conditions or needs indicate negotiation of new provider alignments, the supervisor as administrator must weigh the possible consequences if this category of elderly clients needs services beyond the present scope of cooperating provider agencies. For instance the rape treatment center, small group substance-abuse programs, or other specialized programs extend the service system but generally require agency personnel with higher-level competence and authority to establish the initial, appropriate linkage.

The six dimensions just presented are offered as some of the checkpoints for use by supervisors in decision making for initial case assignments or reassignments to more competent workers. Such risks face case-management agencies at both the client level and the organizational level.

The Supervisor and Agency Training

The success of an agency program depends on a continuous match of available practitioner skills and the job requirements to carry out the aims of the agency. Maintaining the match between skills available and the work requirements must be in tune with changing demands. There are the expectations of the service providers and the commitment of the program to deliver needed services to the client target group. There are also the workers and their desires for work satisfaction. They expect some feedback about the value from the work they do.

The supervisor is in the middle position in balancing the strains between management, the service system, and the workers' performance. It is the latter that produces the accomplishments of the program, depending on the supports and resources at their disposal.

The supervisor is the crucial link in the decisions about the direction of training and the affordable costs. The issue is not whether to develop a particular training program but, rather, what is the best way to achieve this match between skills and needs to carry out the agency's goals.

Training needs change and can be best interpreted when

the agency is starting its program and a group of new workers is hired;

some workers are promoted or are reassigned;

workers are given new duties, a different target group, or must adapt to new staffing patterns;

new knowledge or technology is introduced—say, a computerized information and response system;

policy changes and procedures create significant changes in the usual mode of operation;

the program is stabilized and routine monitoring shows quality has slipped;

monitoring or evaluation shows a discrepancy between the program's level of expectation and level of attainment.

A number of such evaluative question are listed in chapter 7. Identifying shortcomings may trigger a new round of training for the new or modified work skills required. As we all know, a number of steps intervene between the training of workers, the change of worker behavior, and the impact on clients.

The Need for Training. In general, training is of two types, which may overlap: (1) shortrange training or a single episode and (2) continuing training and staff development. Planning for training should take place only when there is a need for it and when it is seen and understood by trainees and other agency staff to be involved, especially the administration.

The popular approach for assessing training needs is often to survey the trainees regarding what is needed. This is useful but not sufficient because workers can report only as their level of experience, language, concepts, and image of future agency needs permit. The heavy burden falls on the trainer or the supervisor to put the inventory of training needs together.

All training programs are based on explicit or implicit assumptions about what tasks or actions the job requires and at what level the worker must perform in order to do the work satisfactorily. The list of work activities and the training needs list may vary in range from how to fill out a short, simple form to what to do on a first investigation interview in follow-up to a complaint of an abused aged person.

Some trainers overemphasize one modality for meeting all training needs. A well-designed training program does not begin with a particular modality but uses the appropriate modality or blend that is best for the training content and objectives.

Training Modalities. More comparable to strategies for defined purposes than to buzz groups and special gimmicks, the most common modalities are described in the following paragraphs.

Agency induction or orientation is a simple, informational type of teaching. An inventory of work tasks or actions is described to trainees, who may have had similar experience but who need to know how this particular agency does it. When possible, these instructional pieces are related to the goals and mission of the organization. New workers are able to recognize the utility of doing the task or following the rules set by the agency. This modality covers the bare basics of agency orientation for employees to begin their work with the agency. It covers the essentials of personnel procedures and explains some of the work boundaries of other related staff positions and the principal program components included in the program. Every agency or program gives some instruction to aid the new employee (or the old employee in a new job) to feel at home in the work setting.

Instructional techniques and explanations include training that is to affect the attitudes, values, and behaviors of workers. The agenda is usually composed of bits of information and pieces of action. Modeling, role playing, and "show and tell," experiential sessions are used. Equipment, types of orthopedic appliances, types of wheelchairs, vision aids, and so on are demonstrated for case managers who are supervising chronically ill or handicapped cases. Crisis telephoning, family interviewing techniques, interdisciplinary conferences, and similar techniques are included.

Prescription for practitioner behavior includes rules or principles to follow in certain kinds of situations. The assessment form for gathering client data prescribes the format to follow. Experienced professional workers may use these standardized forms selectively or incrementally. The less-trained practitioner will be expected to follow the form. In addition, prescription is given for practice behaviors in patterns in the form: "If you run into this kind of client situation, this is what you do", "Our policy says this but under these conditions you may report to your supervisor for possible exception." Prescribed learning often is less than the best because the reality "out there" has many combinations of differing factors.

Action scenarios do not prescribe but are similar to a problem-solving sequence. A problem, a conflict situation, or a case planning objective that failed is used as the springboard for the group problem-solving experience. Planning a sequence of related action steps that focus on one aspect of a case plan is called partializing the problem. Successful results from some of the easier steps that are most important to the client beget the next successful steps. The crisis or barrier problem has a sequence for learning. The partialization of a larger, complex problem situation offers another type of action scenario.

Experiential learning is similar to on-the-job training. This is a traditional modality used in field practice assignments, internships, and mentoring when a junior worker is assigned to an experienced supervisor-teacher. Other variations of on-the-job training are found in all levels of personnel training. The buddy system is frequently developed as a systematized peer teaching approach. In its more sophisticated form experiential learning is directed toward integration of practice theory and practice behavior.

Professional education may be used in agency training, particularly in a well-planned, continuing staff-development program. Professionals who have been out of touch with their practice or who have not been exposed to recent technology or more recent goals and values may have a great need for "catching up on" professional education. Concept teaching, guiding principles, personality theories, practice styles, and theories can be cast into a professional education context appropriate for the paraprofessional who is ready for a more generalizable approach.

The agency supervisor or trainer may work with the local community college or university in developing a sequence of courses in gerontology, working with the aged, and so forth. Released time may be offered by the agency for approved course work or workshop training intensives at conferences. With the tight budgets, workers who find they must pay for their own improvement in education, may obtain a good out-of-agency staff development course by sharing costs across agencies to bring in a qualified expert.

There is no equally matched alternative for the professional course sequence that provides the practice discipline for the graduate. One of our unsolved problems in training is the two-track system created by aide training and the development of paraprofessionals. Those who were trained as aides often face the impossibility of having their past experiences credited to a professional education track. The high staff turnover in health care aides, hospital aides, and social-work aides is testimony to this problem.

Choices and Costs in Training. The life cycle of the program influences modalities. After a new program is stabilized, new workers and position changes may be in such small numbers that intensive orientation training through group methods may be uneconomical. Even the established program with little staff turnover will need to provide periodic training.

New training alternatives are always considered as choices. It may be necessary to change agency goals or lower the preferred standards in order to match workers' capacities with agency goals and values. Upgrading of personnel by adding more professionals or experienced workers may decrease training needs. Doing nothing and allowing future events or problems to come as they may is another choice. Training has sometimes been introduced after the consequences of mistakes and negative publicity have attracted attention.

Restructuring agency program components and job responsibilities sometimes offer a nontraining choice. Finally, another nontraining alternative is to offer a reward (pay raise, conference trip) for workers who individually seek and pay for their own educational advancement. Similarly, an agency can establish a good reputation by supporting competent personnel who advance to better jobs in other organizations.

Training programs are frequently challenged by boards of directors and funding sources. There is only a slight recognition that being a nurse or social worker in one program setting can be quite different from filling that role in another. Training becomes difficult to interpret. For this reason we often find the cost of training activities buried in supervisory time at the expense of resource development or other important supervisory functions. While workers helping their peers is excellent for day-to-day collaboration, it is too costly be used as a replacement for agency orientation or pre-service training. Bringing inappropriate lecturers into the agency may be worse than no training at all, even if they cost nothing.

Training and supervision are valued by workers when they feel the benefits are worth the time even when they will have to catch up with the work backlog. When the budget is cut, training may be the first budget item to go. Interpretation and explanation of training to the money decision makers must be continuous. The satisfied customers—the trainees—are the best interpreters.

Case-Manager Interventions

Clinicians in the various professions engaged in case management work primarily with individuals on a one-to-one basis. Case management cuts across several disciplines but has its own emphases:

home visits and evaluation as to how the client functions in daily living;

outreach and case finding, seeking out clients unable to get along alone;

the medical-social balance for the target group's chronic conditions and the interrelationships with social and often economic barriers;

education for client or family coping, such as information about resources so that those who can handle their own case management are encouraged to do so;

initial assessment (or continuing evaluation), which emphasizes a holistic approach for the multiproblem client;

follow-through with continuity of service for the frail or vulnerable elderly or planning for an expected continued-care program;

emphasis on linkages, coordination, and service procurement rather than on treatment or direct service;

worker aggressiveness as contrasted with a receptive readiness. A client needing protective service or guardianship or one who is neglected, abused, or unable to live at home is not expected to call for help to make appointments or drive to the doctor. The case manager assumes an active stance when serving the frail elderly; and

preventing "learned helplessness" in the client by careful balancing of response to unavoidable dependencies while guiding a rehabilitative independence.

We can embellish this list by adding that case managers are likely to be at their desk only for paperwork and making heavy use of the telephones. A day's schedule full of fifty-minute office interviewing and counseling periods is exceptional. Case managers have heavy field-work duties except in one or two types of agencies where the aides do the field work.

The Professional Stance of Practitioners

What a practitioner does in practice is influenced by two sets of factors, external and internal. The external factors include:

The community setting and the general attitudes about agency coordination and joint planning. Is the new coordination program perceived as an invasion or as a welcomed resource?

The willingness and readiness of provider agencies' staffs to accept the case manager as a peer—not too elite and not obviously below the professional (or administrative) rank of their counterparts for negotiation and cooperation.

Whether the work week set by the agency includes hours or days when most other agencies are closed. If case managers are covering for evening or weekends, their tasks will be expanded.

The degree to which the agency keeps its workers up to date on changing procedures, policy interpretations, and agreements with service providers. If the agency is negligent, the case manager must shift priorities to allow time for searching out the changes before taking case actions.

Sufficiency of supervision or other needed guidance as needed. Uncertainty about which course of action to choose can create frustration when the agency is not clear about what choices are feasible or correct. (On the other hand, in this same context excessive anxiety about making decisions is often a personal problem of the worker.) Peer consultation is to be encouraged. It can reduce anxieties and competitiveness while taking advantage of special areas of competence some workers bring to the agency or acquire on the job.

The agency's procedures, rules, communication channels, support resources personnel practices, and reporting requirements. Most of these implementing devices help to facilitate the work of the agency. When policy changes or new barriers interfere with care-plan implementation the worker is responsible for feedback.

Excessive staff turnover; poor case-finding practices; inequitable case-load distribution; staff involvement in fund raising; community crises such as a flood, fire, other disasters, or unplanned staff vacation schedules. Some of these are to be expected, to be endured and lived with. For others there may be choices. Workers can do more than just complain; they can pose solutions and alternatives.

Poor working conditions, inflexible transportation provisions, frequent ad hoc case-load surveys for legislators or other purposes, staff conflicts and poor morale, excessive staff illness and absence, change of executives and prolonged suspense about next year's funding and personnel cuts.

The internal factors affecting what case managers do are as follows:

The worker's degree of maturity and life experience, previous work experience in the human-services field, general education, and professional education. All these provide a frame of reference that affects the worker's performance.

Motivation. Each worker comes to the agency with some reason for having chosen or accepted the job in a case-coordination agency. Workers' reasons given for working with the elderly run the gamut from "I like to work with older people," "Work with elderly is so greatly needed", "It fulfills a religious and ideological commitment" to "It is a career with a future," "It's where the money is now," "There were no other jobs available."

In addition to such reasons and such factors as professional training and related work experience, there is another category of influences that shapes and directs the work activities of case managers: Parental training, life experiences, and the value system of one's neighborhood, friends, and relatives create a point of view or personal set of beliefs that bear on one's work life. In the next section we shall examine some statements of values that are especially framed for case-manager work direction. The focus is on workers' attitudes and behaviors as clues for further testing and thinking on the part of workers, their supervisors, and trainers.

Values. The worker's personal stance, feelings, and values influence not only the choices of interventions but the feeling quality that accompanies worker–client interactions. These are values necessary as a context for work with the aging:

> *To like genuinely and respect older people, especially the frail and impaired.* Some workers want to avoid contact with the frail or with nursing-home patients because they find them too depressing. Some workers cannot tolerate the deteriorating older person whose earlier life as a respected, interesting person is no longer recognizable.

> *To encourage client participation to the extent of the older person's capacity.* Participation in one's own health care and social program planning is just as good for the aged as for the middle-aged adult. The case manager should be ever on guard against two undesirable behaviors toward clients—infantilizing them and inducing increased dependency.

> *To be committed when finding the vulnerable aged in crisis.* A similar stance is required in child welfare when the worker finds an abused and neglected child: The worker has met a point of no return and must take some action, having seen there is no turning back. The case manager must know what steps to take at once. Empathy helps, but know-how is needed.

> *To individualize the client and the client's particular situation.* The core of a clinical practice is individualization. Although availability of service programs can be mechanized, the matching of services and the appropriate human interactions for individual needs are a long time in the making. In operationalizing this value statement, an important addition is essential. The concern of the agency or case manager to emphasize individualization is lost if the client never gets the message. The way the client is treated in the waiting room, care in returning telephone calls, and consulting the client about a change

in the service plan communicates a special individual interest in an important person.

To reach out to the most vulnerable. The agency may provide a special outreach program to screen in the most vulnerable elderly clients. But getting the client into the agency is not the end of the reaching out. The case manager is actively following through when telephone calls are initiated, when transportation is arranged, or when unfinished steps are pursued in the service plan. If clients are unable to follow through on their own, they should not get lost or fall through the cracks.

To be a humble gatekeeper of resources. One of the first requirements of a case manager is to marshal an adequate range of resources for the elderly and to become intimately familiar with eligibility requirements, procedures, and quality of these services. Access to purchase of service enhances the service inventory. Mobilizing resources is a total agency responsibility, particularly for the administrator. There is always a scarcity of such resources as housing, home care services for the seriously impaired and alone, and transportation to support social interaction. The case manager has the power and authority to allocate these limited resources to some clients and not to others of equal need. Such decisions on the part of case managers cannot be made lightly. The crux of the issue is how to use this power and authority wisely with a well-considered rationale.

To affirm the client's rights of privacy, of confidentiality, and of use of client consent and to protect from indignities. It takes sensitivity to recognize the situations that may embarrass or expose a client to humiliation. Most staff and others having contacts with impaired older people want to be humane and considerate but are not aware of the effects their manner or actions may have on the older persons already embarrassed because aging and illness have made them less than what they used to be. Case managers must also be aware of their own deeply embedded beliefs in aging stereotypes as well as the effects of labeling on the old. If the worker is not wise and aware of this, how can the preference of the adult children (the doctor and others in the client's own network) be assessed by the worker? Premature nursing home placements are frequently the result of stereotyping by the family.

To handle issues of sexuality and death and dying gracefully and kindly. There are deep-seated emotions and attitudes on the part of service providers as well as case managers. Case managers must identify and modify their own "hang ups" and assist others who are experiencing difficulties in confronting outmoded stereotypes about the aged.

The Case Manager's Know-How

This section is devoted to action—the actual practice at a task level. In writing definitions of tasks one can identify work units, small pieces of the job to be done, that can stand alone and have meaning for its accomplishment. The general format is to use action words, explaining how to accomplish something specific and, if possible, giving some standard of performance and level of skill needed. What follows here is not a task definition but, rather, the action words for doing the interventive activites. The first group is focused on clinical activities and the second group on organizational activites required to support the clinical activities.

In carrying out the overall job of assisting the client through the client pathway, the following interventions are used by case managers in their exchange and relationships with clients. They represent a focus on clinical activities.

developing trust and confidence between worker, agency and client (and family);

giving personal understanding to individual client conditions and situations;

listening to the client sometimes just for the sake of listening because the client wants to talk and because the worker is gathering information for better understanding of the client and the situation;

leading clients to participate actively in recognizing their own impairments and in restorative activities;

mobilizing the client's own network of resources—spouse, family, clubs, church—so that older persons become their own case managers within their individual capacity.

seeking client preferences and providing information about possible alternatives;

negotiating conflicts between client preference, relatives' wishes, and doctor's recommendations;

offering a professional (experienced) opinion regarding plan implementation (client, family, and physician have a right to know where the worker (or agency) stands—not to guess about it);

providing support all along the way through encouraging, reassuring, approving, a pat on the back, sometimes cajoling and persuading, sometimes using brief counseling;

using reinforcement techniques of rewarding and withholding praise as well as approval for carefully selected aspects of self-care the client has agreed to perform;

referring for counseling or, if deciding on direct service, formalizing the counseling sessions so that the client can understand the difference and have a choice;

handling barriers and interferences from negative family relationships, other environmental problems, or the client's own anger and hostility;

finding specialized resources such as for treatment of substance abuse, stroke, and other problems beyond the worker's own capabilities;

using a psychological contract approach when appropriate; that is *not* a formalized signed agreement but some reminder notes (client may forget) as to what the worker will do and what the client suggests (or agrees) to do;

providing some concrete aids for client—a pill box for the week, night lights, a ramp, railings, or a wheel chair, or providing special learning sessions when the client has asked for help with handling money, writing checks, paying bills, or otherwise managing money, (this may be done better by an aide or volunteer or other specialist);

using an incremental approach in introducing changes, a new service, or new accommodations expected from the client. Too much change can be more detrimental than no change.

conducting a medication review (or referral to expert) when there are indications that this is needed;

interpreting and explaining to the client what is going on to get the services and help expected (the worker should communicate about the efforts done on the client's behalf, and when a worker fails to deliver an expected service, the client should have an explanation);

educating the client about what the agency does and how it operates;

bringing about closure to complete short and immediate steps which have been partialized. Don't bite off the whole problem at once. A step at a time makes small closures possible. Case termination or reclassification to a case status of holding or inactive is also a form of closure even when the client case is not terminated.

Summary

This chapter has presented a selective picture for understanding the interventions of a case manager. The focus has been on the doing of case management from the perspectives of the administrator, supervisor, and case manager. It is important in a specific program that representatives of these three levels meet together frequently enough to ensure that they are all acting upon a common perception of what case management is.

The chapter has also set forth concepts and principles about case-management practice within an agency or program perspective. Case managers are interested not only in what they bring to their own job but also in how their job is influenced by administrative and supervisory decisions. Their commitment to particular clients ultimately leads to a concern for the revision, expansion, and improvement of quality of the human-service system as it affects the larger group to be served.

Suggested Readings

Aronson, M.; Bennett, R.; and Gurland, B. *The Acting-Out Elderly*. New York: The Haworth Press, 1983.

Cohen, E., and Staroscik, L. *Community Services and Long-Term Care: Issues of Negligence and Liability*. Philadelphia, Pa.: Temple University Long-Term-Care Gerontology Center, 1982.

Collins, A.H., and Pancoast, D.L. *Natural Helping Networks: A Strategy for Prevention*. Washington, D.C.: National Association of Social Workers, 1976.

Kane, R.A., and Kane, R.L. *Values and Long-Term Care*. Lexington, Mass.: Lexington Books, 1982.

Kirschner, C. "The Aging Family in Crisis: A Problem in Living." *Social Casework* (April 1979):209–216.

Lowy, L. *Social Work with the Aging*. New York: Harper and Row, 1979.

Nuttbrock, L., and Kosberg, J.I. "Images of the Physician and Help-Seeking Behavior of the Elderly: A Multivariate Assessment." *Journal of Gerontology* 35, no. 2 (March 1980):241–248.

Perlman, R. *Consumers and Social Services*. New York: John Wiley & Sons, 1975.

Silverstone, B., and Burack-Weiss, A. *Social Work Practice with the Frail Elderly and Their Families*. Springfield, Ill.: Charles C. Thomas, Publisher, 1983.

Tesfa, A. "What Does It Take to Let Them Go Home?" *Journal of Gerontological Nursing* 12, 692–695, 718.

Wasser, E. *Creative Approaches in Casework with the Aging*. New York: Family Service Association of America, 1966.

8

Case-Management Considerations in Information Systems, Accountability, and Evaluation

In a case-management program, as in other human services, the primary purpose of recordkeeping, information systems, data analysis, and reporting is to keep administrators aware of what is happening in the program. An orderly and timely flow of information is administrative self-protection in two ways: (1) it can provide early warnings if the program is not progressing as planned so that corrective measures can be taken; and (2) it provides a basis for accounting to others how the program is using resources and what level of productivity has been achieved. In addition, as noted in chapter 2, a program may need to answer questions beyond its own organizational needs and may contribute to national knowledge building regarding the experiences and outcomes of a particular type of program.

This chapter is an introduction to the multiplicity of questions for which the administrator may need answers and to some conceptual tools useful for obtaining answers. The chapter concludes with notes about technical assistance for information management and for taking corrective action.

The underlying assumption of this chapter is that an administrator should first focus on management questions and collect only the information needed to answer the most salient questions. The chapter does not attempt to deal with the numerous technical issues and skills involved in information handling or in evaluation design but, rather, highlights special considerations that a case-management program poses for the administrator and for any technical experts who assist with these functions.

What Program Feedback Most Administrators Need

The irreducible minimum information that a case-management program needs to keep current is to know who is being served and how much money has been spent of the total funds available. The degree to which a given program elaborates on these questions depends on its unique combination of internal needs and external requirements.

Elaboration begins at the client level. Workers need to know not only the names of the clients but also the presenting problem, impairments, and resources of the client. The worker needs a record in which to file the identifying information and in which to record the case plans, activities performed, the services obtained, results observed, and changes identified over time. Case records may simply be in file drawers or may be stored in computerized information systems. The worker may even be able to obtain computerized daily printouts listing the clients due for reassessment. The case record becomes the primary source for case continuity.

At this point the reader may think that this chapter is merely an elementary review of the obvious. It is unlikely that an administrator would be hired to direct a case-management program without prior knowledge of the basics of agency recordkeeping. Some of the basics are outlined here because too many programs have been overloaded with an over-elegant information system with inadequate phasing in of the essential recordkeeping before workers are diverted from their direct work with clients to do the additional, albeit important, research-oriented paperwork.

An Inventory of Common Programmatic and Administrative Questions

The kinds of questions that emerge concerning a case-coordination program can be so numerous and diverse that an administrator must have some conceptual framework to guide efficient planning. Such a framework becomes necessary whether the administrator is preparing the agenda for staff or board meetings, planning an information system, designing an evaluation, or contracting for technical assistance.

As a first slice at such a framework, we recommend classifying questions at the three levels used in earlier chapters: the client–worker level, the program or agency level, and the service system level. In the following inventory we have organized examples of questions drawn from many information systems, program evaluations, and administrator's agendas according to the three levels of operation. *These questions become evaluative when achievements are compared with expectations.* Analyses of the discrepancies between expectations and achievement may lead either to reducing the expectations or to taking action to increase achievements. In the list that follows, we do not ask questions regarding discrepancies but, rather, for simplicity, list the basic question (such as, Which population are we actually serving?) and ask the reader to project such questions into their implied evaluative question (such as, Is there a discrepancy between the people we intended to serve and our present clientele?). Once a discrepancy has been identified, many subsets of questions will emerge (such as, Is the problem in our outreach, pre-screening, or intake or, rather, in a wrong estimation of who in this community most needed our service?). The overall perspective of this chapter is that information systems are primarily to serve the communication needs of a program.

Examples of Questions Related to Administration and Evaluation

In the following list, common programmatic and administrative questions are grouped into three categories within the three levels (client–worker, program, and system). First are those that take stock of the agency's *resources* (what is going into the program). This category may also be known as "inputs" or raw materials. Second are those questions dealing with *performance* (what is coming out of the program), sometimes referred to as "outputs" or productivity. Third are listed questions about *outcomes* (what are the results of the program), sometimes labeled as effects, benefits, or goal achievements. The various questions are often considered in one or another program. Each program must select whichever questions most pertain to its objectives and for which it can afford to obtain data.

Client-Worker Level

Resource Questions.

Which population are we serving? How do subgroups of clients differ?

What staff do we have to work with clients (quantity, qualifications)?

To what extent are workers oriented to their jobs (knowledge of goals, functions, procedures; attitudes toward clients and program; perceived needs for training)?

To what extent do workers have the program and administrative supports they need to do their job?

Performance Questions.

What activities are being performed (what kind, quantity, quality)?

How many clients have been served and for how long?

Are there time lags in a client's movement through the pathway?

What are the size and characteristics of caseloads?

What problems are being identified (quantity, comprehensiveness, intensity)?

To what extent are clients satisfied with services?

To what extent have informal supports been mobilized?

Are different subgroups of clients receiving equivalent attention?

Outcomes Questions.

To what extent have clients benefited from the program (in problem status, goal achievement, quality of life, costs, improved attitudes)?

To what extent has accessibility for underserved populations been improved?

To what extent has inappropriate use of scarce services been avoided?

Agency or Program Level

Resource Questions.

What funds and other organizational resources have been obtained?

What functions are in place? (See table 1–1.)

What is the composition of the governance body? Is the functioning of the governance body consistent with its mandate?

Performance Questions.

What is level of staff morale, burnout and/or turnover?

What is the pace and distribution of expenditures?

What is the cost of each function and average cost per client?

Is there effective coordination between units of the agency?

Outcomes Questions.

To what extent are program goals being achieved?

To what extent has program achieved credibility and continuing support?

To what extent does the program have internal and external planning processes and conflict resolution mechanisms to ensure continuing improvement of performance and evaluation according to changing needs?

Service-System Level

Resource Questions.

What kinds and quantities of outside services have been obtained for clients?

How are the program and its goals perceived and supported by relevant communities of interest?

What interagency agreements are in place?

What other interagency linkages have been negotiated?

What gaps in available resources have been identified?

Performance Questions.

What obstacles to implementation exist (as experienced within the organization or system *and* by outsiders)?

What unanticipated achievements have emerged?

To what extent are other agencies satisfied?

What actions have been taken to fill gaps in system resources?

Outcomes Questions.

To what extent has community's continuum of care been enhanced or balanced by the program?

What impact has program had on costs of care to the community at large?

What improvements in services of other agencies have resulted from program?

To what extent has program led to improved community awareness and policy?

What has program contributed to national knowledge-building?

Implications for Information Reporting and Handling

Having clarified what questions the administrator most needs to have answered, the next step is to decide which information must be obtained on a *continuing basis* and which information may be sufficient if obtained on *special-purpose basis.* Too many information systems become over-loaded (and consequently overload personnel) by attempting to routinize reporting of events and other data that are only needed occasionally or for a one-time inquiry. The selection of relevant questions and the de-termination of which data must be maintained on a continuing basis are matters that will vary between programs.

The balance of this chapter will review some generic principles of designing an appropriate information system for a case-management agency, then will discuss information systems as a coordinating mech-anism. Finally we will examine some common concerns about the human factors in establishing and maintaining an appropriate system.

Four Types of Information Handling

Whether a program keeps paperwork to a minimum or is committed to a full-blown electronic data processing (EDP) management information system (MIS), there is usually some degree of involvement in four types of information handling: routine individual records, routine summary reports, periodic analyses of performance, and nonroutine inquiries or evaluative studies. In case-management programs the central topics of records and reports, or the "units of observation," are clients, worker activities, dollars, and services obtained.

In common with other service programs, records and reports may also deal with other topics such as governance, support services (pro-grammatic and administrative), and correspondence, which will be dis-cussed only briefly here. For example, the individual records in governance may be in the form of minutes of board meetings, executive orders, and funding agencies' announcements of regulations. A summary report, in the case of governance, would be a policy manual. Periodic analyses of governance may simply be an agenda item in staff meetings, the main subject of an annual board retreat, or the subject of a special-purpose evaluation. Individual records and summary reports of support services may be highly relevant to analyses of intraagency coordination and in rebudgeting. Correspondence files and memoranda of conversations, while rarely summarized, may become pertinent to comparisons of client-related with non–client-related work and accounts of the program's experience in encountering and overcoming barriers to implementation.

The primary units of observation—clients, worker activities, dollars, and services obtained for clients—are the categories of information most often analyzed in relation to each other in programs that aspire to perform some degree of self-analysis or evaluation, processes essential to improving performance.

To illustrate the spectrum of approaches to information we will trace these four units of observation through the previously mentioned four types of information handling. One encounters programs in which, except for a card file of clients' names and addresses, virtually all information is stored and processed in the heads of the personnel, especially in a special unit (of a large agency) that does not have to manage its own funds. At the other extreme are a few programs attempting to collect all its information about clients, worker activities, dollars, and services obtained in a grand electronic data-bank with its accompanying burden of keeping the databank up to date. The latter programs need generous budgets for information handling. They must have access to specialized experts to design and maintain the system and process data in formats that will assist the workers, administrators, and evaluators. This discussion is primarily aimed at the middle-sized program that attempts to go as far as possible in handling useful information within its limited resources of time and dollars.

Clients. The most difficult decisions are concerned with the optimum degree of recordkeeping about client characteristics, events, and status. The first task is deciding what information workers must have on tap to do their job (clinically relevant information). The second task is deciding the data needed for case accountability—that is, what supervisors may need to know in order to monitor and give technical assistance to workers as well as to provide the agency with a frame of reference when there is staff turnover or a legal challenge in behalf of an aggrieved client or family. Some funding sources require case-by-case evidence that there has been compliance with regulations for eligibility. The third task is deciding what kinds of information will be summarized in reports or aggregated in routine analyses of performance and long-term evaluation studies.

Some programs make the mistake of going beyond these three considerations by including in case files or information systems many other bits of information that may be interesting to know or might prove useful someday in as yet unknown ways. Such nonessential bits of information tend to impede the completeness and accuracy of recording and reporting. When and if the need for such additional information arises, it may be obtained on an ad hoc basis.

In addition to deciding how much information should routinely go into a case file (be it manual or EDP) each program must make an explicit decision as to what unit of observation comprises a "case." Is it an individual, a family group, or a household (which may contain more than one elderly person)? For a case-management program these are important considerations in view of the frequency with which there may be a spouse, sibling, partner, or housemate who provides some care to the client but who may also benefit from some of the services. The implications are most apparent when case information must be summarized and analyzed. When each individual is considered a separate case, the program summaries show larger numbers of clients and lower costs per client but fewer services per client. Most programs tend to maintain a single file per household, a practice which makes most sense to case managers and the authors. When comparisons of clients or services are made between programs, however, it must be borne in mind whether the policy regarding what is a case is the same across programs and across time.

Similarly, different programs take different approaches to what is an "active case" that have implications for the interpretation or comparison of summary reports as well as for the equitable distribution of cases between workers. (Even in a program with merely a single worker, differentiation of more active cases from less active cases is useful for prioritizing work.) Few agencies have an effective policy for classifying cases as active, inactive, or terminated. For the most part this omission occurs because most cases are long term, because of time lags in updating the information system, and because workers fear the red tape that may be involved in reopening a terminated case when new needs arise or old needs recur.

Each program must adapt and monitor policies to suit its own circumstances. As an example at least three categories of case classification may be used so that the administrator can maintain a useful perspective on summary data—active, inactive, and terminated. *Active* cases are those for which case managers will need to initiate some activity with or in behalf of a client within the next three months; *inactive* would be those cases in which the next agency contacts are to be initiated by the client within the foreseeable future or for which another agency has assumed primary responsibility. Some programs will find it fruitful to differentiate active cases between those clients who need continuous monitoring by the case manager and other clients who continue to receive referred services and periodic reassessments but do not need continuous contact with the case manager.

Moving from routine individual to routine summary reports it is obvious that the content of summary reports is constrained by what information has been routinely distilled from the case files. Typically summaries of clients include total number and distributions by age, sex, ethnicity, income level, functional status, service needs, and occasionally, type or location of residence.

Such summaries move into the arenas of analysis or evaluation when summaries for one point in time are compared with previous points in time (showing trends) or are compared with the program's stated objectives on target group (showing goal achievement); when subgroups of clients are separately summarized (such as by ethnicity, age, sex) in order to make comparisons between subgroups; or when clients are being compared with a group of nonclients.

Worker Activities. At very least workers generally report in the case file any contact they have had with the client. In addition case files should contain a record of all activities of the worker done in behalf of this case. Since a large percentage of a case manager's time goes into activities other than direct contact with the client (see chapter 7) some agencies require a log or diary of worker activities. This is a cumbersome demand to make of workers except during evaluations of time use, which can be made for a limited period rather than built into the routine information system.

When a time study is desired, data must be included about both case-specific and non–case-specific worker activities. Examples of activities related to active cases include reassessment, home visit to introduce home-chore worker, consultation with client's physician, and so on. Examples of activities not related to active cases but that must be taken into account are prescreening visits that resulted in referrals elsewhere, visits to cooperating agencies to explain the program or to seek new services for clients, and meetings with case aides to review procedures.

When workers' activities are specific to particular clients it is essential that each action be dated. This is to ensure clarity not only about which entry is most recent but also about time lags in the client pathway. The timeliness of each phase of case management should be analyzed at least once a year, which requires tracking of the dates of referral or application, prescreening, intake, assessment, service plan, initiation of service delivery, and so on for at least a sample of cases.

In addition to keeping data on clients and worker activities, larger agencies will need to establish files of the administrator's activities with

funding sources, cooperating agencies, and government officials to ac-
cumulate a record of contacts (such as memoranda of conversation, memoranda of understanding, and correspondence). Some of these activities
may need to be summarized in routine reports, made the subject of
analysis, or included as data in an evaluative study.

Dollars. The recording of fiscal transactions and summaries of fiscal
status usually involves a specialist on the staff who knows at least the
basics of fiscal planning and accounting; therefore little will be discussed
here. There are always unavoidable prescribed requirements for keeping
account of incoming and outgoing dollars. Fiscal data are usually given
priority over recordkeeping about clients or services, with respect to access
to a computerized system or the hiring of information personnel.

Special considerations in fiscal recording must be given by the administrator of a case-coordination program in order to monitor the costs
of particular functions within the program. In functional budgeting, each
expenditure must be recorded according to the defined cost centers for
groupings of similar functions. At the same time, most funding sources
continue to require traditional line-item bookkeeping.

The use of agencywide functional budgeting or cost analysis is
impeded to the extent that programs have multiple funding sources. Each
source requires separate accountability on the basis of line items (salaries,
travel, supplies) or by cases that meet the eligibility rules or entitlements
of that source. In evaluating program costs and taking action to reduce
costs it must be recognized that costs are higher during the start-up phases
of a new program as compared with an experienced, stabilized program.

Services Obtained. Perhaps the most perplexing information issue in case
management is how to record and report the various services being obtained for or delivered to clients. While there are numerous precedents
from research-based demonstration projects, there is little consistency
across projects, with little satisfaction with present methods.

The emergent issue is one of definitions and names. Some programs
use generic service definitions such as can be found in the Older Americans Resources and Services questionnaire (OARS) developed at Duke
University. The use of generic service definitions facilitates comparisons
between communities, between agencies, and between the formal and
informal supports. For example "help with bathing" is quite explicit and
amenable to comparison. However, alone, such phrases do not tell workers with which agency to communicate, or fiscal offices which agency
or individual providers to pay for purchased services. Conversely, using
agency names alone leads to ambiguities regarding which service has
been delivered or at what frequency. Between these two types of defi-

nitions or names are directory-type categories, such as "attendant care, home chore, homemaker, counseling, outreach," which are understood and practiced with such variability from site to site or agency to agency that each program must develop its own, locally acceptable set of definitions of units of services.

In many state governments current attempts are being made to standardize definitions of services and delineate units of service that arise in the programs of Titles XVIII, XIX, and XX. Administrators should begin by obtaining such information from the state agency that handles these titles of the Social Security Act as well as seeing what requirements or prototypes for definitions are promulgated by the case-management program's sponsors. The administrator must then examine the program's needs and constraints and determine at which points in the information system services must be recorded by agency name, by generic service label, or by units of service definition. It would be convenient for personnel to use the same method in all instances, but this is virtually impossible.

To illustrate, let us examine the four types of information handling—routine individualized records, routine summary reports, periodical analyses of performance, and nonroutine evaluative studies. In routine individual records, such as case files, the worker will need to know which service providers are involved and which services each provider is delivering. This need includes not only the service providers who become involved through the case-management program, but also the agencies that were previously and continuously involved and the services being delivered by the informal support system of family, friends, and neighbors. All this information is needed for care planning and coordination, although by far not all current programs require the recording of informal support services.

Routine summary reports usually require only two kinds of information: what kinds and quantities of services (not the providers) are being obtained for clients and, if purchase of service is used, how much should each contract agency be paid for services delivered (both the provider name and the quantity of units of service). Both periodic analyses of performance and nonroutine evaluative studies call for one or several kinds of information about services obtained depending on the degree to which the following kinds of questions are important to the program:

To what degree do the service plans vary to meet the different needs of different clients?

To what extent are service plans comprehensive? (This question must take into account not only the services obtained through the program but also concurrent services from the informal support system and previously involved agencies. If service plans tend to look alike or are rarely comprehensive, then the program must review its investment in individualized, comprehensive assessments.)

To what extent are some service providers being overutilized while other relevant service providers are being underutilized? (Here, agency names are important. Also, case-manager communication grapevines tend to be reliable regarding quantity and quality of providers.)

What service gaps are being identified by the case-management program? (This requires a method for routine reports concerning any service not available to that client by virtue of geography, eligibility constraints, waiting list situations, or total lack of supply in the locality.)

To what extent are less costly services being substituted for more costly service or inappropriate institutionalization? (This requires development of cost figures on nonpurchased as well as purchased services, and in some programs, development of cost equivalents of services provided by the natural support systems as well as considering copayment by clients.)

What are the significant differences in the performance of service providers?

What opinion do key service providers have of the case management program? What actions would enhance their cooperation and performance?

The next-to-last question may relate to important decisions regarding which providers to use preferentially. In such analyses it may be important to compare not only the cost differences per unit of service or per client, but also the amounts of time case managers have to spend in monitoring or other follow-up activities with different providers to ensure quality care, coordination, and timely care. In such a case the information system—or the ad hoc study—will have to be provided with data about worker activities in relation to particular providers, particularly those from whom services are being purchased. The final question suggests an ad hoc survey rather than routinized feedback from providers. Major relevant providers can be readily identified by workers at a staff meeting rather than routinized reporting for this purpose alone. If the program for other purposes maintains summaries of frequency of use of providers, then survey respondents can be identified from summaries.

With increased size, budget, research evaluation, or multiple funding, the data requirements become more sophisticated and demanding. Units reflecting the so-called hard or concrete services are less complex to define, collect, and interpret. We also call these services instrumental. The soft services (affectual and capacity building) are more difficult to define by units and more complex to include in a system for social bookkeeping. The administrator or information system designer will be able to find many references and prototypes for service definitions that may be adapted, but each program must screen its choices according to what questions does it need to answer routinely and which concepts and nomenclature best matches the orientation and language of those who will have to report about the services used, worker activities, and client characteristics.

In the evaluation or comparisons of case-management programs lies a major hazard. When using comparisons of client change, we cannot separate the effects of good or poor case management from the effects of good or poor quality services in the community. No evaluation has yet been able to measure differences in the relative quality of services obtained for the client. A top-notch case-management program that only has available poor services for referrals cannot be expected to achieve positive results. Conversely, excellent service providers may help a poor case-management program appear to achieve successes with clients—successes that might have been achieved without the case-management program. Nonetheless, many millions of dollars continue to be spent on comparing case-management programs without controlling for qualitative differences in service delivery.

Human Factors in Interorganizational Shared Information Systems

In this chapter we have thus far focused on the intraorganizational needs for information handling. As case-management programs increasingly become identified as centerpieces in long-term-care systems, they will expect to confront the problem of initiating or being a key partner in a multiorganizational shared information system for client tracking and for other system chores of communication, accountability, or evaluation.

A formal shared information system is one of the most difficult interorganizational linkages to establish and requires a long period of time before it begins to pay back on the efforts that must be invested by participating agencies. In chapter 9 are described the various data bases of our project, including the literature search, reported in the section Extracts from the Literature. In that compilation of lessons of the past from 217 coordination projects and classified according to 83 topics, the most do's and don'ts focused on interorganizational relations and the second largest category was information systems.

The challenges were not in the area of technical problems of information management but, rather, in the human factors in achieving organizational change. The most frequently recurrent guidelines were as follows:

Shared information systems are usually expensive and always require enormous cooperation between agencies.

Information systems can be designed to meet the critical information needs of a goal-oriented program

if the staff at all levels who are affected have participated in its development and can obtain understandable and useful feedback of information within a reasonable period of time;

if the system leaders are sensitive to the concerns of workers such as duplicate recordkeeping, client confidentiality, incompatibility with familiar professional concepts, repeated reporting of seldom-used or never-used variables, time for staff training, questions that create barriers to relationships with clients, and incorrect assumptions in using the data for evaluation of performance;

if attention is paid to the time and expense of training personnel at all levels in new skills of producing the required data.

Well-installed and continually maintained shared information systems contribute to interagency coordination when they

cause agencies to clarify shared goals and standardize terminology regarding clients and services;

improve the quality and volume of interagency referrals through client tracking, alerting personnel when clients experience discontinuities of care or are scheduled for reassessment;

provide management with information regarding such issues as gaps in services, inequities in staff case loads, costs per client, and program impact;

provide workers with displays of the case loads as an aid to prioritizing work with the client and with other cooperating agencies;

have had two to five years for a smooth introduction without

excessive stress and with key leadership and organization sufficient to ensure that data are accurate and up to date enough to
be trusted by the users.

Computer-based information systems are not necessarily more accurate than well-organized manual files and carefully prepared summary
reports. Whether or not to use computers is a judgment based on volume
of data, comparison costs of manual and electronic processing, and staff
capabilities. Beware of offers from other agencies or jurisdictions to share
computer time and staff expertise when they are already overloaded with
other priorities. The more removed the control of data bases is from the
agency that produces and must use the data, the more risk there is of not
having information available easily and quickly.

In obtaining technical assistance or specialized staff for an interagency
information system as a coordination linkage, it is essential to recruit
experts who understand interpersonal and organizational behavior, as well
as the technical aspects of information management. When all the necessary conditions are present or when the funding source requires a specific information system and has designed it for you, there remains an
inescapable long term of hard work to establish and maintain even the
simplest of systems.

Conceptual and Technological Considerations

This section is directed to some of the issues and considerations affecting
agency decisions in the collection, use, and management of information.
The underlying theme is that the information management plan must
originate in a clear design of a particular program and be compatible with
the processes and events through which work is done.

Relationship of Information System to Service System

The central axis of case coordination and of this book is the client pathway. The eight tables dealing with this pathway have presented it in five
phases: entry, assessment, goal setting and service planning, care-plan
implementation, and review of client status. These case-level functions
do not start, progress, stop and start over, or terminate without the support
of other organizational levels and supplementary agency functions.

A study or review of an operating agency for whatever purpose must
be cast into a perspective that will economically give directions for the
observations and the analysis. A new administrator, a personnel con-

sultant, or a systems expert who is making a proposal for an information system must have in mind a framework for flushing out the information needed for the questions at hand. The big, broad areas of information gathering are understanding the workings of an agency and the influences in its environment to be considered, identifying authority and funding channels, and grasping a structural picture of its organization.

A client-centered information system requires specific data on a case-unit basis over time and a knowledge of the phases of the possible pathways the client may travel in the course of case-management services. Adding to the complexity of mapping the client pathway is the fact that the client may have numerous side trips into other pathways for each service provided.

An information system analyst must first be well grounded in how the service system works before beginning to conceptualize the information system design. While all of the information obtained through this process will obviously not be included in the information system, it is useful in helping the designer to make decisions about what should be included. Mapping the flow of clients as they enter and move through the functional phases of a case management program or a long-term-care system is a fundamental step in beginning this decision process. This step is equally important for

identifying common events for most cases;

determining what forms and procedures will be used at what points in the client pathway flow;

identifying programmatic connections between events and phases;

deciding which of the events along the way should be reportable for the information programs;

deciding which data should be continuously available to groups of workers (staff) in the agency and which information should be made available intermittently; and

clarifying what discrepancies between the client pathway design and actual client experience will be tolerated before the administrator must make adjustments to correct "functional drift" or "program slippage."

Agency Function and Program Reporting

Table 8–1 illustrates some of the types of agency information commonly considered in case-management agencies. The examples are suggestive

Table 8–1
Information System Development in Relation to Program Functions at the Client Level

Entry	Assessment	Case Goal Setting and Service Planning	Care-Plan Implementation	Review and Evaluation of Client and Program Status
Purpose	*Purpose*	*Purpose*	*Purpose*	*Purpose*
To identify and enroll clients most appropriate for objectives and capacities of program.	To understand the client as a whole person and be aware of strengths and needs in client's situation.	To clarify expectations and agree upon an individualized plan of services and other problem-solving activities.	To arrange and ensure that services and other help are provided and utilized effectively.	To update knowledge of client and situation for possible revisions in client plan or for management of agency resources.
Guidelines	*Guidelines*	*Guidelines*	*Guidelines*	*Guidelines*
Outreach	Agency standardized, comprehensive form to be fully completed, "incomplete" items noted; comprehensive form necessary for client to use service system.	Case goals are immediate, long term, and changing; services needed, delivered services utilized, not available or client not ready to use a service can be reported in common units.	Reporting of service arrangements and implementation is generally reduced to what was needed, what was secured according to common definitions.	Case-load management, client tracking, program revisions depend on available current information from central reporting of active and other case status classifications.
report monthly gross count elderly reached by case-finding approach;	Home visit utilized in majority of service cases, record location of assessment.	Coordination agencies usually have a responsibility for both individualized goals and service system goals. The information system needs capacity to track progress of both kinds of goals.	Level of difficulty, types of problems encountered, necessary negotiations, substitute arrangements, locating or developing informal arrangements are worthy of reporting but involve a time and skill investment for precoding.	Prioritizing is not only used with a case load but must be consistent with a declaration of agency case classification and termination policy.
report monthly number of entry cases reaching agency;	The "whole person" assessment takes place on an incremental basis, information system must identify incomplete assessments.	Distinguish three levels in plans (1) service arrangements only, (2) service arrangement and supportive client counseling, (3) service arrangements and supportive counseling	Early in the implementation phase, tickler systems are developed, geared to supervisor–worker needs for monitoring client services and agency policy compliance.	Reporting requires common definitions, such as new admission, readmission, inactive, or service completed (by plan with or without follow-up), active intensive cases, active but low intensity cases, holding/pending until fixed date, case closed by reason of status unknown.
report number cases channeled to intake process.	Assessments that include other expertise information or consultants are considered to improve the assessment process—as compared to a one-person assessment report.			
Intake process reporting—immediate service				
emergency or initial service completed or closed;				
emergency, at-risk case continued for intake process;				
client card index ready for reopening of case.				

Table 8–1 Continued

Entry	Assessment	Case Goal Setting and Service Planning	Care-Plan Implementation	Review and Evaluation of Client and Program Status
Expected continued activities home visit scheduled; referred for comprehensive assessment and continuation; set up checkpoint for assessment appointment follow-through; client consent form, other agency intake forms; other agency forms prior to last assessment phase. Information reporting keep the continuing reporting information at a minimum; use special surveys, sample client panels, and so on for other intermittent information demands; use tally counts, number reached, to account for staff time and evaluate outreach activities;	Assessment tools often limit encouragement for collection and use of information about client preferences, client participation, life-styles, values, changing help from social support systems, and so forth. Analysts of computerized data must remain aware of what is *not* included in formal information system. Begin client-tracking approach as well as worker tracking; continuity in service especially long-term care depends on worker as well as client continuity.	and client capacity-building objectives. Client/family participation and preferences in care planning can influence plans more than client functioning levels scores. Such process information is more suitable for case file recording than for information systems reporting. Common definitions for services is a time-consuming effort for participating agencies but necessary for analysis of services needed and delivered. Reporting always requires a defined unit. Reporting responsibilities essential for accountability and research functions can amount to 5 to 15 percent of staff time.	Monitoring, accountability for continuity, under- or overutilization, case re-evaluation, time and cost limits of some services can be enhanced by the supports provided by a full-blown information system as repetitive events receiving planned attention. Prioritizing and case-load management begin here to avoid later overload. Who wants the information system, who generates the data, and who finds the data useful should be recognized as supporters for the system.	Trained volunteers make good statistical aides checking death notices, use of agency telephone roster for address changes, routine client tracking. Analysis of information system data must be supplemented with other forms of feedback, such as telephone surveys, study the effect of worker vacation and turnover on the clients welfare, contrast studies such as high-risk versus low-risk predictions and consequences. An agency self-study or case studies of a sample of clients will provide a check on the efficacy of the information system as well as of the agency policy and procedures.

have a policy and definitions as to when a case becomes an active service case to be counted.

Summary
Generalization: A reporting system is not a "full blown" electronic data processing information system but a developed information system is built on clear understandings of agency service functions, the delivery system, and the present reporting system.

Summary
Generalization: Differentiate information needed for agency service planning and client practice from data needed for research.

Summary
Generalization: Demographic or other client data that are *not* subject to frequent changes should be identified and handled differently from other "update" data requirements—for example, relocation of client or change in service plans.

Summary
Generalization: If the formal information system is developed as a support system for (1) the workers, (2) the coordinating program, and (3) the development of the community service system (including long-term care) the rewards for time and money invested should begin to appear during the third year.

Summary
Generalization: Feedback that can have an impact on agency or worker effectiveness depends on the appropriate design of the information system, provision for qualified staff to maintain and adapt the system, procedures for continuous update, and administrative support of the system.

rather than exhaustive; they apply to some programs and not to others. In the Entry column, for example, *outreach* may not be a function of an agency which by policy agreements routinely does all assessments for elderly Medicaid patients who are identified by other agencies. Case-management agencies who handle the outreach function need to know the costs and benefits of its outreach program. A disproportionate amount of time and money may be wasted on outreach approaches that do not yield appropriate cases. Inefficient outreach can also unintentionally build up an unnecessarily large information and referral program in an agency.

If the information system is to include changing, qualitative information from assessments then there are problems in coding. As mentioned in the chart's Assessment column, standardized assessment forms tend to discourage attention of the worker to questions which elicit qualitative answers such as client life-style, client preference, personal values, or attitudes. Too often, reporting forms for the information system restrict the framework for case practice. The practitioners may begin to work for the reporting forms instead of the client!

The last column of table 8–1 points to a significant problem of information input and feedback regarding the changing status of clients. When there is no typology or criteria for differentiating cases in the continuing case load, the mixtures of client need levels and of goal attainments remain unknown.

Table 8–2 reviews client-level functions from the perspective of example research issues. Sometimes these research questions have implications for information system development, but often they call for separate data gathering tasks.

A reporting system cannot make a program coherent. It can only reflect the clarity or ambiguities of the coordination program design as it exists. If the responsible agency or the service system is in a state of confusion, then the house should be put in order before investing in a computerized information system or a manual system.

Using Outside Assistance in Information System Development

The start-up of a new information system or the adaptation of an old one to an expanded program may call for expertise beyond the staff. Asking for and using technical help is the subject of many texts elsewhere. Here we will highlight issues that were most often raised in case-management program reports.

As noted earlier in this chapter, the prevailing theme is to keep mindful of the human factors and interorganizational relations of installing

Table 8–2
Research Issues in Relation to Agency Functions at the Client Level

Entry	Assessment	Case Goal Setting and Service Planning	Care-Plan Implementation	Review and Evaluation of Client and Program Status
Purpose	*Purpose*	*Purpose*	*Purpose*	*Purpose*
To identify and enroll clients most appropriate for objectives and capacities of program.	To understand the client as a whole person and be aware of strengths and needs in client's situation.	To clarify expectations and agree upon an individualized plan of services and other problem-solving activities.	To arrange and ensure that services and other help are provided and utilized effectively.	To update knowledge of client and situation for possible revisions in client plan or for management of agency resources.
Guidelines	*Guidelines*	*Guidelines*	*Guidelines*	*Guidelines*
A complex issue in evaluation of service coordination is how to differentiate the effects of case management from the effects of service provision beyond the control of the coordination project.	Much of the controversy about the use of a standardized, common assessment form is due to lack of clarification as to its purpose. A good research instrument is not necessarily the best diagnostic tool for understanding a client and the extent to which services needed will be acceptable and usable by the client.	Case goals that can be expressed in task objectives are amenable to research evaluation on a case-by-case basis.	Search and procurement of services are more easily identified than are activities in the goal-setting and planning phase. Fact finding on service gaps, eligibility barriers, service supply and limitations, and access problems can be readily quantified. Systematic inquiries cross-cutting several agencies are difficult but possible.	Research issues under this column are frequently tied to retrievable data in the information system of the coordination agency (or in the community); investigators tend to reformulate the evaluation questions to fit available data and to hold down cost of the inquiry.
Research on the efficacy and cost of the various approaches can inform choices in case-finding strategies.	The frail elderly, the vulnerable, the at-risk elderly, multiple-problem, multiserved elderly or most needy elderly constitute common terminology for identifying target groups for service coordination and for service recipients. For reasons of social policy and for political reasons and because	Generally when research inquiries are directed to case objectives, plans and implementation, it is necessary to train case-workers in advance on goal formulation and a format for writing plans.	Matching the elderly client with a needed resource opens an important research issue with regard to describing skill levels of staff, client characteristics, and variations in results. Patterns of differences in securing needed services can be documented and analyzed.	Evaluation research can be focused at the various levels—the service system, the agency program (intra-organizational), and the client–worker level.
A researchable issue in client screening is one of validating the worker competence level required for an early screening out of the obviously ineligible clients at the least unit cost. Professional panel review of a decision sample is a simple approach.		In the search for measures of service impact, the developmental theoretical frameworks from psychology, biology, and sociology do not offer a reasonable fit for the elderly. Elderly case goals are seldom the corrective or remedial types. Also change goals of "getting		Evaluation research can also be directed toward immediate performance goals, intermediate program objectives or ultimate case goals such as "quality of life" with a
Intake issues are numer-				

Table 8–2 Continued

Entry	Assessment	Case Goal Setting and Service Planning	Care-Plan Implementation	Review and Evaluation of Client and Program Status
ous—a single-point entry is considered to enhance service comprehensiveness; common intake forms are said to prevent duplication; a central intake center is considered as a convenience to the client; a comprehensive assessment is wanted as a helpful prerequisite for any service, an incremental assessment process overlapping with intake process is considered to be more client centered. These assumptions need testing. A separate intake organizational unit is said to offer more effective controls in admission of clients most appropriate to agency functions. However, many practitioners point to duplication of effort, client disruption, wasted time and loss of service quality by this division of functions.	of limited resources the field is under pressure to produce measurable indicators that will delineate a priority service recipient target group and whether this is a research or linguistic issue. Analyze to what extent information from an assessment tool is actually used, how much and what kind of data are needed to make the best decisions for service planning and implementation for this individual client, and how much is enough. Clients' opinions and reactions vary when they are confronted by an unanticipated lengthy assessment questionnaire. We should know more about client reactions, under what conditions and why.	better'' are too often inappropriate. Research directed toward case planning frequently concerns social policy research issues—for example, social need surveys to redistribute block grants or influence state funding. An important research issue for the researcher to recognize is the fact that case practice does not fit neatly into a distinct five column chart as used here as a communication framework. The "doing" of giving help to the elderly fits this schema only in a general sequence. Much back and forth activity from problems, plan implementation occurs. Process stages are a matter of *emphasis* and boundaries are not rigid in reality.	Another related issue is whether a service coordination program with untrained (or semitrained) case managers works better than *no* coordination program in view of risks and benefits. Often numerous rumors based on few facts create a good research issue. Repeatedly we hear that volunteers, CETA workers, paraprofessionals, and other lower-level workers are frequently "put-off" by the professional gatekeepers of service provider agencies. Scarce resources may often go to the client favored by having a higher status professional worker. Some research focused at service arrangements may be more appropriately investigated at the service system level or the agency linkages level than on a case-by-case basis.	set of descriptors to measure change. The most important issue at the case status level is to test achievement of both agency program and client goals. Questions along this line are tempered to aim the findings at agency or worker practice and other monitoring requirements from funding sources. Research or statistical skills are useful in developing definitions of service units to be monitored, in defining criteria for case prioritization, in setting supports for case classification, and reporting measures for worker intensity in given cases.

Summary
Generalization: The barriers of the entry channel are found within the client's situation (language, family values), the community (unpleasant past welfare agency experiences, lack of transportation), the service coordination agency (poor service interpretation, inept reception arrangements), and the intake personnel (inexperienced, overloaded, expressed disinterest). The issues are broad in scope but amenable to simple fact finding as well as more sophisticated research methods.

Summary
Generalization: The holistic concept which prevails about the client assessment process and comprehensive services may, when tested, fall considerably behind both the philosophy and the goal to be achieved. A better understanding as to the feasibility of a whole person approach for each elderly client for all coordination programs and all levels of workers is needed.

Summary
Generalization: As regards research issues or questions in setting goals and making plans for individual elderly clients, the data sources will likely be nonexistant unless case recording for such research questions is preplanned. The use of interview dyads of workers and clients is a fruitful but relatively costly methodological approach.

Summary
Generalization: The procurement of a needed service with legally defined eligibility makes different demands on worker skill than available professional services where the provider agency requires a "diagnostic entry." Procedures for procurement of instrumental help is more prescribed. Affective help, implementing client capacity building, demarcates the division between the lower- and the higher-level personnel.

Summary
Generalization: Technical assistance on an intermittent basis may be the best solution in assisting an agency to assess its program progress and caseload status after a period of program operations. The possible variations in agency and community settings and other influencing factors are so broad that a collaborative working approach between a specialist and the agency would be more cost effective than an elegant research design applied to a series of noncomparable sites.

a system. Thus, if technical experts are used, they too must be kept aware of the internal and external climate of the agencies involved and the importance of good interagency relations to a case-management program. It is essential that some staff member within the agency serve as the counterpart or anchor of the outside expert. This counterpart arrangement helps to protect the process so that the technical issues and the human factors can be developed concurrently and compatibly and so that the unique characteristics of the particular case-management program are understood. In addition the counterpart can ensure that the technical advice is utilized in a timely, efficient manner by all those in the system who are relevant. The counterpart is usually that ongoing staff member who is responsible for maintenance of the information system after it is designed. When the information technician on staff is not well grounded in human factors and community organization skills, the program director will need to maintain an involvement in each step of information system development.

A number of private firms and university centers with experience in human-services information systems are available as consultants or sub-contractors. It is suggested that the administrator first check out whether the program's funding source has plans to contract a consultant to work on a multicommunity information system. Despite many failed attempts by federal funding agencies during the 1960s and 1970s to have a national contractor for developing a management information system (MIS) to be replicated for all kinds of programs and in all types of communities, more recent efforts acknowledge that systems must be adapted to specific programs and specific communities. In other words there must be a certain amount of "reinventing the wheel" of information system design in each new community if the system is to be well used.

As in all other facets of local program development, the planner or administrator is reminded to seek first technical assistance within the local community—from government, voluntary, and private corporate sources. Such use of help keeps the agency's information system compatible with local practices and standards. So long as expectations about the technical assistance are clarified at the outset, then supportive linkages are developed that can be continued.

One of the most trusted kinds of assistance is that from peers who have faced and solved the same problems in another community. Our project's publication, "A National Directory of Case Coordination Programs for the Elderly," indexes agencies that have experience with information systems. When utilizing written materials from other programs, the reader is cautioned to keep in mind possible differences in program goals and different requirements for research and evaluation. Many reports have an appendix of all assessment and reporting forms but often do not describe the developmental problems of starting an information system or specify which of the reporting forms worked satisfactorily for them. It is up to the administrator to test and revise materials from other programs before putting them to use.

Finally, one "do" and one "don't." Don't oversell the information system as the key innovation in your program. Information systems per se do not create coordination, though well-organized information in the hands of decision makers facilitates coordination and performance. Do attempt to install your information system through an incremental approach. Early payoffs on simple-as-possible first steps will reinforce motivations among all concerned to move toward more complex and costly investments for long-range benefits for clients, personnel, organizations, and national social policy.

Summary

Recordkeeping, information handling, reporting, and evaluation in case management have much in common with other human-service administrative practices. Some special considerations for case management have been discussed in this chapter. The locus of attention will need to span what is happening at the interorganizational or service system level, as well as at the client–worker and organizational levels. Because of its complexity a case-management program can inundate personnel at all levels with an excess of variables to be tracked and questions to be answered. Case management poses special problems in defining and quantifying units of observation such as services, case, and case goals. Therefore, each program must be highly selective in terms of which units of observation are most relevant to its goals, which will be included routinely, and which will be included on an occasional basis. Evaluation of case management has the particular problem of separating the impact on clients caused by the case management itself from the client impact of the services provided in the care plan. Cost–benefit approaches must consider whether benefits to the service system should be in the equation along with benefits to clients receiving case management.

Finally, the handling of information for any of these purposes must be designed and implemented with creativity and vigilance to minimize undesirable side effects on the client pathway or on the network of good interagency relationships upon which case-management programs depend. At all phases and levels attention must be paid to the human factors of making changes.

Suggested Readings

Block, A.H., and Richardson, D., Jr. "Developing a Client-Based Feedback System for Improving Human Service Programs." *Human Services Monograph Series,* 10 (February 1979), Project SHARE.

Bowers, G.E., and Bowers, M.R. "Cultivating Client Information Systems." *Human Services Monograph Series,* 5 (June 1977), Project SHARE.

Branch, L., and Jette, A. "A Prospective Study of LTC Institutionalization among the Aged." *American Journal of Public Health* 72, no. 2 (December 1982):1373–1379.

Cantor, M.H., and Mayer, M.J. "Factors in Differential Utilization of Services by Urban Elderly." *Journal of Gerontological Social Work* 1, no. 1 (1978):47–61.

Carter, G.W. Social Policy and Social Research. In *Social Work Papers.* Vol. 8. Los Angeles, Calif.: University Printing Press, University of Southern California, 1975.

Conly, S. *Critical Review of Research on Long-Term-Care Alternatives.* Washington, D.C.: U.S. Department of Health, Education, and Welfare, Office of Social Services and Human Development, June 1977.

Eggert, G.W.; Bowlyow, J.E.; and Nichols, C.W. "Gaining Control of the Long-Term-Care System: First Returns from the ACCESS Experiment." *The Gerontologist* 20, no. 3 (June 1980):356–363.

Fillenbaum, G.; George, L.; and Maddox, G. "Functional Assessment in a Program Planning, Evaluation, and Resource Allocation Model." Paper presented at the Annual Scientific Meeting of the Gerontological Society of America, Boston, Mass., 1982.

Holmes, D.; Holmes, M.; Steinbach, L.; Hausner, T.; and Rocheleau, B. "The Use of Community-Based Long-Term Care by Minority Older Persons." *The Gerontologist* 19, no. 4 (August 1979):389–397.

Quinn, R.E. "The Impacts of a Computerized Information System on the Integration and Coordination of Human Services." *Public Administration Review* 36 (March–April 1976):166–174.

Steinberg, R.M. Social Program Tracking and Evaluation. In Mangen, D., and Peterson, W. (eds.), *Research Instruments in Social Gerontology.* Vol. 3. Minneapolis: University of Minnesota Press, 1984.

U.S. Comptroller General. *Conditions of Older People: National Information System Needed.* Washington, D.C.: General Accounting Office, 1979a.

U.S. Comptroller General. *The Elderly Should Benefit from Expanded Home Health Care but Increasing These Services Will Not Insure Cost Reductions.* Washington, D.C.: General Accounting Office, 1982 (GAO/IPE-83-1).

9

The Information Bases for this Book

This chapter briefly describes some of the research objectives, methodologies, outcomes, and findings for the various strategies used throughout the three-year project upon which this book is based. The project was initiated with two underlying assumptions. The first was based on a value stance held by the project staff—that at this time case coordination provides a promising approach for securing and integrating comprehensive delivery of services needed by the frail or vulnerable elderly who are unable to manage their own service planning and implementation. In addition, the potential variations in structural and functional designs for service coordination were considerations to be explored rather than explained at the outset.

The second assumption was that a broad-based research stance must become the overarching strategy for the project investigation. This philosophy was based on common staff backgrounds in social planning and established community organization principles. This problem scope needed to be sufficiently broad to include the influencing factors in the community environment on the coordination agency barriers and supports. Yet the focus had to emphasize the case coordination level—the intervention processes and the target groups of elderly.

Major goals, then, were to explore and examine case coordination as broadly as possible; to understand its evolution and development as a service delivery method; to learn how it is accomplished in a variety of settings and communities, what are the processes and practices of coordination at the client level, and what facilitates or inhibits its achievement. An initial objective was to develop models of case-coordination projects, but this soon proved to be futile: The finding that there were no typical configurations or one best way to design and implement such programs pervades the study. Instead, guidelines and recommendations for the development, implementation, and evaluation of case-coordination programs for the elderly were formulated as the major product of the research.

The data that were collected, analyzed, and reported were obtained from a variety of sources from October 1977 to September 1980, primarily from the literature; telephone and mailed surveys; meetings with consultants, practitioners, and administrators; and from in-depth site studies. The following overview of the project research strategies presents a cumulative sequence of activities but not necessarily in chronological order; it describes the intent and some of the results of each research activity undertaken by the project staff.

Research Strategies, Products, and Findings

The various phases of the project are here described under five broad categories: literature search, surveys, data-gathering meetings, in-depth site studies, and dissemination activities that provided valuable feedback. All but the last category are outlined in terms of objectives, methods, outcomes, findings, and products. The products are published by the Andrus Gerontology Center unless otherwise noted.

Literature search

Objectives.

to identify past and current case-coordination programs;

to identify appropriate materials for guideline extraction;

to extract guidelines in the form of recommendations, findings, and lessons to be learned;

to clarify concepts, identify key variables, seek common definitions of terms;

to identify existing measures for evaluation purposes;

to examine historical accounts of coordination efforts for trends, patterns, common issues.

Methods. With the aid of the Andrus Gerontology Center's Information Center, a search of the literature was made to identify relevant documents, articles, reports and books. Books of abstracts were reviewed. Nominations for relevant written materials were solicited from experts in the field. Documents were selected, obtained, and reviewed.

Outcomes. Over 1,000 documents related to coordination were collected and catalogued. A list of past and current coordination programs was developed as a starting point for future surveys. A coding scheme for extracting and storing guidelines was developed.

Examples of Findings.

While volumes of written material are available on coordination, coordination programs and evaluation, little is known about coordination at the client level.

Measures for evaluating the coordination component of projects are virtually nonexistant.

There is a long history of coordination efforts within the human services.

Definitions of concepts and terminology related to case coordination vary considerably.

Few attempts had been made to compile lessons to be learned from past coordination efforts.

Our initial distillation highlighted fourteen guidelines that became subjects for further validating research.

1. No one program model suits all communities.
2. The majority of users of innovative, multipurpose or case-coordination projects are not the at-risk population for which that particular program was designed (it serves more people who do not need it than those to whom it was originally targeted).
3. There is no gain in coordinating incompetent or irrelevant services. A community should first direct its attention to establishing and improving baseline services.
4. The agency that seeks to coordinate the services of other agencies should not operate its own direct services (some sources disagree). An agency cannot successfully coordinate with other agencies until it is able to coordinate within its own agency.
5. Coordination is expensive as well as difficult. Do not try to coordinate too many agencies at once.
6. Public or voluntary agency funding contracts can work, but successful coordination requires moderate stress.
7. Consumer and community involvement is difficult, takes time, and is a double-edged sword. Different types of advisory bodies are indicated for different kinds of objectives.
8. Colocation of many programs in a multipurpose center does not guarantee coordination. Unification of different services under one administration does not guarantee coordination.
9. Authority of one agency over another helps but does not guarantee coordination. Models depending on voluntary cooperation alone rarely succeed.
10. Accountability mechanisms (reporting, uniform service definitions,

and management information systems) are hellishly difficult to install and maintain but can be productive in time.

11. A coordination system should be evolutionary and cumulative (you cannot get all aspects of the program functioning equally well during the first year).

12. The potential efficiency and effectiveness of a coordination program cannot be evaluated during the first and second years. This does not preclude performance monitoring or documenting the experience and the rate of progress.

13. The leader of a coordination project must be a superbeing with optimum political skills, administrative competence, missionary fervor, and familiarity with the entire range of professional interventions and management techinques. In addition, the leader must, during the early phases of the new project, be primarily process-oriented and, in later phases, be primarily task-oriented.

14. At all levels of coordination, it is crucial that there be frequent and genuine interpersonal contact between representatives of agencies who are essential to the program's success.

Products.

Bibliographies.

Downing, R., and R. Steinberg. *Case Coordination Client Assessment Bibliography.* March 1980.

Steinberg, R.M. *Complete Case Coordination Bibliography.* September 1980.

Steinberg, R.M., and R. Downing. *Case Coordination Selected Bibliography.* March 1979.

Steinberg, R.M.; M. White, and G.W. Carter. *A Compendium of Findings and Recommendations for Planners and Implementers of Coordination Programs for the Elderly: Extracts from the Literature.* August 1980.

Thesis/Dissertation Literature Reviews.

Hutson, D.C. A Comparative Analysis of Three Case Management Models Serving the Impaired Elderly. Unpublished master's thesis, University of Southern California, School of Gerontology, Los Angeles, June 1979.

Jurkiewicz, V.C. An Exploratory-Descriptive Study of Interorganizational and Case Coordination Programs for the Multi-problem, Frail and Minority Elderly. Unpublished doctoral dissertation, University of California, Los Angeles, School of Social Welfare, Los Angeles, 1980.

Kuna, J. The Evaluation of Case Level Coordination. The State of the Art 1965–1975. Unpublished doctoral dissertation, School of Social Work, University of Southern California, May 1982.

White, M. Toward a Conceptual Framework for Case Coordination Program Design: Lessons from the Past, Guidelines for the Future. Unpublished doctoral dissertation, School of Social Work, University of Southern California, Los Angeles, June 1980.

Papers.

Carter, G.W. Service Coordination: a Recycling of Tested Concepts. In *Case Coordination and Service Integration Projects: Client Impact, Program Survival and Research Priorities.* Paper presented at National Conference of Social Welfare, Los Angeles, 1978.

Downing, R. Three Working Papers. March 1979.

Downing, R. Staffing Patterns in Case Coordination Programs: Choices and Consequences, a Working Paper. June 1980.

Steinberg, R.M. Case Coordination: Lessons from the Past for Future Program Models. In *Case Coordination and Service Integration Projects: Client Impact, Program Survival and Research Priorities.* Paper presented at National Conference on Social Welfare, Los Angeles, 1978.

Steinberg, R.M. Case Service Coordination: Senior Center Issues. In Jacobs. B. and R. Pflaum (eds.), *Senior Centers: Helping Communities Serve Older Persons.* Washington, D.C.: National Council on Aging, 1982.

Progress Reports.

Carter, G.W., and R.M. Steinberg. Alternative Case Coordination Programs: A Problem of Research Strategies. Research paper presented at 33rd Annual Scientific meeting of Gerontological Society of America, San Diego, Calif., November 24, 1978.

Case Coordination Project Update (newsletter) November 1978.

Essentials of Program Design and Practice in Case Coordination with the Vulnerable Elderly. (Interim Report used as materials for workshop discussion at 32nd Annual Meeting, Gerontological Society, Washington, D.C., November 26, 1979).

First Survey: Telephone Survey

Objectives. Contact was established with identified case-coordination projects still in operation in order to verify that coordination at the case level was part of that project; invite participation in further studies; solicit preliminary guidelines; and determine whether the project had been evaluated. Another objective was to determine the rate of survival of known case coordination projects.

Methods. Identified projects were contacted by telephone. In cases where project status or contact sources were unknown, staff located agencies, former personnel, or others who might know the current status of the project. A maximum of three phone calls were alloted to trace a project. A brief questionnaire was utilized to obtain desired information.

Outcomes. From the original list of 608 projects identified, a sample of 125 case coordination projects was obtained, representing 37 states and the District of Columbia and including all ten federal regions, for participation in a pilot study. A beginning set of guidelines and recommendations for "success" was obtained.

Examples of Findings.

Sixty percent of the projects had survived although all had changed from their original designs.

Almost none of the projects had evaluated coordination at the client level.

Interorganizational relations was considered as the key to program success or failure.

There was no commonality of the concepts or terminology related to case coordination.

Respondents' advice to newly starting programs generally stressed the importance of "a dedicated, high-quality staff," "clear definition of agency and worker roles," "adequate, flexible funding," "advance groundwork to ensure public understanding and interagency cooperation,"—and time, patience, and trust. The strongest area of disagreement was between those who stated that the agency or person who does case coordination should *not* provide direct services and others who asserted that case coordination should be done by the principal provider of care.

Products. A summary of the telephone survey is included in *Project Update*.

Second Survey: Pilot Study

Objectives. To pretest questionnaires for future national study of aging programs, to test the notion of categorizing projects into "models," and to validate a subset of guidelines and recommendations extracted from the literature a pilot study was conducted.

Methods. Twenty-eight administrators from a variety of case-coordination projects responded to two mailed questionnaires: (1) an instrument collecting descriptive data and (2) an instrument seeking a level of agreement with guideline statements. Descriptive data were analyzed for similarities and differences in project characteristics, staff, and methods of operationalizing coordination. Guideline data were compared for levels of agreement to the statements and examined against demographic data provided by the respondents.

Outcomes. Descriptive questionnaires provided the basis for the development of the national survey instrument. The pilot study pretested variables useful for measures of project differences and for the Monika White conceptual framework for case-coordination program design. The overall utility of guidelines from the literature was confirmed.

Examples of Findings.

Program components as described by respondents defied classification into project "models."

The programs in the sample did share some characteristics. Most were initiated by existing agencies through legislation or availability of funding.

A majority operated as the "lead" agency in their coordination network with both client and system responsibilities.

Most stated their objective as providing comprehensive services to multiproblem clients.

Case conferences were the most frequently used interagency linkage, followed by joint planning and joint training.

Most employed professional staff; one-half utilized paraprofessionals, less than one-third used volunteers.

Of the guideline statements presented to respondents, 82 percent of the sample agreed with 80 percent of the statements suggesting that past experiences are relevant to current programs, including

It is important to provide training for coordination staff.

It is important that information be shared among the agencies that work together.

The planning and implementation of coordination efforts is best accomplished with participation from a variety of community representatives who will be affected.

The director of coordination programs must have a variety of skills.

The primary mission of a coordination project should be to coordinate rather than to provide services.

Products

M. White dissertation.

J. Kuna dissertation.

Third Survey: The National Survey

Objectives. The national survey was conducted to determine the extent to which case coordination for the elderly exists, to develop a directory of existing projects; to determine differences among these projects regarding their design, clientele, funding sources, personnel, and environment.

Methods. Contact was made by mail with 823 projects across the country. Projects meeting the study criteria were asked to complete a questionnaire.

Outcomes. Of 365 responses, 333 case coordination programs were included in the directory. Data collected provided the basis for consideration of issues for an in-depth site study (interorganizational dynamics, essential services). These data also provided additional perspectives on the guidelines with respect to clients served and services.

Examples of Findings.

Program design configurations did not divide themselves into any particular models.

The majority of the programs operated case-coordination units within a larger agency or engaged in coordination activities through various agency personnel without a defined unit.

Case-coordination personnel rated eight services as most crucial for their clients: friendly visiting, housekeeping, transportation, community mental health centers, visiting nurses, social or family casework, adult protective services, homemaker services.

Social workers were the principal coordinators in more than three-fourths of the programs.

Interorganizational linkages utilized by more than one-half of the programs included informal agreements, informal interagency meetings, and systematic information exchange.

Products.

Interim Report: Essentials of Program Design.
Jurkiewicz, V. dissertation
Steinberg, R.M., and V. Jurkiewicz. *A National Directory of Case Coordination Programs for the Elderly 1979–1980 with Findings from the National Survey,* 1980.

Evaluation Analysis

Objectives. To determine the extent to which client-level evaluation has been undertaken by programs, to identify what variables have been measured and what measures were utilized, and to develop recommendations for case-coordination program evaluation, an analysis of case-coordination program evaluation was performed.

Methods. Evaluation literature was reviewed for theories, historical trends, and program evaluation documents containing strategies and outcomes of various measures and approaches. The telephone survey and pilot study survey provided initial information on the extent and focus of evaluation activities. A research instrument was developed to collect data from evaluation reports with the intent of capturing the most critical variables measured—to find out what was measured and what data sources were utilized.

Outcomes. A set of variables utilized by program evaluators was identified; included were such items as service utilization, comprehensiveness of problem identification, extent of coordination activities, methods for assuring continuity and timeliness, and client satisfaction. The analysis of the state of the art of case-coordination program evaluations led to recommendations for new measures, which were tested during the site studies.

Examples of findings.

Within a sample of 125 programs, 60 percent had been evaluated.

For the most part, evaluation data focused on processes, performance, and descriptions of program activities.

Generally, case coordination has not been evaluated for client impact.

Current evaluations of case coordination are seriously limited by changes implemented during the life of the project, lack of comparable data in analyzing experimental and control groups, and attributing client changes to case coordination alone.

It is possible to evaluate coordination programs at the client level.

Products.

J. Kuna dissertation.

Interim Report: Essentials of Program Design.

Consultant Conference

Objectives. A conference was held to bring together experts in the field to act as a sounding board regarding research strategies; to identify issues in coordination programs; and to distill coordination concepts.

Methods. A group of policy, program and research experts met with the project staff in an unstructured meeting to share ideas, discuss issues and proposed methodologies during the early stages of the research.

Outcomes. The research design was refined and revised. Both the need for and the timeliness of the questions to be addressed by the study were validated. Sources of informaton from the literature were suggested and known case-coordination programs were identified.

Examples of Findings. The meeting of experts as a method of launching a research project proved to be valuable and productive. The consultants confirmed that the project was needed and well conceived. The initial investment of time and thought made by the consultants resulted in heightened interest, staff confidence, and, in most cases, continuing input into the project.

Product.

> Steinberg, R.M. (ed.). *Selected Readings Related to Study Project in Case Coordination.* November 1977.

Practitioners' Symposium

Objectives. A practitioners' symposium was held to describe case-management practices across a variety of case-coordination programs, to clarify concepts from the perspective of the front-line practitioner, to discover commonalities in the processes and practices of case management, and to probe the personal and professional experiences of the case managers.

Methods. Twelve practitioners were invited to attend the symposium after a selection process seeking experienced workers from programs providing coordination services on the client level for the elderly. Symposium participants met for two and one-half days of structured sessions on selected topics, small and large group discussions, and individual debriefing interviews with project staff.

Outcomes. Information obtained during the symposium influenced the planned in-depth site studies. The issues and unresolved dilemmas that emerged provided clues to questions needing further examination and exploration. Discussions among participants and project staff further clarified concepts and terminology.

Examples of Findings.

> Despite variations in agency and community settings, case-coordination practices share more similarities than differences.

> Workers' perceptions of individual clients ("easy" versus "difficult," "successful" versus "unsuccessful," "motivated" versus "unmotivated") provide direction in working with the clients and characterize the perceived potential outcome for the clients.

> While there is agreement to the need for and content of a comprehensive client assessment, there is great variation in the process of assessing due in part to individual agency policies and procedures.

Planning for services is a complex process that begins at client assessment and includes consideration of client needs, potential, preferences, and support systems as well as the constraints of the service network itself with respect to availability and procedures.

Ongoing contact with clients appears to be preferred on an indefinite basis in order to permit workers to keep informed about changes in client status and service needs.

Successful coordination activities require strong agency supports and availability of community resources.

Role definitions of the coordinators are shaped by their tasks and activities, agency job descriptions, and the perceptions of clients, coworkers, and the coordinators themselves.

Case coordination is viewed as a service.

Products.

Carter, G.W.; R. Downing, D.O. Hutson; and B.S. Ishizaki. *Case Coordination with the Elderly: the Experiences of Front-Line Practitioners.* Proceedings and summary of findings from the symposium held January 20–22, 1979.

Administrators' Task Force

Objectives. The task force was formed to test project staff formulations with the realities of program operations, to seek recommendations regarding policy and administrative problems, to gain insight into the administrator's perceptions about the major issues in coordination agencies and their community setting.

Methods. Considering agency size, organizational type, and variation in program goals, sixteen executives of case coordination programs were invited to form a task force with the project's research staff. The task force met for one and one-half days to discuss management issues and policy recommendations related to case-coordination programs.

Outcomes. The variations and contrasts in concerns expressed by the participants aided in the clarification of concepts for the project staff. A list of principles for coordination and recommendations for programs was developed.

Examples of Findings.

The most forceful influence, as well as the most demanding factor in program management are the requirements, uncertainties, and lack of continuity of funding sources.

The case coordination agency needs a strong organizational base; building the program onto an existing agency with historically good performance and a good reputation is desirable. If a new agency is needed, it should "buy into" established organizations.

There was general consensus that approximately 5 percent of the elderly (60 years and older) need case management.

In spite of remarkable differences among programs and priorities and styles of administrators, there was general agreement with the concepts, approaches, and priorities of the University of Southern California project including the abandonment of "models" in favor of differentiation by such variables as organizational base, goals, program components, funding, and interorganizational linkages.

Products.

None, except as utilized in this book.

In-Depth Site Studies

Objectives. The purpose of the studies on site were to examine in depth what case managers do; to discover how worker activities and services plans vary at different sites and with different clients and different staffing patterns; to understand interorganizational linkages and how they relate to community context; to understand how variations in goals and goal clarity effect case management practice; and to assess the impact of environmental contingencies on program operations.

Methods. Data were collected at three levels—community, agency, and client groups in six communities. Through a nomination method, leaders of the human-services segment of the community were selected and interviewed. Agency workers interviewed clients (no workers interviewed their own clients) who were first sampled on the basis of long- and short-term (3 months) cases. Workers were queried using case-record materials for some of the information.

Outcomes. Project staff attained a richer understanding of worker activities as they vary between different cases. The importance of influences on work with clients that come from the community and organizational context was confirmed. The importance and feasibility of evaluating programs at all three levels (community, agency, client) were reinforced.

Examples of Findings.

Agency or program goals affect worker activities and service plans.

There was no significant difference between worker activities or comprehensiveness of services between minority and nonminority clients.

Communities with a longer history of community interaction and a strong interest in target groups tend to develop formal case-coordination programs.

Among clients receiving case management, the health status of the young-old is poorer than that of the old-old; age criteria for eligibility would be counterproductive.

Clients with supports and previous service utilize recommended services more and better; client values and personality have greater impact on service plans than needs.

Case-management programs vary so much that they defy classification into models. However, case-manager practice does tend to follow three patterns outlined in Downing's working paper on case-manager roles.

Products.

V. Jurkiewicz dissertation

Steinberg, R.M.; G.W. Carter; and M. Walsh. *A Comparative Study of Case Coordination Programs in Six Cities: An Analysis of 140 Cases.* (In process).

Dissemination Activities

A variety of activities have served to disseminate information and findings to interested individuals and groups. Project staff have participated in conferences, training sessions, and agency meetings. Working papers were written and delivered to a wide range of audiences. A mailing list was developed and newsletters containing project updates were sent to practitioners, agency administrators, and researchers throughout the country. The extensive document collection obtained by the project is accessible and available for use by professionals and students. Most products are available at cost of duplication through the Andrus Gerontology Center's Information Center. The dissertations and theses are available through normal channels and the final edition of the book is expected to be available through book stores after publication.

Brief summaries of project conclusions have been published in such specialized national media as *Human Development News* and *Older American News* (both January 1982) and in case management manuals produced by other projects such as Senior Care Action Network (SCAN), Long Beach, California, and the Iowa Assessment Project (University of Iowa). Most project products are also available through the National Clearinghouse on Aging (AoA) and Project Share (U.S. Department of Health and Human Services).

In addition, presentations were made at annual conferences such as those of the National Conference on Social Welfare, the Gerontological Society of America, the National Council on Aging, state units and area agencies on aging. These dissemination activities were two-way communication channels in that they provided opportunities to obtain feedback on the applicability of our findings and uncovered new sources of information.

Suggested Readings

Carter, G.W.; Downing, R.; Hutson, D.; and Ishizaki, B. *Case Coordination with the Elderly: The Experiences of Front-Line Practitioners*. Los Angeles, Calif.: Andrus Gerontology Center, University of Southern California, 1980.

Downing, R. *Three Working Papers*. Los Angeles, Calif.: Andrus Gerontology Center, University of Southern California, 1979.

Steinberg, R.M. (ed.). *Case Coordination and Service Integration Projects: Client Impact, Program Survival, and Research Priorities*. Los Angeles, Calif.: Andrus Gerontology Center, University of Southern California, 1978.

Steinberg, R.; White, M.; and Carter, G. *A Compendium of Findings, and Recommendations for Planners and Implementers of Coordination Programs for the Elderly: Extracts from the Literature*. Los Angeles, Calif.: Andrus Gerontology Center, University of Southern California, 1980.

The dissertations and theses listed in this chapter are available through traditional sources (see Hutson, Jurkiewicz, Kuna, and White).

Index

Index

About the Authors

Raymond M. Steinberg, D.S.W., has conducted research and training activities at the Andrus Gerontology Center since mid–1973. He currently serves as research associate professor of the Leonard Davis School of Gerontology; deputy director for Service System Design and Evaluation, Institute for Policy and Program Development; training director at the Rehabilitation Research and Training Center in Aging (in cooperation with Rancho Los Amigos Hospital); and senior staff associate and fellow of the UCLA/USC Long Term Care Gerontology Center. Dr. Steinberg's earlier projects at the center focused on training of directors of area agencies on aging, research on implementation of the Older Americans Act, and evaluation of policy research dissemination and utilization in the field of aging. His career has included front-line work in intergroup relations, social work, rural and urban community development, and area planning as well as administrative leadership positions in program planning, international development, and grants management.

Genevieve W. Carter, Ph.D., is Professor Emeritus of the University of Southern California School of Social Work. After many years as research director and executive director of Los Angeles' Welfare Planning Council, Dr. Carter spent the 1960s in Washington, D.C., as a top-level research administrator in the U.S. Department of Health, Education, and Welfare. Upon her return to Los Angeles in 1970 she established and directed the Regional Research Institute in Social Welfare. She is currently a consultant to the Andrus Gerontology Center as well as to local, state, national, and international programs in human-service planning and social research.

While Dr. Steinberg initiated and served as principal investigator for the research project leading to the publication of this book, Dr. Carter was the principal partner in the formulation of the research strategies and the execution of the study throughout all its phases, and she was a consultant to the entire staff. Upon completion of the research and dissemination requirements of the AoA-funded project, the two authors worked on this book part-time, between other professional assignments. Although each originally drafted distinct chapters, this final version has undergone many exchanges so that there is joint authorship in all chapters.

Date Due

AUG 0 7 1996			